Following in the steps of

Following in the steps of Jesus

1Peter 2:21, For to this you were called, because Christ also suffered for us, leaving us an example, that you should follow His steps:

2Titus 3:15, from childhood, you have known the Holy Scriptures, which are able to make you wise for salvation through faith which is in Christ Jesus.

Caution

> **Articles in this book are my views and opinions. You may disagree with them.**

Hari Patel

Published in 2020

A CIP catalogue record for this title is available from the British Library.

ISBN 9798681429432

Also by Hari Patel

- Bhagavad-Gita
- Duality of Bible (NT) and Bhagavad-Gita
- Spiritual Sanctuary. The Hereafter according to major scriptures
- Following in the steps of Jesus (Limited edition)

I am well aware that no one is infallible. Please, read my articles relating to scriptures with caution. Where there is a discrepancy with the Holy Scriptures' overall theme, you should discard such items.

Following in the steps of Jesus

Property of Author, on Temporary loan to Recipient. I would appreciate feedback on my book; please return to Author or next of kin on request harxpatel@gmail.com

Limited edition of 195 books for distribution in England & Canada.

Book Number...**E...149**

Terms of loan.

1.   I want as many people as possible to read this book. Please pass on the book to another church leader within seven months.

2.   In the 7th year (2026), please return my book with your comments below.

3.   Book No 7 is the only book on sale. The first page of chapter 1 and the last page of the chapter are handwritten by the author, to be sold in 2027.

Isaiah 55:11, so shall my word be that goes out from my mouth; it shall not return to me empty, but it shall accomplish that which I purpose, and succeed in the thing for which I sent it.

	Date	Comments	Initials
1.			
2.			
3.			

4.

5.

6.

7.

8.

Author's Note

As I was walking towards my home, this scripture came to my mind.

Acts 10:5 "Now send men to Joppa, and send for Simon whose surname is Peter.

'Lord,' I prayed silently, 'what is it you are trying to tell me from this verse?

The Holy Spirit breathed on this verse, and it came to life as, 'Go to the house of your friend Ken.'

I changed direction and headed towards Ken's house. Five minutes later, I knocked on his door, but there was no reply. I knocked again. No reply. I thought I must have made a mistake and started to walk home.

I took a different route for home. I walked 200 yards and turned a corner. Parked on the side of the road was a car with its hood up. As I approached the car, I saw Ken staring at the engine.

Together we worked on the car engine, and soon Ken was on his way.

Throughout this book, I have used scriptures, not in their historical context, but as they came alive and spoke to me in a personal way to transform my life and those around me.

Hari Patel   **H. Patel** .

I will be happy to receive any corrections from you. Your contribution would be appreciated.

harxpatel@gmail.com

Judgment Day

Mystic

Chapter 1 – The Judgment Day (Revelation 20:12)

1 Corinthians 1:27 But God has chosen the foolish things of the world to put to shame the wise, and God has chosen the weak things of the world to put to shame the things which are mighty;

The Lord commanded me, 'Come and stand on my right. You were not like other men; when you prayed, you asked specific things, names, dates, hours.' I stood on his right. Before us stood the **church leaders**[1] of England and Canada. The background was the New **Heaven,**[2] New Earth, and the holy city New Jerusalem, coming down from God out of heaven.

He looked at them and said, 'It is time for you to give an **account**[3].'

They were hard-working, decent, honest men. Wonderful, kind, compassionate men who had worked hard to bring relief to their flock. Men of honour. They saw the high quality of workmanship required to pass through the fires of **Judgment Day**[4-5]. Their works and effort flashed

---- ☆ ----

Bible, (NKJV) New King James Version, (NRSV) New Revised Standard Version, (NLT) New Living Translation

[1] *James 3:1 Dear brothers and sisters, not many of you should become teachers in the church, for we who teach will be judged more strictly.*

[2] *Revelation 21:1-2 And I saw a new heaven and a new earth: for the first heaven and the first earth were passed away; And I John saw the holy city, new Jerusalem,*

[3] *Romans 14:12 So then every one of us shall give account of himself to God.*

[4] *2 Peter 3:10 But the Day of the Lord will come as a thief in the night, in which the heavens shall pass away with a great noise, and the elements shall melt with fervent heat. The earth also and the works that are therein shall be burned up.*

[5] *Revelation 20:12 And I saw the dead, small and great, stand before God; and the dead were judged out of those things which were written in the books, according to their works.*

.........x...x......

before them.

I saw the fear on their faces. Their legs shook. Many were unable to stand, so great was the fear of missing their full inheritance on this day. They had assumed this day would be easy, a day of joy. Now confronted with the realities of the written scriptures, their hearts sank.

However, this was not a day of condemnation or fear, far from it. These people had stepped out and responded to the lord's call, when many others had walked away, to enjoy the pleasures of material life. Our wonderful lord and the whole church recognised the great sacrifice and contribution they had made to the kingdom. The entire creation was thankful. It was a day of awards, of acknowledgement and giving each man the glory and crowns they **merited**[6].

The Lord said, 'You will give me an **account,** minute by minute, of your time. You will account for every word you uttered and for every soul on your parish, and I will test your Works in the **fire**[7].'

Their works were **tested**[8].

The Lord addressed the church leaders that stood on his right. There was praise, gratitude, and acknowledgement in his tone. 'You helped build my kingdom, to bring all things under my control. You chose to go hungry, sacrificed the comforts of the home, your health, and your families. You went out in all weather into your parish to seek the lost, the hungry, and the vulnerable. You spent long nights in prayer, learning from the Holy Spirit to take every **thought captive**[9] to obey Me (Christ). You helped build my kingdom, to bring all things under my control.

---- ☆ ----

[6] *Revelation 22:12, "And behold, I am coming quickly, and My reward is with Me, to give to every one according to his work.*

[7-8] *1 Corinthians 3:13, each one's work will become clear; for the Day will declare it, because it will be revealed by fire; and the fire will test each one's work, of what sort it is.*

[9] *2 Corinthians 10:5, and we take every thought captive to obey Christ. ...x..x...*

'You were **baptised**[10] in the Holy Spirit and given time to learn to take every **thought captive** to obey Me. You have not failed Me.

'I called you to the wedding, and I find you have the **garments**[11]. You have reached the **full stature of Me**[12]. You are **heirs**[13] of God with me. I have a special place for you in my city, and there you will receive your crowns according to your **works**[14A].

'Stand at my right hand. I have much to share with you.' He smiled, and they relaxed, glad the day had gone well.

The whole of creation shouted in joy as they beheld the **New heaven**[14B] and New Earth descending towards them.

On the **left hand**[15] of the Lord stood thousands of church leaders from all over the world who were given multiple chances to transform into the image of Jesus. They had chosen to go their **own way**[16].

---- ☆ ----

[10] *Acts 11:16, "Then I remembered the word of the Lord, how He said, 'John indeed baptized with water, but you shall be baptized with the Holy Spirit."*

[11] *Revelation 3:5, "He who overcomes shall be clothed in white garments,*

[12] *Ephesians 4:13, till we all come to the unity of the faith and of the knowledge of the Son of God, to a perfect man, to the measure of the stature of the fullness of Christ;*

[13] *Galatians 4:7, Therefore you are no longer a slave but a son, and if a son, then an heir of God through Christ.*

[14A] *Revelation 22:12, "And behold, I am coming quickly, and My reward is with Me, to give to everyone according to his work.*

[14B] *Revelation 21:1, And I saw a new heaven and a new earth: for the first heaven and the first earth were passed away; and there was no more sea.*

[15] *Matthew 25:33, "And He will set the sheep on His right hand, but the goats on the left.*

[16] *Matthew 25: 1-12, Then shall the kingdom of heaven be likened unto ten virgins, which took their lamps, and went forth to meet the bridegroom... Afterward came also the other virgins, saying, Lord, Lord, open to us.*

...x..x...

They saw the holy city, **New Jerusalem**[17], coming down out of heaven from God, prepared as a bride adorned for her husband.

They were gloomy, disappointment as the angels led them **outside the city gates**[18]. The Archangel Gabriel said, 'You mislead yourself and thousands of others. You do not have the wedding **garments**[11]. You will dwell outside the Holy **City**[18]. You were offered the privilege to walk within the city gates but failed to meet the requirements.

'You chose to live in ignorance, in darkness or chose to neglect the **scriptures**[19]. Whatever the reason, you have forfeited the privilege. It will go to others who were not called but have proven themselves more worthy. Here, outside the city, you will set up your kingdoms among your followers, but not within the Holy City.'

I stood and beheld the tears in their eyes as the realisation hit them of their eternal loss. These men cried out in their thousands. 'Lord, we have **lost our inheritance**[20]. You called us to serve you in your city as **priests**[21] forever. Why did you not send a mystic to warn us about the requirements of this day?'

--- ☆ ----

[17] *Revelation 21:2, Then I, John, saw the* holy city, New Jerusalem, *coming down out of heaven from God, prepared as a bride adorned for her husband.*

[18] *Rev 21:27,   But nothing unclean* will enter *it, nor anyone who practices abomination* or falsehood, *but only those who are written in the Lamb's book of life.*

[19] *Hebrews 2:3, how can we escape if* we neglect *so great a salvation? It was declared at first through the Lord, and it was attested to us by those who heard him,*

[20] *Colossians 3:24, knowing that from the Lord, you will receive the reward of the* inheritance; *for you serve the Lord Christ.*

[20] *Ephesians 1:18, so that, with the eyes of your heart enlightened, you may know what is the* hope to which *he has called you, what are the riches of his glorious* inheritance among the saints.

[21] *Revelation 1:6, and has made us kings and* priests *to His God and Father, to Him be glory and dominion forever and ever. Amen.*   ...x..x...

Jesus looked at me, "Hari, you look gloomy."

I stood there with a heavy heart, 'Lord, please give me a chance to go back in time and speak to them. Every sheep matters; we have to bring every lost sheep back into the fold.'

He replied, 'They will not listen to **you**[22]. You are not equipped for this task.'

'Let me try,' I begged.

Our Lord Jesus said, 'Hari, when you are back in time, remind the church leaders that those who make enormous sacrifices for the Kingdom and are **overcomers**[23] will enter the New City. I went **hungry for forty days**[24] waiting upon our father and Holy Spirit. I spent long hours in prayers seeking our **father's will**[25]. I left them an example that they should follow in my **steps**[26].

'These good, righteous people standing on my right side also fasted and put their calling before their families. Like me, they spent **many nights**[27]

---- ☆ ----

[22] *Luke 16-30 -31, The rich man replied, 'No, Father Abraham! But if someone is sent to them from the dead, then they will repent of their sins and turn to God.' v31 "But Abraham said, 'If they won't listen to Moses and the prophets, they won't listen even if someone rises from the dead."*

[23] *Revelation 21:7, "He who overcomes shall inherit all things, and I will be his God, and he shall be My son.*

[24] *Matthew 4:2, And when He had fasted forty days and forty nights, afterwards He was hungry.*

[25] *Hebrews 5:7-8, While Jesus was here on earth, he offered prayers and pleadings, with a loud cry and tears, to the one who could rescue him from death. And God heard his prayers because of his deep reverence for God. V8 Even though Jesus was God's Son, he learned obedience from the things he suffered.*

[26] *1 Peter 2:21, For to this you were called, because Christ also suffered for us, leaving us an example, that you should follow His steps:*

[27] *Luke 6:12, Now it came to pass in those days that He went out to the mountain to pray, and continued all night in prayer to God. ...x..x...*

In prayer, waiting upon our father.

These saints offered up prayers and supplications with fervent **cries and tears**[28] to our heavenly father, and their cries were heard because of their godly fear. They learnt from suffering to bring every thought into captivity to the obedience of our father. Their lives were not comfortable.

'Hari, go back to your time and remind them to follow in **our steps**[29], and they will **walk in my city**[30].'

Colossians 1:28, Him we preach, warning every man and teaching every man in all wisdom, that we may present every man perfect in Christ Jesus.

---- ☆ ----

[28] *Hebrews 5:7 -8, While Jesus was here on earth, he offered prayers and pleadings, with a <u>loud cry and tears</u>, to the one who could rescue him from death. And God heard his prayers because of his deep reverence for God. V8 Even though Jesus was God's Son, he learned obedience from the things he suffered.*

[29] *1Peter 2:21, For to this you were called, because Christ also suffered for us, leaving us an example, that you <u>should follow His steps</u>:*

[30] *Revelation 22:14, Blessed are those who do His commandments, that they may have the right to the tree of life, and <u>may enter through the gates</u> into the city.*

Chapter 2 – Heir of God through Christ.

Galatians 4:7 Therefore, you are no longer a slave but a son, and if a son, then an __heir__ of God through Christ.

The Great American Evangelistic, Billy Graham, Haringey stadium, North London, England. March 1954

Billy Graham filled the 11,400-seat Haringey Arena for 12 weeks.

He began. "I am calling upon you to pray as you have never prayed before. I believe there is a hunger for God. I long to see new life and fire in the Church. I believe it can happen in answer to our prayers."

Hundreds of People stepped forward to give their lives to Jesus.

....

22 Years later, Oct 1976.

I was twenty-three years old. I move into Haringey, a place where 22 years ago, Billy Graham had preached and led hundreds of people to the Lord.

I took my shoes off and knelt before our Lord. He placed his right hand on my shoulder.

In a soft, gentle voice, he said, 'You will not be like other men. You are not in the flesh but in the **Spirit**[1]. You are my **heir**[2] (in Christ). You will learn to ask me specific things in others' presence for a date, time, hour, and I will honour it. I have called you to be my **watchman**[3]**, my mystic**.'

---- ☆ ----

[1] *Romans 8:9, But you are __not in the flesh; you are in the Spirit__ since the Spirit of God dwells in you. Anyone who does not have the Spirit of Christ does not belong to him.*

[2] *Galatians 4:7, Therefore you are no longer a slave but a son, and if a son, then an __heir of God__ through Christ.*

[3] *Ezekiel 3:17, "Son of man, I have made you a __watchman__ for the house of Israel; therefore hear a word from My mouth, and give them warning from Me:*

...x..x...

Haringey Congregational Church.

Green lane, London N8.

Cancer – Miss Staking

3 Dec 1978. It was evening, and I went to a church meeting. During the meeting, Rev Jim Hammond asked if we could pray for Miss Staking, who had been taken to the hospital with an illness.

The Holy Spirit said, 'Tell Rev Hammond Lord will heal her.'

I was standing at the back of a room full of people. I raised my hand.

Rev. Hammond looked at me.

My heart was racing with fear. In a timid voice, I said to Rev Hammond, 'Our Lord had told me she would be healed.' All eyes were on me. He nodded and said, 'thank you, Lord.'

....

Two weeks later.

Rev Jim Hammond went to see Miss Staking at the hospital. As he prayed, a cancerous growth the size of a tennis ball on Miss Shaking's hip began to shrink, and about ten minutes later, it had disappeared. She was 95 years old!

(**Appendix 1**: Miss Staking. Refer to my notes on next page

---- ☆ ----

Some of my original notes. Appendix   Healing of Miss Staking

3 Dec 1978

Miss Staking.   2

The sick sheep.   3

                                                  0

                                                  0

                                                  0

11·00 am I came to one of my sheep. She   8

was very sick. There was nothing I could   9

do to help her. I couldn't understand   7

where the sickness came from   5

I looked up and saw the elder   7

standing, watching my concern.   4

"Go, I shall heal her." Note A few   9
                                   01

minutes later she was healed and returned   7

to her flock. — HP.   4

                                                  0

Note 01 That evening I went to Haringey   8
                                        meeting +2 NR
United (congregational) church meeting. During the lw 7

Jim Hammond asked if we could pray for Miss   9
                     had been
staking as she was taken to hospital with illness 11

I said to Jim that the lord had told me   10

she would be healed. He accepted and thanked the lord 10

Two weeks later Jim went to see her at the   10
                                          Tenis ball
hospital. As he prayed, a cancer growth the size of a 12

on Miss Staking hip dis-appeared. She is 95 yrs! — HP. 10

16

Paul's Friend in Hospital July 1980

It was Saturday.

I was at a church prayer meeting. One of my friends, Paul, looked tense and worried. He asked if we could pray for his friend who was in the hospital, in a very critical state, and could pass away any day.

By now, I was part of a close-knit group. While people were praying, I looked up at the Lord, 'Lord, will you help?'

He looked at one of my **angels.**[1]

I knew the angel; I used to call him Benis. He said, 'It will take a few days to go to the throne and come back with the healing **leaves[2].'**

I looked at him. 'When?'

'Thursday,' he answered.

My heart was racing. Did I imagine this?

I wasn't brought up as a Christian. Having grown up in Africa as a Hindu, I was still uncomfortable with church practices. I could barely speak. I was petrified.

Could some people see angels?

---- ☆ ----

[1a] *Acts 8:26, Then an angel of the Lord said to Philip, 'Get up and go towards the south to the road that goes down from Jerusalem to Gaza.'*

[1b] *Hebrews 1:14, Are they, not all ministering spirits, sent forth to minister for them who shall be heirs of salvation?*

[2] *Revelation 22:1-2, And he showed me a pure river of water of life, clear as crystal, proceeding from the throne of God and of the Lamb. In the middle of its street, and on either side of the river, was the tree of life, which bore twelve fruits, each tree yielding its fruit every month. The leaves of the tree were for the healing of the nations.*

..x..x...

Appendix   Paul's Friend Healing

Lord Heals Paul Hooper friend.	5
July 80 I was with some friends from Horingey	8
church. Amonge them was Paul Hooper. He asked	8
if we could pray for his friend who was in	10
hospital in a very critical stage and could possibly die.	10
We prayed.	2
	0
	0
I looked up at the Elder, "Sire, will	8
you help?" He looked at one of my Angels.	10 ml 4
I Knew he would by that look.	7
Angel, "It will take few days to go to	9
the throne and come back with the Healing Leaves. Rev 22:2	+1 ml 9
"How long?" I asked.	5
"Till thursday." he answered.	4
"Lord," I prayed, "Let the doors of the Ward	9
open on Thursday 3.00 O'clock and the man be	9
healed. In Jesus name." The others believed.	7
Later at home I continued to pray," Father	8
Let the Angel's names be written in the Book of my	11 ml 10
Angels. One day I shall (Judge) reward him for his	12 ml #
good deeds. He shall be called Agape. Angel of love.	10
— x r. —	0
3 weeks later at Paul's House, heard his friend was	10
miraculously healed. Thursday afternoon doctors had said he was	9
healed. It was a miracle! He is back home.	10
— v u —	----

18

Our Lord had asked me to be very specific in prayer. But what if I had fabricated it in my mind? There was one way to test it.

I prayed aloud, 'Let the doors of the hospital ward open on Thursday at three o'clock, and the man be pronounced healed. In Jesus name.' To my astonishment, they all believed and said amen.

---- ☆ ----

Result of our prayers. *Three weeks later, at Paul's house group.*

Paul informed us that after our prayers, a few days later, doctors had checked his friend's test results and on Thursday afternoon sent him home as I had prophesied.' [**Appendix)**

---- 👑 ----

Chapter 3 Gall Bladder Stones.

A few days later, another church prayer meeting. Rev Hammond read a list of people to be prayed for. Among them was his assistant, Neville. He had gall bladder stones and was due for an operation. People prayed.

There was a quiet spell. My heart was thumping. I broke out in a sweat. I prayed with a quavering voice, 'Lord, thank you, when he goes for the operation, his stones will have disappeared. I ask in Jesus name.' *(John 14:13 "And whatever you ask in My name, that I will do, that the Father may be glorified in the Son.")*

I waited for 'amen' from the others. I should say - I was nervous, my voice was trembling. Most of the people present said amen.

---- ☆ ----

A few days later, Rev Hammond announced in the church that when Neville went to the hospital for his operation, they took an X-ray to locate the stones' position. There was no sign of the stones, so he was sent home.

Uganda

A few years earlier, in 1977, we had a prayer meeting for Uganda at Haringey church. President Idi Amin had brought death and destruction to his country. The president was Muslim, and he persecuted Christians.

We had a mission connection to a church in Uganda, which was being persecuted. Amin's soldiers had arrested the church minister.

We were holding a prayer meeting in support of fellow Christians in Uganda. People prayed.

In my mind, thoughts of someone taking a pot shot at him or one of his disgruntled bodyguards shooting him surfaced. That's what I would like to happen. I almost started to laugh.

I just felt the Lord say you cannot pray such nonsense. I suppressed such thoughts.

I waited upon the Lord. Then I prayed, 'Lord, I want to thank you. He (Idi Amin) will flee the country. He will wander from one country to another. He will finally seek refuge in a Muslim country. Amen.'

There was a big Amen from Mr Hammond repeated by others.

---- ☆ ----

Appendix   Uganda. Idi Amin. His downfall

Years later, on review of my prayer, I found on internet

Idi Amin. History.Com Editors
Nyerere mobilized a counter-offensive to recapture the land and drove the Ugandan Army out with Ugandan exiles' help. The battle raged into Uganda, and on April 11, 1979, Amin was forced to flee when Kampala was captured. Although he initially sought refuge in Libya, he later moved to Saudi Arabia, where he lived comfortably until his death of multiple organ failure in 2003.

My Prayer for Israel and Palestinian people in 1989. Answers for prayer for items hundreds of miles away is often hard to verify.

He shall en power a member of Isreali 7
Govt to champion the palastian cause. He shall 8
cause a resolution to be passed thro the Govt to 10
stop robbing the land of Arabs. This will be sat 10
In motion within Six weeks. 37

Note Added on 8|8|89. Did I make a mistake + 19
Could it be six years i.e. by Oct 1992 .....

A few days later, I saw this in Daily Mail 1989 newspaper

Words from the wise

1989. Daily Mail. Newsp op

Amos Oz: Bravery

ISRAEL'S government of occupation in the territories has become a monster which has removed its mask and even boasts of its monstrosity.

Not my words. If they were, hundreds, maybe thousands, of Jews would accuse me of anti-semitism, although we have all seen more than enough to know the words ring with a terrible truth.

They are the words of Amos Oz, the bravest and most honest of Israeli writers, in a speech in Tel Aviv addressed to President Herzog, Premier Shamir, and all the leaders of Israel:

"If you do not take steps with all possible speed to rehabilitate the law which is being perverted and justice which is beginning to falter, on the basis of the absolute principle of one and the same law for Arab and Jew, if you do not do this at once, our blood is on your heads, and at the end of the road your own blood also.

'Without one law and equal justice for everyone you will have to give up not only Ramallah and Hebron; you will have to give up the State of Israel, because the State of Israel cannot live without one law and equal justice.

'Nothing can exist here without one law and equal justice. Not Judaism. And not the State. It will be a jungle here: Beirut.'

Amos Oz asks God to preserve Israel from stepping into the shoes out of which the PLO is trying to step.

---- ♔ ----

22

Chapter 4- Authority Over Spiritual Powers

St James Church, Muswell Hill, N London. Marko.

It was early May 1983. On Sunday at church, the vicar mentioned that Marko had gone missing from the church we supported in South America. He wanted the church to engage in intercession for his safekeeping. A prayer meeting for Marko would be held on Monday evening at the vicarage.

Later on, I saw a vision. Marko was in a dangerous situation held in captivity. Then I saw a captain. He had the authority to release Marko. I saw angels assigned to escort him home. He would return home in two to three days.

Monday evening, I attended the prayer meeting held on behalf of Marko. There were about nine people, and the vicar's wife led the prayers. While people prayed for Marko, I waited upon our Lord and received more clarity in a vision. (**Appendix** Marko)

I had joined this church recently. I was mindful that I was a stranger in this close-knit group. I did not know how to present my vision, so I prayed the best I could. It is fair to say my voice was stressed. I was very nervous. I did not know how my prayer would be received.

I just prayed, 'To the captain, I command you in Jesus' name to release Marko. I request/command the angels to look after Marko and guide him home.

'On Tuesday (tomorrow), he shall be brought before the captain. He will be released. For three days, he will wonder. His life shall be in danger. On Friday morning, he will arrive home safe. Thank you, Lord. In Jesus name, I pray.'

Nobody in that prayer meeting said amen. I was nervous, sweating, and they sensed my tension. I could understand their lack of trust in me.

---- ☆ ----*About a month later, our vicar said a letter from South America had arrived, saying that Marko was safely home.*

A few weeks later, a visitor from South America came to our church. He was from the same church as Marko, and I spoke to him after church.

He was amazed when I asked him if Marko had been brought before a captain on Tuesday and returned home on Friday. He confirmed my prayers. He said to me, 'You know more about Marko's situation than I do. Where did you get your information?'

My initial vision was partly wrong. I wrote that Marko would return home in two to three days. That worked out as Wednesday or Thursday. By the time of the prayer meeting, I had had time to think, and the lord had time to correct me.

Appendix Marko

1983 At church — VISION of Marko received on 9ᵗʰ MAY 1983.	12
Saw a Captain. To him was granted	7
authority to release Marko. Angels to escort	7
him home, surrounded by danger. He shall	7
return Home in 2/3 days.	7
	0
	0
At st James, the Vicar Micheal Bunker	7
mentioned that a person called Marko in	7
South America had gone missing. Would the	7
church pray for his safe return.	6
10ᵗʰ MAY 1983	9
The next day on Monday at	
Vicarage there was a prayer meeting for	7
Marko. At this meeting there were about	7
9 people and the Vicar's wife.	6
People prayed for him. Then I	6
prayed for him. I spoke in Spirit	7
To the Captain I command you	6
in Jesus name to release Marko. I	7
command / request the Angels to look after and	9ʷᵉ 8
guide Marko back Home.	4
I prophecied. On Tuesday he would	6

be brought before the Captain. He will
be released. For 3 days he ⨯ shall wounder,
His life shall be in danger. On Friday
⨯ morning he shall arrive home safe.

    I felt in my spirit that Marko
wanted to die. Then I saw his family
pleading for him. I prayed for his safe
return.

    Lord,' Your eyes shall see that which
the prophets and kings and princes have
longed to see and did not.

    Nobody in that prayer meeting said
Amen to my prophecy.

    About 2 month later Micheal said
that a letter from S. America arrived. That
Marko was safe home. A few weeks later
someone from S. A came to our church
    South America

    He knew Marko. I spoke to him after
church. He was very suprised when I
asked him if Marko had been brought in
captivity before a Captain on Tuesday... etc

    He confirmed my vision. I knew more
about Marko's situation than even he did

    He asked, "Where did you get such
detailed information from?' I said from the Lord!

---- ❧ ----

Chapter 5 - Grief of a Family

*Romans 8:35, Who shall separate us from the love of Christ? Shall tribulation, or distress, or persecution, or famine, or nakedness, or peril, or sword? 8:39 nor height nor depth, nor any other created thing, shall be able to separate us from the love of God (*or from his people*) which is in Christ Jesus our Lord.*

I was at a house group. The middle-aged group leader and his wife, a lovely couple, were sad. A decade ago, their only daughter had suddenly passed away. She was only 17 years old. Her best friend was a great comfort to them in their time of grief.

They kept in touch with her during her university days and built a close relationship with her. She became part of their family. They began to regard her as their daughter. She was a great comfort to them. After graduation, she moved to another part of the country where she had found work. They lost touch with her. They made efforts to find her. Years went by, and they had not received any news. Their grief mounted.

They had developed affection for her and greatly missed her. They asked if we could pray for her. They wanted to hear from her. We felt their grief and sorrow.

In my mind, I asked the Lord to help them. His reply was simple. 'Make it happen. Use my angels to bring it about. Learn to work with them.'

I looked at his angel and silently asked him, 'Can you get the young girl to write to this couple using **Zak's tenet**[1]?'

He nodded.

I asked, 'Can we fix a date?'

---- ☆ ----

[1] **Zak's Tenet;** - Guide you with my eye. I can reason with you. I respect your privacy, so I will not press you nor persuade you without your consent."
Tenets are the principle of belief learnt from my fellow Christians.
...x..x...

26

He nodded. I prayed, 'Lord, thank you; they will receive a letter next Tuesday morning from the young woman.'

---- ☆ ----

The following Wednesday at the house group, their faces were radiant. They had received a letter from her on Tuesday morning.

The Baptist minister

For a short while, I left Haringey church and went to a couple of Baptist churches in North London. I wanted to see what they were like, and I was on the lookout for a nice Christian girl. I went to one church, and I should say - solely because I fancied a girl.

This Baptist minister was too clever. He was also tall, handsome, and well built. He would preach to us about the Trinity, the sinfulness of humanity, the fall, crucifixion, redemption, all way above our heads.

He had taken a dislike to me, probably because he knew my ulterior motives and would try to provoke me whenever possible. One evening after church, as we sat around a table with tea and biscuits, he wanted to belittle me in front of the church and the girl I fancied. I took offence at his sneering remarks, and as he smiled at me mockingly, I quoted a scripture,

Matthew 10:8 *Heal the sick, raise the dead, cleanse the lepers, cast out demons.*

I asked him, 'Can you show me two cases where you have applied this scripture and seen the healing power of the scriptures? Could a panel of non-Christians give merit to your evidence?'

That mocking smile disappeared from his face. His face went bright red, and he walked away. He could speak with much passion and conviction about theological concepts that he did not practise. Book knowledge gained in a Bible college, but not at the feet of the Lord.

I do not have a fraction of his theological knowledge. I have a simple faith in the bible. It says in **John 10:27,** *"My sheep hear My voice, and I know them,* *and they follow Me.* It's fair to say -I know that voice, and I have proved it several times in a precise way in the presence of a packed church.

My knowledge is based on my walk with the Lord. I illustrated some examples earlier, and I will state a few more. Verses the Lord has breathed on, and they have come alive with the power to transform lives.

That evening in prayers, as I brought before the Lord the day's event, the Holy Spirit said, 'On the Judgment Day all his works will burn to ashes, but he shall be saved. A child of Esau.' **Genesis 25:34** *Esau despised his birthright.*

God describes such worldly unsuitable shepherds in a very vivid way in **Ezekiel 34:1-31**[1]. At one time, it applied to me. I was a house group leader in Rev Hammond's church. One evening after the house group, as I sat down in prayer to account for the day, the Lord spoke to me from the above verses.

I was not up to the level the Lord required. I gave up the house group leadership and spent five years seeking, learning what it takes to be an anointed leader.

---- ☆ ----

[1] Ezekiel 34:1-31 (and at one time, it applied to me).

V1 Then the word of the LORD came to me, saying,

V2 Son of man, prophesy against the shepherds of Israel (me), prophesy, and say to them, The Lord GOD says this to the shepherds; Woe to the shepherds of Israel who have been feeding yourselves! Should not the shepherds feed their flocks?

V3 You eat the fat, clothe yourselves with the wool, and kill the fattened animals: but you do not tend the flock.

V4 You have not strengthened the weak, healed the sick, or bound up broken limbs, nor have you brought back those who were driven away or looked for those who were lost; but you have ruled them with force and violence.

---- ⚜ ----

Chapter 6 - Healing of Silvia's Cancer

1 Corinthians 4:20 For the kingdom of God is not in word but in power.

7th **Jan 1981**, I was Alan's guest at his house group, part of the North London community church.

This was not my house group.

Alan's talk was about, 'the kingdom of God is in power.' (1 Corinthians. 4 v 20)

It was also about the need to be sensitive to the Holy Spirit, Angels, Christ, and the Father. *John 10:27 My sheep know my voice.*

Next, his friend Adrian stood up and said, 'We need to be sensitive to the spirit. The carnal man has no desire to stand firm.' (*Galatians 5:25 if we live by the Spirit, by the Spirit let us also walk*).

Adrian continued, 'The spiritual man is determined, proven, approved of God, and trusted by the angels. He is a man of authority. (*1 Corinthians 4:20)* The kingdom of God is not in words but in power.'

The next day, Thursday 8th **Jan 1981, at Bible Study. [Appendix: Silvia]**

There were about 18 people present.

Colin asked if we could pray for his wife, Silvia. She had cancer of the throat.

I Prophesied: **'On 15**[th] **Jan,** she will begin her healing treatment.' I did it according to the things shown to me by the Lord. [*Revelation 22:2 leaves from the tree of healing.*] This is the number of days it would take the angels to walk up to the tree, whose leaves are for healing and return.

I continued, 'Also, she will be better by the end of the month, possibly healed. God will do this on account of his grace, not due to our prayers, good deeds, etc.'

Confirmation of prophecy.

A week later, on Tue, at Bible Study

At the start of the meeting, Silvia's husband Collin said, 'they had received a letter from the hospital requesting Silvia <u>attend the hospital on</u> – **15**[th] **Jan**.*'*

An hour later. At prayer time, we prayed once more for Silvia.

I looked to the Lord, inquired about his thinking.

The Lord said, 'Ask me a specific prayer. I will reveal I am among you.'

I prayed, 'Lord, let Silvia be back in her home by the 3rd of Feb.'

The Lord said, 'Be more specific.'

'Lord,' I prayed, 'let it be at 10 a.m. that she arrives home.'

<u>Note:</u> 4 weeks later. 10th **of Feb. Confirmation of prophecy**

At our Bible study,

<u>*Colin said, "Silvia had returned home,*</u> **on 3**[rd] **Feb at around 10 a.m.***" The hospital treatment had worked. She was free of cancer.*

The whole congregation praised God. The Lord became so much more real and alive to the people.

Appendix   Healing of Silvia from cancer with date, time, and hour.

Tuesday 8ʰ Jan 1981

      <u>Bible study Silvia.</u> | 3

                                      | 0

Adrians Hse Walthamstow . Lon. E | 5

18 People present. | 3

                                        | 0

      To-day on 8ʰ Jan at Adrians house group | 9

we prayed for Collin's wife Silvia. She is suffering | 9

from Cancer of throat. There were about 18 people present | 10кp. 9

      Prophecied. on 15ʰ Jan she will begin her | 9

healing treatment. [Rev This is the time required by Angels | 11

to walk up to the tree, whose leaves are for healing | 11

and return] I talked to the Angels and agreed | 10

on this & date. I did it according to the | 11

pattern of things shown to me by the Elder. | 9

      Also that she will be better by the | 8

End of the month. (Possibly healed) God will do this | 12

on account of his Grace, not due to our prayers | 10

good deeds etc. | 3

13 JAN 81
(Again at hse gp) The following Tuesday 13ʰ JAN 1981 Collin | 12

Said they had received letter from hospital requesting | 8

31

Silvia to attend the hospital on 15ᵗʰ JAN.

I looked at the lord, Inquired about his mind.

Lord: "Ask me specific prayer. I will reveal I am among you."

I looked at the Angel. They said they would have brought and finished their ministry by (3ʳᵈ) Feb ie. the ministry of healing

I prayed, "Lord Let Silvia be back by (3) Feb 1981 to her home."

"Lord," I prayed, "Let it be 10.00am when she arrives home."

Early around 10ᵗʰ Feb at our Bible study Colin said Silvia had returned home well on 3rd Feb 10.00 am.

The whole congregation praised God. The Lord became so much real and alive to the people

HP.

---- ♛ ----

Chapter 7 - Intercession for Silvia

Saint Paul encourages us in *1 Corinthians 2:4, And my speech and my preaching were not with persuasive words of human wisdom but in demonstration of the Spirit and power.*

Our life should demonstrate this power.

Prayer is hard work. It is like tilling and ploughing a field and then a long wait for the harvest.

In my intercession for Silvia, I was given the dates and times in front of about 18 people. I did not ask people to write down their testimonies to my prophecies. I did not see any importance to it.

When I came home after the house group, I gave an account of the evening to the Lord and prayed for Silvia. Our Lord said he would heal her, but he had a particular thing he wanted me to do. I had to learn to walk in the spirit and learn to exercise authority. I had to claim this victory on behalf of the Lord and church.

It would have been easy to ignore the small voice and go to bed. I did a demanding 8-5 job, plus commuting time to central London. I had an excellent excuse to go to bed, rollover, and fall asleep. Instead, I spent a couple of nights in prayer, sleeping perhaps 2-3 hours from exhaustion, learning the art of spiritual welfare.

In my intercession, as I prayed, I recognized my place on the **cross with Christ**[1]. I acknowledged any wrongdoing that I was aware of. I put all my thoughts, deeds, and unrighteousness since my last prayer on the cross. I was dead to the world, foes, and self. I claimed the **blood of Christ**[2] to cleanse me of all wrongdoings and unbelief, then put on the whole

---- ☆ ----

[1] *Galatians 2:20 "I have been crucified with Christ; it is no longer I who live, but Christ lives in me; and the life which I now live in the flesh I live by faith in the Son of God, who loved me and gave Himself for me.*

[2] *1 John 1:7 But if we walk in the light as He is in the light, we have fellowship with one another, and the blood of Jesus Christ His Son cleanses us from all sin.*

Appendix. Years later, on review of intercession for Silvia and lessons learnt.

Intercession for Silvia (Prayer). Sabbatical review

(Prayer)

22/7/11 In my Intercession for Silvia, I was given the Dates | 14

and times in the House group in front of about 18 people | 12

It's sad, that I did not ask people to write down their | 12

testimonies to my prophecies, but at the time, I did not | 11

see any importance to it. | 5

When I came home after the house group I | 9

was to their laid in intercession. It was made | 11

clear to me that the lord would bring this prayer | 10

to fulfillment but I had to Learn to walk in | 10

the Spirit and Learn to excercise Authority. | 7

To do this, first I had to claim the blood | 10

of christ to clense me of all. Then put on the | 11

whole armour of christ, walk up to the tree of | 10

healing (Rev 22:2 Book of Rev) take its fruit and bring it to | 14

Silvia with the help of Angels. I had to calculate | 10

(note) the days it took me to walk in Spirit to the | 14

Tree of Healing and back. It worked out that by | 10

3 Feb, we would be back. Then Sat 10.00am as the | 11

time we would apply for her return home. The | 11

Angels were to arrange this with hospital discharge and | 9

Journey time home. It took a huge amount of my time | 11

and energy for a couple of days. | 7

Note Added | 2

22/7/11 This was one of my early prophecy. | 8

When it came to pass, I was so excited | 9

that I could not sleep, eat but waited | 8

for the next bit which soon followed, no. | 8

armour of God[3].

I was grateful for the people that had come in my life, to the Lord for making me a **priest[4]** in his temple. In spirit, I stood my ground against the **principalities and powers[5]** and then walked to the **tree of healing/life[6-7]** With the help of the angels, I took its fruit and brought it to Silvia.

I calculated (note) the days it took me to walk in spirit to the tree of healing and back. Added those days and worked out the actual date of recovery. Then I set 10 a.m. as the time we would apply for her return home. The angels were to arrange this with the hospital discharge team and factor in the journey time home. It took a considerable amount of my time and energy for a couple of days.

This method works for me. It may not work for others since it's based on a **covenant[8]** between the Lord and me. We all need to find out what works for us, that is, between the Holy Spirit and us.

---- ☆ ----

[3] *Ephesians 6:11, Put on the* <u>whole armour of God</u> *that you may be able to stand against the wiles of the devil.*

[4] *Revelation 5:10, And have made us kings and* <u>priests</u> *to our God; And we shall reign on the earth.*

[5] *Ephesians 6:12 For we do not wrestle against flesh and blood, but against* <u>principalities, against powers</u>, *against the rulers of the darkness of this age, against spiritual hosts of wickedness in the heavenly places.*

[5B] *Colossians 2:15 Having disarmed* <u>principalities</u> *and* <u>powers</u>, *He made a public spectacle of them, triumphing over them in it.*

[6] *Revelation 22:2 In the midst of the street of it, and on either side of the river, was there the* <u>tree of life</u>, *which bare twelve manners of fruits, yielded her fruit every month: and the leaves of the tree were* <u>for the healing</u> *of the nations.*

[7] *Revelation 2:7, "He who has an ear, let him hear what the Spirit says to the churches. To him who overcomes I will give to* <u>eat from the tree of life,</u> *which is in the midst of the Paradise of God."'*

[8] *Covenant: As a learner, I have Covenanted with the Lord, whereby he amends my mistakes or errors, provided I learn from my mistakes on my sabbatical review of notes. ...x..x...*

Note: God would answer specific prayers if Christians were to engage in the spiritual battle and **disarm principalities**[9].

Ephesians 6:12 For we do not wrestle against flesh and blood, but against principalities, against powers, against the rulers of the darkness of this age, against spiritual hosts of wickedness in the heavenly places. Colossians 2:15 Having disarmed principalities and powers, He made a public spectacle of them, triumphing over them in it.

There is a big difference between prophesying and making it happen. Old Testament saints prophesied, and God made it **happen.**[10] On the other hand, heirs in God have the power and authority to make it happen.

We are born again through the **WORD**[11-12] **of God.** When we exercise this WORD that abides in us with the Holy Spirit's help, it has the power to disarm principalities. It gives us access to the fruit of victory, to eat from the **tree of life**[7]. With power comes responsibility and accountability. This WORD **abides forever**[12]. Once released, it will remain alive forever.

As an heir of God, I have an eternal responsibility to lift in prayer every 7th month, **7th year**[13] these WORDS, so that they continue to produce the fruit until Judgment Day, and maybe ever after.

---- ☆ ----

Note: Even **Balaam's** donkey could speak (and prophecy) on behalf of God. It is not an outstanding achievement. *Numbers 22:28, Then the LORD opened the mouth of the donkey, and she said to Balaam, "What have I done to you, that you have struck me these three times?"*

[9] *1 John 5:4, For every child of God defeats this evil world, and we achieve this victory through our faith.*

[10] *2 Peter 3:5 For this they wilfully forget: that by the word of God the heavens were of old, and the earth standing out of water and in the water,*

[11] *Luke 8:11, "Now the parable is this: The seed is the word of God.*

[12] *1 Peter 1:23 having been born again, not of corruptible seed but incorruptible, through the word of God, which lives and abides forever.*

[13] *1 Timothy 6:19, storing up for themselves a good foundation for the time to come that they may lay hold on eternal life.* ---- 🐝 ----

Chapter 8 - Good works.

Ephesians 2:10, For we are His workmanship, created in Christ Jesus for good works, which God prepared beforehand that we should walk in them.

God remembered the good works written in his book for me before he gave me life. Each good work was carefully chosen to teach me a specific thing about God and my role in his kingdom on Earth and Heaven.

Some of the good works he had planned for me:- Authority over government (Uganda), authority over sea, rain, aid (Ethiopia and Korea), spiritual powers (Marko), healings (Paul's friend, Colin and Silvia, Miss Staking), angels (timing of delivery of letters, healing), money/material, and spiritual tabs (Raymond/ caravan).

This is my understanding, and it works for me. I have to say my knowledge is limited. That does not deter God from working with us. At times we lack knowledge or understanding, and God carries us forward as a way of encouraging us to keep on seeking, learning, and amending our errors.

He gave me an idea of his plans. Showed me the principle, *[Hari's Tenet 1][1]- The law of the cosmos dictates: No one has a right to gain at the expense of others, not even **God**[2]. Your conscience demands that you have a moral conscience for all life, i.e., thou shall not steal.'*

Moreover, God has undertaken to make everything and everyone **whole**[3-4]. Anyone that has contributed intentionally or not to establish his

---- ☆   [1] *Hari's Tenet 1.* **Tenets are the principle of belief learnt from my fellow Christians.**

[2] *Lamentations 3:33, For He does not afflict willingly, Nor grieve the children of men.*

[3] *Ephesians 2:16, and that He might reconcile them both to God in one body through the cross, thereby putting to death the enmity.*

[4] *Colossians 1:20, and through him, God was pleased to reconcile to himself all things, whether on earth or in heaven, by making peace through the blood of his cross.   ..x..x..*

kingdom, will eventually be made **whole.**[5] And we have a moral obligation, to do everything in our power to bring about the process of reconciliation of all things in Heaven and **Earth**[6]. By starting on our Patch (Parish) and continue this work until Judgment Day.

While our Lord walked on this Earth.

The Good works his father had ordained for him the following day did not fall into his lap. It was hard work to seek them out and suppress his desires and wishes.

There was a choice between waiting upon his father all night or seeking the allure of a warm, comfortable bed. It is a question of obedience, iron will, firm discipline, and commitment to a higher calling.

We all have to make a choice every day if we are to follow in the footsteps of Jesus. *(1 Peter 2:21, For to this you were called, because Christ also suffered for us, leaving us an **example**, that you should follow His steps.)*

The Lord God gave Lord Jesus visions about his past glory, his place in the WORD (John 1:1) and took Jesus back to the beginning. Through such revelations, his father showed him things and good works (Ephesians 2:10) he had prepared for Christ to carry out the next day, i.e., the ten lepers would come to him for healing, only one would go back to thank him.

Jesus then prayed and discussed with his father what he ought to say to them and do. To heal all of them, or just one? His father would give him

---- ☆ ----

[5] *Revelation 21:1, Now I saw a new heaven and a new earth, for the first heaven and the first earth had passed away. Also, there was no more sea.*

[5] *Colossians 1:20, and by Him to reconcile all things to Himself, by Him, whether things on earth or things in heaven, having made peace through the blood of His cross.*

[6] *Ephesians 2:16, and that He might reconcile them both to God in one body through the cross, thereby putting to death the enmity.*

...x..x...

visions about the heavenly realms; insight into Judgment Day and beyond. This physical healing would confirm things and understanding he had gained into the spiritual world, strengthening the father-son bond.

Evidence

I like to proclaim a date, time, and particular things in public, before a crowd, so there is no mistaking the hand of God in my life.

As far as I know, the laws of physic do not apply to spiritual things. How does one test what one sees in a vision?

For me, it makes sense to say the primary reason for the display of God's healing power was to convince me to walk in spirit with confidence in heavenly places. Observe what was going on there, learn from it, and he would use specific healings to convince me of the spiritual world's reality, for example, Silvia's healing.

 Secondly, to encourage me to continue to seek the path of good works he had prepared for me since each good deed had a lesson for me. To spiritually build and make me more worthy of my spiritual inheritance in God. To mould me and perfect me for a role he had in mind in his coming kingdom. All this training was for the future, not the present world.

The full inheritance would go to the best, strongest, most determined and those that had overcome/passed all tests. Such would be <u>tested to the utmost as Christ was</u>. And God would even take the weak things like me to prove that anyone could meet this test with his help.

Thirdly, to bless others.

Imagination and spiritual reality

There is no line between imagination and spiritual reality. The only way to prove to oneself the reality of visions is to ask God for an external means to verify what is going on in our spiritual or mental minds. That needs a lot of research, trial and error experiment, making notes and finally testing if it works. If it is from God, it will happen.

I would test every vision and have it confirmed by external means, a confirmation that even an atheist could accept and admit the explanation was outside the scope of physics. I have attached as evidence (**Appendix**).

The Lord was clear. 'You are to build my kingdom with the aid of the indwelling Holy Spirit and not with your hands and feet. Men build churches with their hands and with stones; God builds his church within us.' *Luke 17:21, "nor will they say, 'See here!' or 'See there!' For indeed, the* <u>*kingdom*</u> *of* <u>*God*</u> *is within you."*

Our Lord's expectations

Jesus expects us to exceed him, to do incredible things here on earth and in Heaven, like building his Spiritual Sanctuaries (more about it later).

Exodus 25:8, "And let them make Me a <u>sanctuary</u>, that I may dwell among them.

John 14:12 "Most assuredly, I say to you, he who believes in Me, the works that I do (Lord, building his spiritual sanctuaries in Heaven) *he will do also; and* <u>*greater*</u> *works than these he will do, because I go to My Father.*

He expects us to build his spiritual sanctuaries. It is his will. It requires commitment, an iron will, and determination and the whole heavenly crowd is watching

Ephesians 2:19. Now, therefore, you are no longer strangers and foreigners but fellow citizens with the saints and members of the household of God.

Isaiah 65:25 The wolf and the lamb shall feed together, the lion shall eat straw like the ox; but the serpent—its food shall be dust! They shall not hurt or destroy on all my holy mountain, says the LORD.
Isaiah 66:1-2Thus says the LORD: Heaven is my throne, and the earth is my footstool; what is the <u>house that you would build for me</u>, and what is <u>my resting place</u>? These things my hand has made, and so all these things are mine, says the LORD. But this is the one to whom I will look, to the humble and contrite in spirit, who trembles at my word.

He has many vacancies for these posts. Church attendance is falling; it is in his interest to go out of his way to empower you.

I hope my testimony will encourage you to step out in faith. The Lord needs courageous, dedicated people to build his kingdom.

The Bible requirements are simple. You should be prepared to spend all night in prayer, willing to regularly account for every prayer and sermon until the words (whatever you spoke in spirit) fulfils what they were sent out for.

You have to be prepared to tend to your words until that great Day of Judgment for the result *(Revelation 2:26 "And he who overcomes, and keeps My works until the end, to him I will give <u>power</u> over the nations —).*

That is if you firmly believe your <u>Words</u> are from the indwelling Holy Spirit and have the same ability as the WORD of God by which creation came into being.

This is the kind of commitment required from leaders who have received a calling to eternal life.

1 Corinthians 1:26, For you see your calling, brethren, that not many wise according to the flesh, not many mighty, not many noble, are called.

The race set before us is the most demanding race ever devised on Earth or in Heaven. Fortunately, the Holy Spirit runs with us, carrying us most of the way. All he needs is our consent, willingness, courage, and iron will.

1 Corinthians 1:27, But God has chosen the foolish things of the world to put to shame the wise, and God has chosen the <u>weak things</u> of the world to put to shame the things which are mighty;

Many Christians have said to me, 'I am doing fine; I don't want scriptures *(God)* to change my life.' What a shame. On the Day of the Lord, they will regret it.

I am glad I have run the race set before me. Join me.

---- ----

Chapter 9 – Under the African Sky. Kenya, Outskirts of Nairobi

I was about 16 years old, when late one evening, I inserted the key into the front door, but it was locked from inside. A clear message from my father: give up the Bible if you want to stay in this house.

It's fair to say that I was shunned by my parents and by our community. I had no friends, no place to go. Shivering with cold and fright, I stood looking at the clear African sky, full of stars. I thought maybe God wanted me to be like John the Baptist, walk out into the African bush and live off the berries. The scripture rang through my mind. *Matthew 3:4, and the same John had his raiment of camel's hair, and a leathern girdle about his loins; and his food were locusts and wild honey.*

I stood there looking at the calm, clear cloudless sky with hundreds of shining stars. So beautiful, yet a few hundred steps away lay the wilderness and ferocious wild animals, predators like lions and hyenas.

I had made up my mind to walk into the African bush. It wasn't the most welcoming of places. I had no choice. I had lost my family, and now I was an outcast from our community. We lived in Kenya on Nairobi's outskirt, an eight-minute walk, and I would be in the wilderness.

I felt alone. I felt like I had no one in the world I could turn to. I sat on the steps, tucked my head into my lap, and folded my hands over my head. I closed my eyes and started to cry. How nice it would be to crawl into a hole in the ground and let it swallow me.

Right then, the angel of death was a friend, a relief from all my inner pain, despair, and loneliness.

The Bible says love, faith, and hope are eternal. I didn't feel its comfort. They were just words. Months of isolation and family rejection flooded into my mind. It was a time of such despair that my mind just blanked out. I could not cope with it. I had reached the end of my rope. Young, single, jobless and no family or friends. I buried my head in my lap.

As I sat there crying, the Lord God breathed new life over verses of the Bible, and they began to come alive. *Job 29:12, I delivered the poor who cried out, the fatherless and the one who had no helper. James 1:27 pure religion is to visit the fatherless.*

God spoke to me from these Bible verses, making them relevant to my current situation: **Genesis 9:11** *And I will establish my covenant with you.* 'Because you have given up your family for me, you are an orphan. I will be a father to you. Write this down. If it is from me, it will happen. By the time you are twenty-two and a half, you will have gone through college, and you will have your own house.'

I got up, took a deep breath, and climbed down the three steps, ready to walk into the wilderness and follow in the footsteps of John the Baptist.

I heard a low metallic noise. My young sister opened the door. 'Hari,' she whispered, 'don't make a sound.'

She sneaked me into the house. I am grateful to my little sister. She lifted my spirit. At least one person cared.

For the next few months, I kept out of my parents' way. The atmosphere in the house was tense. They didn't speak to me; we avoided all eye contact. I was lost, emotionally a wreck. I suffered from anxiety, loneliness, and insecurity. I had no place to go. I did not qualify for a work permit, as I didn't have Kenyan citizenship. I was unable to sleep. Physically and emotionally, I deteriorated.

My father, who I had adored and greatly loved, respected for his charitable good works and deeds for the needy, stood on the other side of an invisible barrier from me. He had instilled in me the ethos that to care for the vulnerable was a noble act. Maybe that was why he had wanted me to be a doctor. Now a book had put a barrier between us. My mother avoided eye contact, but she was courteous, caught between a mother's love for her child and an angry husband.

I had no resentment or ill feeling towards them. I had put them in a complicated situation in a close-knit Hindu community by reading the

Bible. Reading the Bible was considered conversion to Christianity. Arranged marriage was still a common practice in our community. No one in our community would want to give their son or daughter to a family that had a heretic.

There were days I felt suicidal. But even in the depth of my despair, it never occurred to me to give up the Bible.

I was a complete failure in my parents' eyes, a great disappointment to them. All their hopes of seeing their son become a respected member of our community had gone.

Months of isolation from my family took a further toll on me. Outwardly, I looked calm, smiley, but inwardly I was a wreck. My self-confidence, my self-esteem continued to plummet. My mother would stand next to me, and I would cry out for a hug or a calming word of comfort, but a book had put a barrier between us.

I would glance at my father, a man who had brought so much joy to my early life. In whose bosom, I would crawl when I had trouble sleeping; now he stood at a distance, avoiding eye contact. I had an overwhelming love for him but could not express it. That door was closed. I could feel the hurt he felt, but neither of us was in a position to reach out to the other.

There were times I felt suicidal. I started to build an emotional wall of isolation around me. I began to sink into my own world of despair. I could not share my deep unhappiness with anyone as if caught in the depths of ocean currents, swelling up and down uncontrolled.

These deep emotional currents would leave their wounds. They say time is a great healer, and yes, wounds heal in time – but the scars remain. Scars that even the Lord could not heal because they had become part of who I was. For the Lord to take away those scars would be taking away part of me that had shaped the person I had become.

It is hard even today for me to talk about this period of my life.

Some people feel very strongly that they are not cut out for this world. They think they are square pegs in round holes. That was how I felt. I resented that God had created me, allowed me to be conceived. I developed a hostile attitude to God, and yet, strangely, I still clung to the Bible. A contradiction in my life. Perhaps it gave me hope when I had nothing else to grasp at. A desperate clinging to some hope. It was as if some unknown strong power held me glued to this book.

Slowly this mental illness takes over. Some people will struggle all their life trying to fit in this world. Others will try and try. One day, sadly, they may walk into a wall and take their own life. My soul reaches out to them, for I know how it feels to be in a world at the wrong time in a wrong place.

When someone goes through such deep despair, a part of him or her dies. I became distant from everyone, including the Lord, unable to trust or share. I sank into my own little hole.

How can anyone who has a happy childhood, surrounded by a loving family, enter the mind of one who was traumatized by persecution and religious bigotry? Someone crazy enough to give up a loving family, friends for a book.

I took that decision and paid the price for it.

There are some scars that I feel will never heal properly. Not in this life. I am aware that these deep scars mar my judgment, which has become impaired, distorted. It governs the things I do. I am an imperfect being, called by Christ to be forged into perfection.

While I am aware of my weakness, I am also mindful of the beautiful gift of God: that the mind of Christ, which we have received, is clear, forceful, focused, and that as long as I follow him, I have clarity and my weakness subsides through leading of the indwelling Holy Spirit.

Galatians 2:20 *I have been crucified with Christ. It is no longer I that live, but Christ is living in me: and that life which I now live in the flesh I live in faith, the faith which is in the Son of God, who loved me and gave himself up for me.*

A disgrace to my family.

In our family, it was a difficult time for all. My parents were under duress from the community. In desperation, my father wrote to my elder brother in England and asked if I could join him.

They sent me to England to join my brother. I was a disgrace to my family and my community, and I felt utterly dejected.

At the airport, my kind and gentle mother wished me well. My father, a man I had loved and adored, stood at a distance, still avoiding any eye contact. My father, who had taught me so much about caring for the weak, now stood apart. A gulf had developed that would last until he passed away.

He was like a stranger to me, someone I now feared—someone I wanted to flee from.

Years later, when I had children, I started to realize the pain and anguish I had brought upon a wonderful father. In my youth, he had cherished me, delighted at my being, but I had destroyed all that. My action, my faith, and the reaction of the community had heaped years on him.

Matthew 19:29 And everyone who has left houses or brothers or sisters or father or mother or children or fields will receive a hundredfold and inherit eternal life for my name's sake.

God may be able to give a hundred-fold, but what's taken away, destroyed, is gone forever. There is no way that the hurt I inflicted on my father/mother or the anguish they felt can be mended. Perhaps in the hereafter, they may be compensated, or restitution made a hundredfold. Nevertheless, how can you replace a broken heart? What was it all for? So, I could read a book.

England. A beautiful country: one big garden with green pastures and rolling hills.

Mid-august 1972, I arrived in England. I was 18. My brother was warm, welcoming, kind and supported me until I could stand on my own feet. He encouraged me to join a polytechnic and enrol for a three-year technical Engineering course.

The words of the Bible and Bhagavad-Gita gave me hope while the flame of life in me was dying. These books were like a pilot light, keeping the flame alive. One of the reasons I wrote this book was that it might give others hope in times of despair and, when they are more robust, they may reach out to others.

--- ----

Chapter 10– Early Life

During British colonial rule, I was born in Kenya when the Mau Mau rebellion was beginning. A traumatic time in Kenya's history.

My parents were from Gujarat, India. They had settled in Kenya. My father migrated to Kenya around 1938. At the end of World War II, he returned to India looking for a wife. My great grandparents had migrated to Gujarat from the north. In the village, my father's family was still considered as foreigners. No one was keen to give his or her daughter to him in marriage.

In desperation, my father made a deal with a 16-year-old boy. This young boy had become head of his family when his father passed away. He sold groceries from a small stall in the village and just about managed to keep his family alive. The deal was that my father would marry his 12-year-old sister, but she would stay with her brother until she was 16. My father would return to Africa and, when she was of age, he would come back and take her to Africa. Meanwhile, my father would send a monthly allowance to support them.

When she was 16, my father went to India to collect her. My poor mother has no recollection of their marriage. I wonder what hardship and anxieties she faced as she set off for Africa with a stranger. A year later, in 1951, my brother was born, and three years later, I was born, followed by a sister and a younger brother.

The second time my mother was pregnant, carrying me in her womb, my father had invited a priest to bless the pregnancy.

The words of the priest had a massive impact on my early life. His blessings were from Bhagavad-Gita, our Holy Book. These words were meant to be a blessing, but my father's wrong interpretation led to misery for all of us.

He told my father that the child would be exceptionally blessed. I was to be set apart for God. My hair was not to be cut until I was five. It would be a reminder to them that God had set me apart and destined me for great things.

Numbers 6:5 *'All the days of the vow of his separation, no razor shall come upon his head; until the days are fulfilled for which he separated himself to the LORD, he shall be holy.*

My father was an intelligent man. He wanted to be a doctor, but the opportunity never came his way. My grandfather sent him to East Africa to earn a living when he was 19 years old. With no family around, my parents struggled to make a decent living for most of their life.

When he heard the priest, he assumed I was meant to be a doctor. My brothers and sisters had an easier time. From an early age, I had to learn the Hindu Vedic religious customs. At the weekend, while my siblings played, I sat in front of a priest and learnt the Vedic teachings and the Bhagavad-Gita.

My father taught me to read and write before I was ready for school. I could read English, Hindi, and Gujarati by the age of four. I was my father's favourite. He would let me cuddle up to him until I fell asleep. Then he would take me to my room; gently lay me on my bed. There was a glow of radiant happiness on his face. He had wanted to be a doctor, but I would fulfil his dreams.

First day at school

On my first day at school, my father walked with me to the school gate. He stopped, stooped down, and looked me in the eyes.

'I want you to study well. You are going to be a great man, a great doctor. The priest said you would change many people's lives.' They were prophetic words, which would happen, but not in the way he had meant.

At this stage of my life, I adored my father. I just nodded and held his warm hand. He squeezed it.

My father had enrolled me early in school in his keenness to see me educated. I was underage, and I was smaller than the other children. At PE, even the girls did better than I did. They outran me. I was teased.

Academically I did not fare well either. My father accepted this since I was the youngest in my year group.

A thief in our house

I was about eight when, one day, my mother caught me stealing biscuits from the larder. Money was tight, and there were days when we went hungry. My mother used to bake biscuits and store them in a tall tin in the larder. Occasionally, she would give us some biscuits as a reward for being good, but the biscuits were for guests for the most part.

I was hungry, and I stole some biscuits. The next day I did it again. I knew if my mother opened the tin, she would notice it, so I got some paper, stuffed it at the bottom of the container, and re-filled the container with the biscuits. A few days later, we had guests. My mother opened the tin and noticed the paper. When the guests had gone, my mother was fuming. She looked at my siblings and me. Her face red with fury, she demanded to know who had been so wicked. My legs shaking, I confessed.

She bent down so she could look me in the eyes. **'One day,' she fumed, 'you will stand before God and account for your actions. You'd better change your ways while you have time.'** *Bhagavad –Gita Ch 11:25. I see your fearful nature with your wide-open mouth afire, swallowing the whole cosmos. O Lord, the refuge of the Universe, be gracious to me and have mercy upon me on that fearsome day (Judgment Day).*

It was a rebuke I would never forget.

This child has additional needs

In the last year of primary school, my exasperated teacher marched me to the head teacher's room just before the lunch break. This happened a few weeks before the final exams, which would determine which secondary school I would be eligible for.

My teacher said, 'this child is a retard (has additional needs). I don't know what to do with him. I don't want to take the blame if he fails his exams. I want to warn his father.'

50

He demanded the head call my father from his work. My father came. There was a big argument between the two teachers and my father.

At that tender age, I knew I did not have the high intelligence, good memory, and other skills required to be a doctor — something my father could not grasp. He was tall, good-looking, extremely bright, and had all the qualities to be a fine doctor, though that opportunity had not come his way.

I did achieve enough grades to make it to the local secondary school. There, my results improved, and my father's hopes ignited. Perhaps the prophet was right.

By now, I had physically caught up with the rest of the children. I was very good at sport and won trophies on sports days. I excelled at volleyball, cricket, and athletics. However, academically I was average — I had improved from being called 'a retard.' Nevertheless, there were no signs of me being a doctor.

Butcher's Shop

I was about ten years old when, one day, I walked past a new shop on my way to school. Someone had opened a butcher's shop. We were vegetarian from a Hindu community and brought up to respect all living things, especially animals. We did not eat meat, fish, or animal products like eggs.

Bhagavad-Gita 3:30. Arjuna, fix your mind on me and surrender all your works unto me. Fulfil my divine plan to improve the welfare, interest, and happiness of all creatures. Do it without any desire for personal gain.

I looked at the dead carcasses of the animals. I remember crying as I walked to school. Why would God allow innocent animals to suffer, to have their throats cut?

On the other side of our school fence lay the wilderness. There was an underground spring where all the wild wildebeest, zebra, and antelope came during the dry season. A few days later, I walked up to the spring. As I gazed at the herds of wild animals, I was angry (*Why?*). *Bhagavad —*

Gita 5:7. They that follow the path of selfless service, who are pure in soul and control their senses and mind, see the divine in all creatures. 6:30. I am ever-present to those who have realized me in every creature. Seeing all life as my manifestation, they are never separated from me.

I was angry. I cried out, 'If there is a God, I will make him accountable for all the suffering and the pain in this world.' This cry has been at the core of my spiritual drive and reflected in much of my writing.

I believe he heard my cry, and over the years, he has sought to respond via visions and other means. He has tried to bridge the gap, to make amends. **Amos 3:3,** *Do two walk together unless they have agreed to do so?*

Give me a man of God

One whose faith is master of his mind,

And I will right all wrong

And bless all.

Meeting God of Abraham and Isaac

When I got to secondary school, I became interested in reading about different faiths. I read about Hinduism, Buddhism, Islam, and Confucianism and finally read the Bible. As soon as I read the first page of the Bible, I knew this was the book for me. We lived in a Hindu community, so the Bible was my only access to Christianity for the next seven years.

My initial prayers were addressed to the God of Abraham and Isaac. I had problems with some of the Old Testament books, things to do with war and animal sacrifice. Taking any form of life was against our Hindu creed, living in harmony with all creatures.

When I read in Genesis 1:29-30 that God gave us all the green things to eat, it appealed to me. Later in Genesis 3: 21, I read the killing of animals to dress Adam and Eve. This upset me.

It affected me deeply. It still does. No innocent creature or person should pay for the wrong deeds of others. If Adam and Eve sinned, they should be made accountable and face the consequences. It was not fair that generation after generation of innocent animals and descendants of Adam and Eve should pay for their sin. It is against natural justice.

I never blindly accept the teachings of others. I am independent-minded and want to find my own answers.

Each morning and evening, I sat before the Lord and read the Bible. There were no churches or Christians around us. The Bhagavad -Gita and the Bible were my only source of God's Word.

At secondary school, my teachers made it clear that I did not have what it took to be a doctor. My father and I drifted apart. I was a big disappointment to him.

'Mtu wa Mungu.'

Two things from my secondary school have stayed in my memory. The first was when I was in my 3rd year at secondary school. It was lunchtime. Outside our class, we had our lockers. The corridor was empty. I opened my locker and took out the books I would need for the afternoon class. I felt someone behind me.

He grabbed me and locked his strong muscular arms around me. I was frightened. I could feel his heavy breathing on the back of my neck. Was someone going to rob me? I turned my face sideways and saw a big African boy, his hands holding me firmly in a tight grip. His dark face was smiling.

My heart was thumping hard. I tried to appear calm. I did not have anything in my pockets. Fight or run; I did not have either option.

I was praying someone would come down the corridor and break the stalemate. The stranger whispered in my ears, *'Mtu wa Mungu,'* in Swahili – 'A man of God'. Then he released me and walked away. I breathed in relief. I don't recall ever seeing him at our school. The words he spoke have stayed in my memory. It's a strange thing to say to a stranger. --- 🕸 ----

Chapter 11– "Vengeance is mine; I will repay, says the Lord."

Romans 12:19 Beloved, never avenge yourselves, but leave room for the wrath of God; for it is written, "Vengeance is mine, I will repay, says the Lord."

A few days later, two school bullies cornered me in an empty lobby. As I walked past them, one of them gave me a mocking smile. I ignored him. The smaller of the two boys, who was in my class, blocked me. He hurled a four-letter word at me. I was scared. They saw the fear on my face and took great pleasure in it.

The bigger boy grabbed me and locked his arms around me in a tight hold. The other boy was laughing as he hurled more insults at me. The big boy put one hand around my private parts and started to pinch them while he held me with the other arm. They were both laughing as I struggled to get free.

Then the big boy kicked me in the back, and I staggered forward, fell to the ground. They laughed and walked away. I didn't sleep all night, dreading another confrontation with them at school. The next day I stayed close to my friends. Again, that night, I had trouble sleeping.

The following day at lunchtime, a few boys from my class had gathered around. They were solemn. I asked one of the boys what the matter was. He said two boys from our school had died in an accident. A day after they had bullied me, they were dead.

Usually, I would have said it was a coincidence. Over the years, as I reviewed my diaries and went over events where people had mistreated me, I began to see a pattern of disasters following these people. I began to realize why the Lord said to pray for those that persecute you.

Matthew 5:44, *but I say unto you, love your enemies, and pray for them that persecute you.*

Mark 9:42, *But whoever causes one of these little ones who believe in Me to stumble, it would be better for him if a millstone were hung around his neck, and* *he were thrown into the sea.*

Desperate cry for help

When I was in primary school, I was usually last in races. I was a year to eighteen months younger than the rest of the children in my class. By the time I was 15 years old and ready for my O-level exams, I had caught up with the others and started to win prizes on sports day. I had won the first prize in the javelin, second in discus and third price in two other events.

I passed my O-level exams and enrolled for the A-levels. By now, I was stronger than many of the boys. I excelled at cricket and volleyball.

However, home life was traumatic. Reading the Bible had cost me the support of my parents and extended family. Everyone had stopped talking to me, apart from my sister. Losing the emotional support of my family and neighbours had traumatized me. I started to get into trouble with my teachers. I began to be defiant. Teachers suspended me a few times from classes.

There were two other boys like me having difficulties at home. They were strong and well built, and we started to bully others. We enjoyed intimidating the teachers. We were expelled from a class; the next day, the teacher would find his car tyres sliced. They soon got the message to leave us alone.

We had girls at school, and we bullied them. One particular pretty girl that I fancied got the worst of my bullying.

I am ashamed of that period in my life, especially as I knew what it felt like to be bullied. We rebelled, but it was a desperate cry for help. Our inward traumas were coming out negatively, and it was hurting others and us.

Years later, I brought this shameful period of my life before the Lord. I was genuinely ashamed of my conduct. I regretted the hurt I had caused people. From this sad episode of my life, the Lord would teach me one of my two central tenets in life, Zak's and King David's Tenets: sensitivity to other people's needs and to respect others.

Consequences of Reading the Bible

My parents knew I read the Bible. At first, they said nothing, but as I reached my early teens, the word spread in the community that I was reading the Bible, and pressure began to mount on me to give it up. I started to get the cold shoulder from my uncles and the community.

My parents faced hostility from our neighbours. My uncles were concerned. If I continued to read the Bible, my family would lose favour in the community. Once again, no one would give their sons or daughters in marriage to our family. My parents were concerned about my younger sister and brother. An arranged marriage by parents was still part of our culture.

My father had worked hard to be accepted into the Hindu community. Once someone had opened a door for him to marry into the community, it opened the doors for his brothers and sisters to find partners. It was a hard-won victory. Now my conversion to Christianity put all that in jeopardy.

My youngest uncle, called Banu, was most vocal. He had two young daughters and was concerned about their marriage prospects. He was furious at the thought of me reading the bible and jeopardising our good standing in the community.

My parents were caught in a difficult situation. They wanted to protect me, but they needed to look after my siblings' affairs as well. I was too young to understand the difficulties I had placed them in.

They tried to persuade me to give up reading the Bible. In frustration, they stopped talking to me. To appease our neighbours, they told them I was a hot-headed, rebellious teenager, unwilling to listen to anyone. Only my younger sister stood by me.

Eventually, the pressure from the community was too much for my father to bear. He sent me to join my older brother in the UK.

My Uncle Banu

Years later, his life would take a drastic twist. He joined a Hindu order and became devoted to the study of Vedic books. He, who had once persecuted me vehemently, would proudly sit with me and spend all night in a discussion about the workings of the Holy Spirit. He was Hindu, yet his knowledge about the Holy Spirit gained from Hindu Holy Vedic books was profound. He could speak on a level that would put most Christian ministers to shame.

He had read the gospels, and he would point out God's duality in Bhagavad-Gita and the New Testament. *John 1:1-3, In the beginning, was the <u>Word</u>, and the <u>Word</u> was with God, and the <u>Word was God</u>. He was in the beginning with God. All things were made through Him, and without Him, nothing was made that was made.*

*Behaved-Gita ch 8:3. In my imperishable nature, Brahman (Word) resides the breath of life, and it resides in every creature as the highest self, atman. With my blessing, <u>Brahman (Word)</u> is the creator and giver of life. 13:12. They know what knowledge is needed to gain **eternal life**. Eternal life is to know the Supreme Lord and his subordinate, Brahman (Word), one who is without beginning and said to be neither being nor non-being. 13:17. Brahman's breath of life, bequeathed to him from the Supreme Lord, dwells in all. It is the source of knowledge, light, and life to all. Unity with Brahman and the Lord should be the object and goal of all.*

---- ----

Chapter 12 – College

In August 1972, I flew from Kenya to join my brother in London. He encouraged me to join a college. I applied and was accepted into a three-year technical course.

The first year of polytechnic was a remarkable period. No longer under the gaze of my father, I did well. During the summer holidays, I worked in a factory. At the end of the summer holidays, I got a letter from the polytechnic. Now that I was 19 years old, I had to pay for college fees. My brother could not afford it. I applied for full-time work with a couple of electronic companies. I managed to secure employment from the telephone company.

While my friends returned to the polytechnic for their second year, I began work. I kept in touch with my friends. Months passed, and soon it was mid-spring. I had passed my probation period at work and nearly finished my training. Meanwhile, my friends were getting ready for their final exams for the second year.

My brother went to India for a holiday and came back with his bride. He had an arranged marriage.

London house prices were outside their scope, so they moved to Leicester, and I lodged with some friends of his in London.

One evening the words of the Lord came to me. 'Apply for the third year.'

'But Lord, how can I enrol for the third year without having done the second year?'

I just trusted the Lord. I applied for the third year. I took my application directly to the head of the electronic department.

He was a kind, fair-minded person. He asked me a few questions. He said if I sat for the 2nd year exams with the others and passed all three exams, he would enrol me for the third year.

I sat for the exams. I passed two out of three, and he allowed me into the third year.

At work, I applied for unpaid time off during the college term. My supervisor sent my application to the head office. The polytechnic started, and no one at head office had yet opened my file.

My boss shrugged his shoulders and said, 'Go to college. I will sort out your leave.'

I went to the college during term-time and returned to work during the college holidays. My wages were paid during my time off. I was nearly 21 years old when I finished at the polytechnic.

A house

The Lord said to me, 'I have taken you through college. I have kept my word. I want you to start collecting money for a house.'

I started collecting. A year later, I had a small deposit to buy a house. I started looking for a little place to buy. My brother rang me. He asked, 'Are you thinking of buying a house? If you are, I have a proposition for you. You know, Mother and Father have come here from Canada and are staying with me. They are looking for a temporary place to stay before they migrate back to India. Could they stay with you for a few months?'

I hesitated.

He went on, 'Father is willing to give you some money towards your deposit.'

I accepted the money. A few months later, I had a bigger deposit for a three-bedroom house. I found a house in North London, and my offer was accepted, but six weeks later, the sale fell through. I started looking for another small home. A few days went by.

One day I went to a Greek estate agent in Finsbury Park. He showed me a small house in poor condition in a rough area of North London, just within my price bracket.

I was concerned about repairs. He stood beside me and asked me how much deposit I had. I told him.

'Come,' he said, 'get in my car. I will show you a house you will like.' He took me to a nicer part of North London. He showed me a well-kept large terraced six-bedroom three-reception, two bathrooms Victorian house with a cellar and a large garden.

We went around the house. He gave me ample time to inspect it on my own. I loved this gorgeous house, but it well outside my pay scale. It was about four in the afternoon as I stood in the hallway. There was a skylight on the roof. The golden sun streamed through the skylight, filling the hallway.

I was speechless. I could not afford it. I stood in the big hallway with this golden light coming through the skylight. Then I heard the Lord ask, 'Do you like it? I want you to have this house.'

'Lord, you know I cannot afford it.' I was shaking my head. I said to myself, *I am imagining this. I am so desperate to have this house; I can almost imagine the Lord's wishing me to buy this house!*

I was so preoccupied with my thoughts that I had not noticed the Greek Estate agent walk up to me. "Well, what do you think? You like it?" He asked. The estate agent placed his hand on my shoulder. "I see you like this house. Come with me to my office, and we will get all the papers sorted out."

We went to his office, and I signed some papers. I was young and naive. I have no idea what they were. He asked me for a small deposit to secure the house.

He gave me a receipt and said, 'The house is yours. It will take a few weeks for the paperwork to go through.' He shook my hand and said, 'and you can have all the furniture in it as well.'

A few weeks later, in the summer of 1976, I moved into my new home. The Greek estate agent handled the repairs required by the bank and had the outside windows re-painted.

It was a gorgeous house, fully furnished with bed linen, beds, curtains, carpets, kitchen units, all the utensils, even a kettle, plates, knives and forks. All I brought with me was a small bag of clothes and a toothbrush.

The first few nights, I could hardly sleep. I was alone in this big house in London, not even 23 years old yet. Was I the owner of this fantastic house?

A few months later, my parents moved in. They had the upper two-bed flat, and I had the ground floor 2-bed flat with two extra rooms on the mezzanine floor. It was a beautiful house with a large garden. It was a perfect fit for us. Had the Lord started a process of reconciliation within my family?

Colossians 1:20, *And through him to* <u>*reconcile*</u> *all things to himself, whether on earth or in heaven, having made peace through the blood of his cross.*

I felt the Lord had kept his word. It was time to join a church. I joined the local Haringey congregational church.

Unauthorised leave.

A few months after I had moved into my new home, my boss called me into his office. He asked me to sit down.

He said, "I have bad news. Head office has found your application for polytechnic leave. The paperwork has just surfaced after two years. No one had approved your leave! The accounts department has no idea how they could have paid you without your timesheets."

He was embarrassed. "Hari, you have to pay back the money you received during your leave. Since it was their fault, they have suggested you pay back half of the money. They suggest you pay back in small amounts from your salary each month for the next two years."

I agreed.

Forty-two years later

On my 6th sabbatical year, as I reviewed my diaries, I noticed that I had moved into the house when I was 22 years and 9 months old. My earlier offer on a 3-bedroom property was accepted, but the seller had pulled out later on. Had it gone through, it would have been my home by the age of twenty-two and a half, as the Lord had said.

Did the Lord view the 3-bedroom house as a gross error on my part and overrule it?

My offer on the bigger house was accepted just before I was twenty-two and a half, but the completion took a few more weeks, three months longer than what the Lord had stated.

I thought about this. Something the Lord had said came to mind.

In Jan 2017, while I was reviewing my diaries, I had noted another matter.

Hari's Tenet 3; The Lord said, 'Hari, sometimes, to take a loss can be the right thing to do. Your word gave him solace. Breaking someone's misplaced trust (faith in you, expectation) should not be done if you can absorb the pain (loss). Your actions should not cause wounds and scars if you can help it.'

Hari's Tenet 4. (Genesis 9:11 And I will establish my covenant with you). Lord, 'Because you have been obedient before me, I will honour your misplaced expectations even at a loss to me. I corrected the errors during your Heart and hip operations.

What could I learn from this? Had I made an error in choosing the 3-bed house, and the Lord had corrected it, but it meant a delay in house acquisition?

On the other hand, had he taken the date of my offer accepted by the Greek estate agent on the more significant property as fulfilling his time limit?

---- ----

Chapter 13 – Church

John 14:12 *"Most assuredly, I say to you, he who believes in Me, the works that I do he will do also; and greater works than these he will do, because I go to My Father.*

1976-1989 N London. Haringey congregational church, St James Church and Baptist church in Muswell Hill.

This is our birthright: to be able to do what **Jesus did**[1] and more.

I spent 14 years in North London. The gist of what the Lord God taught me was, 'Walk in the spirit, follow the Holy Spirit's lead. I will breathe over the verses of the Bible, and they will come alive. You will state when prayers will be answered, what day and time events will happen. You will pray for particular things as the Holy Spirit leads you.

Lord continued, 'that is the simple part: to state the day and time, work my servants, the Old Testament prophets, did. Even **Balaam's donkey**[2] could prophesy. It is no great achievement.' The Lord God continued, 'A lot more is expected from you. You are the **heir**.[3] The Holy Spirit and I will teach you to make things happen. You will do all the things I did and greater because we are with you. When you have learnt this, you will show others the way.'

It took me decades to do this, and I am still learning. I pray that by reading my testimony, the Lord God will be able to open up your

---- ☆ ----

[1] *John 14:12, "Most assuredly, I say to you, he who believes in Me, the works that I do he will do also; and greater works than these he will do, because I go to My Father.*

[2] *Numbers 22:21-34 And Jehovah opened the mouth of the donkey, and she said unto Balaam, What have I done unto thee, that thou hast smitten me these three times?*

[3] *Galatians 4:7, so you are no longer a slave but a child, and if a child then also an **heir**, through God. ...x..x...*

understanding, and inspire you to claim your rich inheritance in Christ, rather than let you settle at the spiritual level Balaam's donkey achieved.

This is our birthright: to be able to do what Jesus did, and we have to claim it. Of course, you could choose to be like **Esau**[4] and sell your birthright.

...x..x...

[4] *Genesis 25:33 And Jacob said, Swear to me this day; and he sware unto him: and he **sold his** birthright unto Jacob.*

---- ✿ ----

Chapter 14 - My Problems with many of the church's teachings.

I had read the Bible since I was 12 years of age. Years of isolation had formed my unique biblical thinking, not shaped by centuries of church teaching.

As soon as I stepped into the church, I had problems with many of the church's teachings; I was uncomfortable with Christmas, Easter, Lent. There is no mention of them in the Bible. Why do we have to kneel or always close our eyes when we pray? In the *Psalms 123:1, Unto You, I lift up my eyes, O You who dwell in the heavens.*

Why don't we pray with open eyes like the psalmist? I do it all the time and people in the church find it discomforting.

Messiah

A big problem for me in the church was its teachings about the trinity. It says in *1 Corinthians 8:6, for us there is one God, the Father, from whom are all things and for whom we exist, and one Lord, Jesus Christ, through whom are all things and through whom we exist.*

In Africa, I had read the Old Testament many times over. The thought of one God was firmly established in my thinking. *Exodus 34:14, For you shall worship no other god: for the LORD, whose name is Jealous, is a jealous God.*

In Bhagavad-Gita (Hinduism) and Islam, there is one Supreme Being. The idea of a trinity troubles me.

Walk around obstacles.

Rather than make this an obstacle for me, I tend to walk around it until the Lord, in his own time, decides to reveal the truth. Other obstacles I have chosen to walk around.

Messiah.

Like many Jews, after reading the Old Testament, I waited for the coming of the Messiah. When I read the New Testament, I took to heart the concept of Jesus as the **Messiah.**[1]

Matthew 16:20 *Then he warned his disciples not to tell anyone that he was the* **Messiah.**

John 4:25, *The woman said to Him, "I know that Messiah is coming" (who is called Christ). "When He comes, He will tell us all things." v26 Jesus said to her, "I who speak to you am* **He.***"*

Jesus himself claimed to be Messiah. Yet, I have never heard a sermon on Jesus as the Messiah.

The term 'Trinity' was a problem for me. It came from the church's teachings, but I could not find it in the Bible.

Seven-day creation

Another big, controversial issue: evolution or seven-day creation? I do not have an answer.

I have seen our Lord, angels, things in Heaven and predicted to the day and hour something that will happen in the future. I have given some examples that are contrary to the laws of physics. Science cannot explain such phenomena.

Therefore, what is relevant for me is to follow our Lord's teachings, to unleash the power of his words and for the Holy Spirit to transform me as stated in the Bible. It is not to change the world but to change me and release that power to assist others.

The Bible and some of my personal experiences are things that the laws of physics cannot explain. The teachings of the Bible have worked well for me.

---- ☆ ----

[1] *John 20:31 (NRSV) But these are written so that you may come to believe that Jesus is the* **Messiah,** *the Son of God and that through believing you may have life in his name.*

[1] *Matthew 1:18 Now, the birth of Jesus the* **Messiah** *took place in this way.*
...x..x...

66

In the Universe, we have Black Holes where the laws of physic do not apply. Scientists are willing to explore this area and believe in quantum mechanisms that have laws outside our knowledge of physic. Why not use the same open mind to explore walking in spirit?

A foolish person ignores things he does not understand and chooses to live in ignorance.

Challenged. 'How does this apply to me?'

When I read a passage from the Bible, my mind would be challenged. How does this apply to me? Am I willing to give the Holy Spirit the time to bring this passage to life and change me?

When Moses stood before the burning bush *(Acts 7: 33 Exodus 3: 5), the Lord said, 'Do not come any closer. Take off your sandals, for the place where you are standing is holy ground.'*

In the church, when we pray, the Bible says, *Matthew 18: 20, 'where two or three come together in my name, there am I with them.'*

In my biblical thinking, where the Lord is, the ground is holy. He doesn't need to tell me at home or in the church to remove my sandals. He waits and watches to see how I respond to his written words.

Therefore, when I pray, I remove my shoes. It is simple; I believe I stand before the Lord on holy ground/presence. It is also a mark of respect and acknowledgement that the Lord is present. Fortunately, our church was small. I was the only person to remove my shoes, and after a while in a prayer meeting, a few other people did the same.

Wait upon the Lord.

Another problem I had at church was prayers. The bible says *Matthew 6: 8, For* your Father knows the things you have need of before you ask Him.

Shouldn't we listen for an answer instead of bringing before him a long shopping list of needs?

Each morning and evening, I read the Bible for about ten minutes, then

I prayed. I thought, 'the Lord knows what I need, so I will ask, to clarify in my mind what I want, and then wait patiently for fifteen minutes.' I wanted a clear answer. Just as my mother would answer; she would clearly say yes, no, or something specific.

In my early days, my thinking was that I should hear him if I am in God's presence. Daily, I waited for an answer. I didn't hear anything. I had a pen and paper ready to write down his reply. Months went by, and nothing happened. The page remained blank. The temptation was always there to pray and walk away, and the lure got stronger and stronger as time went by.

I was determined, so I kept quiet and waited and waited.

Finally, after months of waiting, I saw him in a vision. He started to speak clearly with precise instructions: names, dates, times, and my life changed. I prophesied dates and times when people would be healed and tested these prophecies' accuracy in others' presence in my public prayers. If what I said was not from the Lord but my imagination, it would put me to shame and ridicule.

I have given some examples in earlier chapters.

Deuteronomy 4:29, and if you search for him with <u>all your heart and soul</u>, you will find him.

---- 🕉 ----

Chapter 15 – Judgment Day

Acts 2:17 & Joel 2:28, And it shall come to pass afterwards, that I will pour out my Spirit upon all flesh; and your sons and your daughters shall prophesy, your old men shall dream dreams, your young men shall see visions:

The Lord has to breathe over the scriptures to give them life; otherwise, they are dormant seeds.

One of my earliest visions, which would have a lasting effect on me, was based on the above verse.

Vision. Early in 1977. I had recently joined Rev Hammond's church. I was coming home from work. Specific thoughts flashed through my mind. A voice seemed to speak to me.

'Mortal man, lift your eyes and tell me what you see.'

'Sir,' I said, 'I see before me a multitude of people as far as the eye can see. They come from every nation, every race.'

'Tell me, o mortal man, what do you see now?'

'I see vessels of gold, silver, and precious stones all around me.'

He put a shield around me. Then he went and stood in the middle of the vessels. There was a flash of light. From the centre of him shot out four arrows of brilliant light.

Each travelled straight and fast. The centre of the light started to glow, and the intensity was unbearable.

The shield seems to protect me.

Suddenly the light faded. The shield was removed. The Lord stood before me.

'Tell me, what do you see now?'

I walked around where the vessels used to be. I began to cry. I picked up the ashes in my hand.

'Why do you cry?'

'Sir,' I said, 'that which was precious only a short time ago has become ash. That which I thought were vessels of gold and silver have burnt to reveal that its substance was false. The fire has burnt it.'

'Count the vessels that remain.'

There were three very poor gold sticks, reaching my waist—five sticks of silver and a few precious stones.

That Sunday, I was distraught. So much so that I went to Rev Jim Hammond and told him about this vision.

He took out his sermon from his pocket and **showed**[1] me.

The title was, 'Vessels of Gold, silver and precious stones.'

I shared this vision with the church, and Mr Hammond preached about gold and silver vessels.

Soon after these visions, things started to happen. Healing begun to take place in our church. People would have scans showing cancer or gall bladder stones.

During the week, people in need would ring Mr Hammond and make known their prayer requests. He would compare the verses I had received with his prepared sermon. He would wait upon the Lord to get instruction as to what to pray for and when.

At midweek prayer meetings or in Sunday services, one of us would prayer, often stating a date and time for the healing. When the people went to the hospital for scans or tests before their operations, these illnesses would have gone.

Other times, people would ask for prayer for work or for their mortgages to go through. We would state which interview would result in a job offer

---- ☆ ----

[1] *2 Corinthians 13:1, In the mouth of two or three witnesses shall every word be established. ...x..x...*

or the amount of mortgage the bank would lend. If the mortgage offer were low, it would give people time to work overtime and gather a bigger deposit. God was very real to all of us.

Prayers became joyful. I could not wait to get home from work for the next revelation and write it down in my books. I would get all excited and long for the mid-week bible study or Sunday service to confirm the disclosure.

Review of this vision on my 6th Sabbatical year

Every seventh year, I would open my diaries and review all my work from the previous years.

I had assumed the three gold and five silver vessels were members of our church. Forty-two years later, when I reviewed my diary, the Lord showed me that the numbers had a completely different meaning. I am glad I made notes and gave the Lord the time to feed and weed his teaching.

Change in my conduct.

Prayer was also a time when the Lord started to correct my conduct. One day in the evening prayer, as I was going over the day with the Lord, I gave an account of my time. I had put up some new curtains in my bedroom. I thanked the Lord for the money to buy the curtains. I was delighted with my work.

As I slept, I felt uneasiness around me. These scriptures started to come alive. *Luke 16:10* "*Whoever is faithful in a very little is faithful also in much; and whoever is dishonest in a very little is dishonest also in much.*

Luke 16:12 *And if you have not been faithful with what belongs to another, who will give you what is your own?*

I had a box of screws in my work toolbox. I had used these to put up the curtain poles. These screws belonged to my employer. That weekend I bought a box of screws and replaced the screws I had used. From that day, I made sure that I utilised nothing from my employer for my personal use. ---- ☆ ----

Early 1977   The Judgement Day   Received on way home on Wightman Rd about 5pm

If I recollect properly it was as I was coming from work one evening (I think Thursday) I was caught up in thoughts flashing through my mind. A voice seem to speak through me.

"Mortal man, Lift up your eyes and tell me what you see."

"Sir," I said, "I see before me multitudes of people as far as the eye can see. They come from every nation, every race."

This person put a shield round me

"Tell me O mortal man what you see."

"I see vessels of Gold, silver and precious stones all around me."

There was quitness as this person went and stood in the middle. There was flosh of light. From the centre shot out four arrows of brilliant light

Each travelled straight and fast. The centre started to glow and the intensity was unbearable. The shield seam to protect me.

Suddenly the light faded. The shield was removed. This person came to me.

"Mortal man walk around and

72

tell me what you see."

I walked round where the vessels used to be. I began to cry. I picked up the ashes in my hand.

"Why do you cry?"

"Sir," I said, "That which was only a short time ago alive has become ash. That which I thought was vessels of Gold and Silver has burnt to reveal that it was only outwardly Gold and Silver. It's real substance was unreal. The fire has burnt it."

"Count the vessels that remain."

There were three very poor sticks of Gold reaching up to my waist. Five sticks

of silver and a few precious stones.

That Sunday I was very troubled in my Spirit. So much so that I went to Jim Hammond (lay) and told him about this vision.

He took out his Sermon from his pocket and showed me. The Title was

"Vessels of Gold, Silver and precious stones 6/6/11 five sticks. At that time I thought they were members of our church. Years later, they would on my Sabbatical review, shed new light to its meaning.

---- ❦ ----

73

Chapter 16 – The Final Judgment

Forty two years later.

Jeremiah 30:2, "Thus speaks the LORD God of Israel, saying: 'Write in a book for yourself all the words that I have spoken to you.

At the end of my 6th sabbatical year, I finished an account of my past few years, starting from the day the Lord had called me to the present. I put my dairies and my books away. I had given him an **account**[1] of every word, prayer, church meeting, and house group I had visited. All logged in my dairies and updated every 7th year. I accounted to the best of my ability for all the people I had come across. I asked the Lord what he wanted me to do.

The Lord said, 'Come follow me,' meaning in a vision. I followed him. It was **Judgment Day**[2], my second vision of Judgment Day.

I stood before his throne.

The Lord said, 'You will give me an **account of your life,**[3] of every idle word, of every prayer and your time (hour by hour, day by day). I will examine the result of all your church sermons and Bible studies, one by one. What did you do with your life? And I will test its **fruit**[4]. I will require an account of it all this day.'

--- ☆ ---

[1] *Ecclesiastes 12:14, For God will bring every work into judgment, with every hidden thing, whether it be good or whether it be evil.*

[1] *Matthew 12:36 And I say unto you, that every idle word that men shall speak, they shall give account thereof in the Day of Judgment.*

[2] *2 Corinthians 5:10 For we must all be made manifest before the judgment-seat of Christ; that each one may receive the things done in the body, according to what he hath done, whether it be good or bad.*

[3] *Hebrews 9:27, And inasmuch as it is appointed unto men once to die, and after this cometh judgment;*

[4] *Colossians 1:28, Him we preach, warning every man and teaching every man in all wisdom, that we may present every man perfect in Christ Jesus. ...x..x...*

I knelt, fixed my eyes on the ground, and started with the day he had called me. 'Lord, the day you called me, I–.'

The Holy Spirit stopped me. 'Hari, we have already gone through that, every day, morning, and night, hour by hour. Every seventh month and seventh year. You gave me an account of your time and deeds, and I **guided**[5] you, rebuked you and corrected your ways. All according to the requirements of the scriptures and according to the ways of the Lord.

'You worked hard and **amended**[6] your ways as you walked under my guidance. You are only required to give an account of the last three hours. These are the only hours unaccounted for.'

I gave an account of these missing hours.

Fruit of your work

Books[7] were opened, and the divine fire **tested**[8] all my works. When the fire died down, I walked on the ashes. The fire had burned most of my works, but the months, years spent accounting had given the Holy Spirit the chance to rebuke me, guide, correct and amend my ways. The things he had taught me, the scripture he had breathed upon, had come

--- ☆ ---

[5] John 16:13, However, when the Spirit of truth comes, he will _guide you into all truth_: for he will not speak on his own; but whatever he hears, he will say: and he will _show you things to come._

[6a] Jeremiah 26:13 "Now, therefore, _amend_ your ways and your doings, and obey the voice of the LORD your God; then the LORD will relent concerning the doom that He has pronounced against you.

[6b] Romans 8:14, For those who are _being led by the Spirit_ of God, are the sons of God.

[7] Daniel 7:10 A fiery stream issued and came forth from before him: thousands of thousands ministered unto him, and ten thousand times ten thousand stood before him: the _judgment was set,_ and the _books were opened._

[8] Revelation 20:12 And I saw the dead, small and great, stand before God. The _books were opened_: and another book was opened, which is the book of life: and the dead were judged according to _what they had done,_ as written in the _books._
...x..x...

alive to change my ways and the ways of others. The Holy Spirit had led me to take every thought captive to obey Christ.

With the Holy Spirit's help, the accounting and the prayers we had upheld for my "Patches (my parishes)" were put on the fire. Every atom, grain of sand, leaf, soul, we supported in the morning and the evening prayers passed through the **test of the fire**[9] and now lay as works of gold worthy of his calling.

'Come,' said the Lord, 'stand on my right. You are my witness of the high quality of workmanship required to pass through the **gate**[10] into the New Jerusalem.

If I can achieve this, so can others.'

--- ☆ ---

[9] *1 Corinthians 3:13 His work will be shown for what it is: for the day will bring it to light because it will be tested by fire; and the fire will reveal the quality of each man's work of what sort it is.*

[10] *Revelation 22:14 Blessed are those who do His commandments, that they may have the right to the tree of life, and may enter through the gates into the city.*

Chapter 17– Vision of a Garden

Acts 10:-3-4 About the ninth hour of the day, he saw clearly in a vision an angel of God coming in and saying to him, "Cornelius!" When Cornelius observed him, he was afraid and said, "What is it, lord?" He said, "Your prayers and your alms have come up for a memorial before God."

One evening I was sitting in my room. It was late afternoon, the sun shone through the window, and the room began to fill with a haze. A face seemed to materialize from the window.

'F**ollow me[1]**,' he said. 'What you see is a **vision[2]**, one which will change your life.'

We travelled through the tunnel and came out into a **beautiful garden[3]**, a clear stream running through the middle of it. We sat on the bank of the **stream[4]**. From the opposite side, a **majestic lion[5]** strolled towards us.

The Angel said, 'This is the garden of prayer. You will dwell here. This is your home. There are **no tools[6]** here. You will use the scriptures as your

--- ☆ ---

[1] *Ezekiel 34:15, I myself will be the shepherd of my sheep, and I will make them lie down, says the Lord GOD.*

[2] *Acts 18:9 Now the Lord spoke to Paul in the night by a vision, "Do not be afraid, but speak, and do not keep silent;*

[3-4] *Psalms 23:2 He makes me lie down in green pastures: he leads me beside the still waters.*

[5] *Isaiah 11:6, The wolf will live with the lamb, the leopard will lie down with the baby goat; and a little child will lead a calf, a young lion, and a fattened animal. V7: and the lion will eat straw like the ox.*

[5] *Hosea 2:18 And in that day will I make a covenant for them with the beasts of the field, and with the birds of heaven, and with the creeping things of the ground: and I will abolish the bow and the sword and conflict from the earth. I will make it possible for them to lie down safely.*

[6] *Exodus 20:25 If you use stones to build my altar, use only natural, uncut stones. Do not shape the stones with a tool, making the altar unfit for holy use....x..x...*

tools. The **Word of God**[7] has built everything you see. Learn to use the WORD to fashion and maintain this garden.

'You will walk here as Adam did. I will not shield my **face**[8] from you. I want you to learn. I want to change you, convert you (**your thoughts**[9]), not the **world**.[10] Remember the story of Adam and Eve and what I taught you.'

'The Holy Spirit will dwell in your **body**[11]. You will learn to hear his voice and follow his guidance. He moves in a cleansed **temple**[12] of the believer.'

From that day onwards, I found myself living in two worlds. I would see things in this garden, and they would happen on Earth. I have used some examples of these in the book.

In the second vision, I saw a bird land on the Lord's shoulder. He touched her, and she fell to the ground. She was full of joy. The scripture, being

--- ☆ ---

[7] *Hebrews 11:3, By faith, we understand that the worlds were prepared by God's word so that what is seen was made from things that are not visible.*

[7] *1 Peter 1:23. Born again, not of corruptible seed but incorruptible, through God's word, which lives and abides forever.*

[8] *Ezekiel 39:29, 'And I will not hide My face from them anymore; for I shall have poured out My Spirit on the house of Israel,' says the Lord GOD.*

[9] *2 Corinthians 10:5. Casting down imaginations and every high thing that exalts itself against the knowledge of God and bringing into captivity every thought to the obedience of Christ.*

[10] *John 17:9. "I pray for them. I do not pray for the world but for those you have given Me, for they are yours.*

[11] *1 Corinthians 3:16. Do you not know that you are the temple of God and that the Spirit of God dwells in you?*

[12] *Romans 12:1, Therefore, I urge you, brethren, by the mercy of God, to present your bodies as a living sacrifice, holy, acceptable unto God, which is your reasonable service. ...x..x...*

baptized in the **spirit**[13], came to my mind. That Sunday, the sermon was about the baptism of the spirit.

In the third vision, I saw a calf ill. The Lord touched her and healed her. I shared this with Rev Hammond. He said he knew what it meant.

Two weeks later, Mr Hammond paid a visit to Miss Staking at the local hospital, he prayed for her, and she was healed of her cancer. [**Appendix 1: Miss Staking**]

--- ☆ ---

[13] *Ac 11:16, "Then I remembered the word of the Lord, how He said, 'John indeed baptized with water, but you shall be baptized with the Holy Spirit.'*

Chapter 18– Armour of God

Learn to put on the armour of God. *Ephesians 6:13, Wherefore take up the whole armour of God that ye may be able to withstand in the evil day, and, having done all, to stand firm.*

What's meant by the helmet of salvation, breastplate of righteousness, the belt of truth, sandals of good news, shield of faith, and the sword of the spirit? Add to it zeal and prayers. What do these mean in practice?

I Bow down in prayer and enter the holiest of holy in Christ. **Hebrews 10:19,** *Having therefore boldness, brethren, to enter into the Holiest by the blood of Jesus.* Time to find my position and my role here.

Some questions to which I needed answers.

Why did he make me? What was in his mind before creation?

I need to pray and find out about my future place in **New Heaven.**[1]

We shall judge the **angels.**[2] How, why, when? How can we use their talents?

Why was my name in his book before the foundations of the world were **laid**[3]**?** Why did he choose me? What are his expectations? What were the selected works for me before the foundations of the earth were laid? If he chose particular good works for me, he had good reasons.

What were the reasons?

--- ☆ ---

[1] *1 Revelation 21:2 And I, John, saw the holy city, New Jerusalem, coming down from God out of Heaven, prepared as a bride adorned for her husband.*

[2] *1 Corinthians 6:3 Do you not know that we shall judge angels? How much more things that pertain to this life?*

[3] *Ephesians 1:4 just as He chose us in Him before the foundation of the world, that we should be holy and without blame before Him in love.*

...x..x...

What equipment will I need to fulfil **his calling**[4]?

James 5:7, Therefore be patient, brethren, until the coming of the Lord.

How can I learn to account for every grain of sand on my PATCH (Parish) so that when he **returns**[5], I am adequately equipped to rule with him?

To rule, I need wisdom, maturity, the ability to account and make a sound judgment that will bring fruit on Judgment Day. Every breath, every act I engage in, should be geared to get fruit on judgment day. Anything that does not bear fruit on judgment day, is wasted effort. A life wasted.

A friend of mine was an aircraft engineer. He told me every bolt, every screw in an aircraft is numbered and logged so that it is possible to trace the faulty part to the original batch of manufacture in a crash. God is a lot more thorough, and we need to follow his example. He has clothed us with the Holy Spirit to do it.

What will happen to us at the end of time? What will happen to our families? Why are we prepared to be priestly people in Christ for eternity?

Jesus said, '**Seek**[6], and you shall find, knock, and the door will be opened to you.' We are **heirs**[7], we should know all about our background, our inheritance. WE need to claim and give a good account of its use. That is

--- ☆ ---

[4] *Revelation 21:27, But nothing unclean will enter it (New Jerusalem), nor anyone who practices abomination or falsehood, but only those who are written in the Lamb's book of life.*

[5] *Revelation 1:7, Behold, He is coming with clouds, and every eye will see Him, even they who pierced Him. And all the tribes of the earth will mourn because of Him. Even so, Amen.*

[6] *Matthew 7:7, Ask, and it will be given to you; seek, and you will find; knock, and it will be opened to you.*

[7] *Romans 8:17, and if children, then heirs — heirs of God and joint-heirs with Christ, if indeed we suffer with Him, that we may also be glorified together. ...x..x...*

if we have set all our heart, mind, and strength towards God's calling. After many months of waiting upon the Lord and Holy Spirit, I had my answers, and I **build**[7] my life on it.

I started my life on assumptions about God, but those assumptions were replaced with sound scriptures and the Holy Spirit in my life as I progressed.

Return of the Lord.

If a person has no desire, expectancy, and thirst to return with the Lord, then there is no need for the Lord to train him for that journey.

The need to learn to account for every leaf; every person in their parish will have little value. Nonetheless, this is part of our inheritance, a gift of God that should be embraced with all our heart, mind, and strength.

Be prepared for hard work. The starting point is ensuring the gospel message is delivered to every householder in the local parish, not once but several times. Then on Judgment Day, stand beside our Lord and me, and testify that the gospel was preached/ made available to every home in your parish.

I did it several times while doing a demanding secular 8-5 work. Many of you are employed solely for the church.

John 17:18, "As You sent Me into the world, I also have sent them into the world.

--- ☆ ---

[7] *Luke 6:48, "He is like a man building a house, who dug deep and <u>laid the foundation on the rock.</u> And when the flood arose, the stream beat vehemently against that house and could not shake it, for it was founded on the rock. V49, But he who heard and did nothing is like a man who built a house on the earth without foundation, against which the stream beat vehemently; and immediately it fell. And the ruin of that house was great."*

Chapter 19 – What Was Required From Adam and Eve?

Lesson 1. This is the gist of what the Lord taught me. It was a start, a gold nugget that would be refined and purified as the years went by.

In the garden, Adam and Eve walked with the Lord (Genesis 2). There was no sin, and there were no people to convert. What was the Lord looking for? What kind of relationship/attitude did he want from them?

He asked me to think about this matter. 'Don't be trapped by some Christians besotted with the idea of converting others, enforcing their thoughts. They have book learning, but they lack the discipline to wait upon the Holy Spirit to bring the scriptures to life and walk in truth and holiness before **God**.

John 4:23, "But the hour is coming, and now is, when the true worshipers will worship the Father in spirit and truth; for the Father is seeking such to worship Him."

Lord, 'They will pray, but nothing will happen. You will not follow their example. I am with you, and I will honour your words.

'Ask yourself, what did I want from Adam and Eve? Seek that. I want to convert you. When I have converted you, you can help your brothers.'

Lesson 2. Sometimes, when I prayed, a passage from the Bible would open up to me with a new light. For example, on reading **Gen 3: 6-13,** the story about Adam and Eve and how they disobeyed God.

Genesis 3:8, And they heard the sound of the LORD God walking in the garden in the cool of the day, and Adam and his wife hid from the presence of the LORD God among the trees of the garden.

V9, Then the LORD God called to Adam and said to him, "Where are you?"

v10, So he said, "I heard Your voice in the garden, and I was afraid because I was naked; and I hid."

v11, And He said, "Who told you that you were naked? Have you eaten from the tree of which I commanded you that you should not eat?"

When I read this, the question arose: what do I learn from this? How is this going to change my attitudes, my conduct in life?

For me, it was not crucial whether Adam and Eve were real or it was a story. The important thing was what kind of conduct our Lord was seeking from me.

This is my understanding and how it went on to change my attitude and conduct. Adam and Eve hid when they heard the Lord. They had made a mistake and were probably very frightened.

Our Lord knew they had disobeyed him. He came to see them in the evening. He had given them time to reflect on their actions. He asked, 'Who told you that you were naked?' He had not judged them yet. He waited on them to own up. What can I learn from this?

They both fail to own up, and that led to their fall. For me, the lesson was clear. There is nothing I can hide from the Lord. In life, there will be many occasions where I will find myself doing the wrong thing, saying the wrong words, getting caught, and, in panic or fright, lie. That is part of my being. I do not feel ashamed about it. I accept it. However, I am not satisfied with my attitude and want God to transform my thinking, my behaviour.

*Romans 12:2, do not be conformed to this world, but **be transformed** by the renewing of your mind, that you may prove what is that good and acceptable and perfect will of God.*

Our Lord expects me to share any inappropriate conduct in the evening prayer and seek help to learn to remedy the situation. For this to happen, I need to give him the time to change my behaviour, which could be hours.

For me, prayer is not only about seeking help for others. It is about accountability and learning to obey the scriptures in the presence of the Holy Spirit to make scriptures part of my life. To build the foundations of my life on the Word of God, on sound solid ground.

Romans 12:2, Do not be conformed to this world, but be transformed by the renewing of your minds, so that you may discern what is the will of God—what is good and acceptable and perfect.

Matthew 7:26, "But everyone who hears these sayings of Mine, and does not do them, will be like a foolish man who built his house on the __sand__:

Prayer is a workshop, a place and a time set aside where the Holy Spirit can change my thinking. It could be a few minutes or hours. In my early years, I often spent three or four hours <u>learning in prayers</u>, guided by the written word and the Holy Spirit.

My mind is also like a fertile field given to the Lord to plough it and sow the seeds (word of God). The more I yield, the more he can plough to get a bigger harvest each time, i.e. until my mind reaches the fullness of Christ.

Ephesians 4:13 till we all come to the unity of the faith and of the knowledge of the Son of God, to a perfect man, to the measure of the stature of the __fullness__ of Christ;

Change in attitude

Each evening, I gave the Holy Spirit the time to point out the mistakes I had made that day. He would then teach me to respond differently. That would take me well past midnight after I had a full day's work. Hours spent learning to <u>renew my mind</u>.

Psalms 86:11, Teach me your ways, O LORD, that I may live according to your truth!

My experience of him is that he delights in those who wait upon him. Moreover, yes, he will answer their prayers in a precise way.

Romans 9:17, For the scripture says, "I have raised you for the very purpose of <u>showing my power in you</u>, so that <u>my name may be proclaimed</u> in all the earth."

Job 34:32, 'Teach me what I do not see; If I have done iniquity, I will do no more'?

I may have to go back to people and admit my mistakes, and if I had wronged them, the Lord would teach me a way to make restitution.

Sometimes, I did not have the resources or strength to make amends, like when relationships failed or fell out with family or friends. I still needed to admit that to the Lord. When I do not have the resources, usually in emotional matters, I say to the Lord, 'it is a hill too steep for me to climb. I cannot deal with it now. I need more time.' He understands.

He taught me to lay such things at his feet. There will be another time when I am strong enough to make amends, but for now, I need to go around the hill and continue on the journey.

The Lord says, 'You matter more to me than what we do.' *[Kathy Cochrane's Tenet 1 – a person, or a relationship, is of more excellent eternal value than the things we participate in.]*

He taught me that the things we do or the times we spend in prayers builds better relationships with him or with others.

Often I am with my family or friends, and getting somewhere seems all-important. We are late, anger and frustration build up, and tempers flare. It is so easy to forget that loved ones should matter more. In stressful situations, we need to subdue our emotions and learn to calm down and unwind.

What is the point of destroying loved ones' companionship because we are a little late, or an accident by a loved one has cost us an item? It can be replaced. Loved ones – the love and happiness they bring cannot be replaced.

Lesson 3, What I learned from *Matthew 18:3, Verily I say to you, Except ye be converted, and become as little children, ye shall not enter into the kingdom of Heaven.*

Keep things simple. If I come across a hill (an obstacle) that is too high, I admit it to the Holy Spirit and go around it. I do not try to figure it out on my own. In his own time, the Holy Spirit will help me climb/overcome it.

Hills that were just too high for me to climb.

1. Was it Seven-day creation or seven periods of time?

2. Adam, Eve, and the Garden. Was it real or a story? Jesus told parables to convey a message.

3. Trinity or One God? In the Hindu holy book Bhagavad-Gita, there is only one Supreme Being, **chapter 10:12-13.** *Arjuna to Lord; you are the supreme Lord of the universe, the truth, the light, the eternal one.*

In Africa, without any Christians around, I read the Bible and the Old Testament says there is only one God, and this was ingrained in my belief. However, in the New Testament, Jesus says he is the Messiah. *John 4:25 Jesus said unto her, "I that speak unto thee am He (Messiah)."* Is he the Messiah, God, or both?"

4. **Revelation 22.** New Earth, New Heaven, and the tree whose leaves are for healing. Is it real or just a vision. Is it a simple story to convey a more profound spiritual truth that I am not mature enough to grasp?

5. **Revelation 1:8.** Alpha and Omega. Past, present, and future are one to God. Is God outside time?

I made a simple prayer. 'Lord, I bring these questions and lay them at your feet. These are hills too high for me to climb. One day in the future, I may be able to understand. For now, I just want to follow your teachings. Help me walk in the spirit. Teach me to live a simple life that is pleasing to you.'

Lesson 4. Give them time.

What I learned from the Lord helped me a lot with our children. As they were growing up and made mistakes, rather than confront them, I would give them time to overcome their fears and, in their own time, tell the truth.

For example, one of the children had spilled orange juice on a new carpet. They would naturally be scared to admit it, and they would be apprehensive of my reaction. It was for me to create an atmosphere where they did not feel afraid to come to me for assistance.

I would ask the children to help me clean up the carpet. I may have been angry, but I was the adult. It was for me to remain calm. There would be no need for accusation or confrontation with the children. We would clean up the mess.

It was for me to give them space and time to overcome their fear. A day later, perhaps when they were relaxed, I would raise the issue. If they felt loved, secure, and cared for, they would find the courage to admit they were responsible. At this stage, it was necessary to praise them for their honesty and affirm: They mattered more than the carpet.

It was for me to assure them that their trust, confidence to share and own up, mattered more than the item they may have damaged. To cultivate that environment of calm, trust, gentleness so that they, of their volition, would be free to admit their mistakes.

That is how God has dealt with me, and I have tried to pass it on to my children, family, and friends. I am glad to say my children have grown up to be honest, straightforward, mature adults. It is the way the Lord wants us to grow in his kingdom.

---- ----

Chapter 20 – Taking Ted the Missionary Home

Our church had sponsored a small mission in Zambia.

A kind elderly widowed person called Ted had opened up a mission to look after young African orphans. Most of them had been left at the orphanage by poor parents, and the children often needed medical care. Our church, together with a few others, sponsored his mission.

About once every two years, he would come to England with some children who needed medical care. He would spend about two or three weeks in England. During this time, our church would arrange a mid-week talk for him, and the church would take a collection for him. He would also attend the Sunday evening service and talk to individuals to build a support team.

I went to his evening talk with my friend Liz. After the talk, there was tea and biscuits. People chatted to him. As the evening drew to a close, people started to leave. Liz and I were washing up in the kitchen. We finished and went into the church hall. There was just one other person from our church left. He had stayed behind to lock up the church.

Ted had jackets in his hand and was helping his young charge with them. It was mid-autumn, very dark around 11 in the evening. It was freezing and raining. There were strong winds.

I asked Ted, 'Do you have transport to get you all to your accommodation?'

He shook his head. 'We will take a bus.'

I looked at Liz's alarmed face and then at the tired faces of the young children.

Liz said, 'Ted, stay here. We will be back in five minutes. We will take you home.'

I had an old unreliable car. I didn't have a full driving license, but Liz did. We walked up to my house, got in the car, and Liz drove me to the church. They were waiting outside the church. We picked them up.

It was raining heavily, and visibility was poor. Liz drove for about three miles, and then my old car stalled in a dark country lane. I got out in the rain, lifted the hood, and changed the plugs. We drove for another mile and came up to a caravan in a field. Ted and the children got out.

Liz and I just sat in the car as they went in. We drove back in silence. Once more, the vehicle stalled. In the cold rain and darkness, I again changed all four plugs. It was well past midnight when we arrived at my home. Liz lived just around the corner from me. I walked her home. She whispered, with tears in her eyes, 'They were going to take a bus!'

As I walked home, I looked up at the sky. About 70 people were at the gathering, and about 15-18 people had driven to the church. Rev Hammond had preached and encouraged us many times about sharing and caring for one another. To follow in the footsteps of early disciples of Christ.

Acts 4:32, Now the multitude of those who believed were of one heart and one soul; neither did anyone say that any of the things he possessed was his own, but they had all things in common.

'Lord, how is it that not one person in the church cared to inquire?

Matthew 25:44, Then will they also answer him, saying, Lord, when saw we thee hungry, or thirsty, or a stranger, or naked, or sick, or in prison, and did not minister to thee?

--- ☆ ---

Note: *This taught me that I was just as capable of ignorance of others' needs. If I was to be lead by the Holy Spirit, I needed to keep my eyes and ears open.*

Chapter 21 – Two Hindu Families: the Salt of the Earth.

Mark 9:50, "Salt is good, but if the salt loses its flavour, how will you season it? Have salt in yourselves, and have peace with one another."

There are some defining moments in life when an incident shapes our future conduct for good or bad. This incident with Ted brought back some memories from my past that had affected me, shaped my behaviour.

One of these incidents took place around the end of my first year of secondary school. My father had to go to Mombasa on a business trip. It was a school holiday. He took me with him, and we were there for a few days. During the day, I was on my own. On the second day, I walked up to the beach. It was a hot day, about 11 a.m. I sat under the palm trees on the white sand.

Two Hindu boys were playing on the beach. They saw me and invited me to join them. I was delighted and accepted their invitation. We had lots of fun. Around lunchtime, we stopped, and they started to gather their belongings. They invited me to their home for lunch.

It was a humble bungalow. I met their parents; they were lovely, modest people, and they welcomed me into their home. We had lunch. I felt happy, comfortable with them. After lunch, the boys said they had some work to do, and it would take about an hour and a half. If I had time, I could join them. I accepted their offer.

I thanked their parents on our way out. We walked up to an old pickup van. The older boy, who was about 18 years old, had a cotton bag in his hand. He stuffed the bag under the driver's seat and drove us to the harbour.

There was a big passenger ship docked, and the last few remaining passengers were disembarking. Soon the dock area was empty. We sat for another ten minutes.

I asked the boys why we were there. The older boy explained. Their father had sent them to **seek out**[1] any new migrant who seemed lost. Their family owned a chain of hotels, and the boys were to seek out anyone in need. Their family provided free accommodation to anyone in need and helped them to find work.

We did not see anyone in need, so we left.

He drove us to a bank. We walked in, and the older boy gave the cashier the cotton bag. It was full of money. I had never seen so much money. They were wealthy, but there was no display of it. They took me home.

Their **conduct**[2] left a lasting impression on me about care, thoughtfulness, and compassion for the less fortunate in life.

A Kind, Generous, Elderly Couple

A few months later, my parents were invited to a wedding in Kisumu, about six hours' drive from us, a town on Lake Victoria's shores. My parents could not attend, so my father arranged with a young couple to take me with them.

It was dark when we arrived at Kisumu. They asked me with whom I was staying, and I gave them a name. Then, they asked for the address, but I didn't have that information. They looked up the name in a telephone book. There were three addresses with the same name. They drove me to the first address.

The owner did not know me, so the young couple drove me to the next person's home on the list. An older person opened the door. The young couple had a word with her.

She glanced at me, looked at the dark sky above us, and beckoned me into her home. I followed her into the house and met her husband. They

--- ☆ ---

[1] *James 1:27, Pure religion and undefiled before God and the Father is this, To visit the fatherless and widows in their affliction, and to keep himself unspotted from the world.*

[2] *Psalms 82:3, Defend the poor and fatherless: do justice to the afflicted and needy. ...x..x...*

had already eaten, but she cooked for me while the husband ran a bath for me.

The next morning the young couple arrived and took me to the wedding. In the evening, they dropped me at the elderly couple's home.

The following morning they came to pick me up for our return journey. As I put my small bag into the car's boot, the elderly couple asked me my father's name and our address. I supplied the information. I noticed the blank look on their **faces.**[3]

They had no idea whose son I was!

These two families' kindness and hospitality left a lasting impression on me. Rarely have I met a Christian family to match the kindness and goodness of these Hindus. I have struggled in church. Why should Christians be given any privilege in God's kingdom above people of other faiths whose lives reflect more of Christ's character?

I have met a few Christians on par with the kind families above: my close friends' Ray, Kate, Malcolm and Jessica, Liz, and Maggie, to name a few. People who, when asked to walk a **mile**[4]**,** would walk two or three.

For example, **Liz** was about the same age as me. She had joined the

---- ☆ ----

[3] *Matthew 25:37-40, Then the righteous will answer him, 'Lord, when was it that* <u>*we saw you hungry*</u> *and gave you food, or thirsty and gave you something to drink? And when was it that we saw you* <u>*a stranger and welcomed you,*</u> *or naked and gave you clothing? And when was it that we saw you sick or in prison and visited you?' And the king will answer them, 'Truly I tell you,* <u>*just as you did it to one of the least of these*</u> *who are members of my family, you did it to me.'*

Matthew 7:20-21, "Therefore, by their fruits, you will know them." Not everyone who says to Me, 'Lord, Lord,' shall enter the kingdom of heaven, but he who does the will of My Father in heaven."

[4] *Matthew 5:41, "And whoever compels you to go* <u>*one mile,*</u> *go with him two."*

...x..x...

church at about the same time I did. Liz had inherited two houses from her grandmother. She donated the bigger home to a charity that ran a women's refuge.

Sometimes it is easy to write a cheque and walk away. Liz was different. She rolled up her sleeves, helped the charity set up the refuge, and worked there for a year.

Liz was a good Christian who would gladly walk the second or even the third mile for someone in need. She was my first love, and she encouraged me to pursue my visions. I am so grateful I met her.

Chapter 22- My Father. An Incident That Shapes my Future Conduct.

I was about eight years old, and we lived in a council house. One day my father asked me to go with him. We walked up to a prosperous part of the town, up to a big detached house with a lovely garden.

My father rang the doorbell, and the owner of the house greeted him. He invited us into his large home. They talked for a while, and then they started to shout at each other. My father was furious with the man. They yelled some more. Then the owner began to cry. He sat down and buried his face in his lap as my father hurled a torrent of rebukes at him. The man was weeping loudly. His wife entered the room, and my father had a go at her; she started to cry.

I should say - I was terrified. I loved my father, and at this tender age, I did not like to see him so agitated. I was also scared that he might be in some kind of trouble. We left the house. I looked at my father's angry face and kept quiet.

Later that evening, my father explained. A friend of his was in trouble and needed the house owner's aid, a lawyer. The lawyer had quoted a fee that the poor man could not afford. This rich man had refused to accept a lower sum.

My father had been furious with the rich man. He had told the couple off for being selfish. A poor man could end up in jail, his family could end up on the streets, and they had shown no compassion. The rich man had argued that he didn't do charity. That had set my father off.

We were not well off, but people turned to my father for help. They knew he could persuade others to help them. He was tall, handsome, passionate, and much respected in the community. He had a furious temper, and people were afraid to upset him.

He cared for people, and I know he was very disappointed that he had not had the opportunity to be a Doctor. He was brilliant, had an excellent memory, and a logical mind that his opponents found hard to confront. Unfortunately, I did not inherit his intelligent genes, and my low school results grieved him. Nevertheless, I did inherit his passion for reaching out to others, or perhaps it was something I picked up from observing him.

I admired his passion for the underdog, intelligence, good looks, furious temper, and penetrating eyes that reduced greater men to tears.

One day those qualities I adored and admired in him would be directed at me, for the worse, a course that neither of us could control because of a book.

Chapter 23 –Jury

Roman 13:9-10, "You shall love your neighbour as yourself." Love does not harm a neighbour; therefore, love is the fulfilment of the law.

How do I read this? I waited on the Lord. He reminded me of the vision of Judgment Day. The vessels of gold and silver and those of straw and clay. But this time, the picture changed.

I saw a multitude of people pass before the judgment seat. Among them were my neighbours.

They cried out to the Lord, 'Why didn't someone warn us?'

They passed me. I saw the looks of fear and missed opportunities written on their faces. It sobered my view of that great day.

The Lord said, 'If a jury were to view your life in Haringey, how would you prove you have loved your neighbour?'

These scriptures came to my mind, *1 John 3:18, Little children, let us love, not in word or speech, but in truth and action. 1 John 4:20, If someone says, "I love God," and hates his brother, he is a liar; for he who does not love his brother whom he has seen, how can he love God whom he has not seen?*

I got the gist of what he was saying. I was new to this area. Apart from a few people in the church, I did not know anyone. I borrowed the church printer, made leaflets, and printed my name, address, telephone number, and a short piece about how I'd found Jesus. If anyone needed help or wanted to talk to someone, I was available. From that day, my home was a sanctuary; I turned the mezzanine floor into a bedsit for anyone in need.

In my leaflets, I wrote a short message and asked people to invite Jesus into their lives. Then, I added our church address and service times.

I would come home from work, pray, go over in prayer which streets I would deliver leaflets, and then drop them in the letterboxes. After I had done this, I would come home, have another quick word of prayer, then sit down, and have a meal.

One night the Lord said, 'When you post the leaflets, you should respect other people's properties. You cannot jump over the dividing barriers or walls. You will close the gates. In winter, you will not deliver the leaflets in the evening after six-thirty.' (In respect of older people who can get alarmed when they hear strange noises in their front garden at dusk.)

A few weeks later, Rev Hammond took me to a side room. He looked glum. He said, 'I am sorry, Hari, but you cannot put the church address on your leaflet.'

He explained that the deacons had had a meeting. Someone showed them my leaflet with the church address on it. They found some spelling errors and did not want the church's good name associated with such poor quality workmanship.

I was shocked. It's fair to say I was fuming. How dare these couch potatoes who loved their undemanding lifestyle and avoided the rain and hunger to do the Lord's work criticise my work. But I just nodded, thanked him for his honesty. I got up and was about to walk out of the room when he said, 'Hari, sit down. I am with you. You are doing the Lord's work.' He smiled. 'They didn't say you couldn't use the printer.'

Still, the rejection was a severe blow to me. For a few days, I felt low. Then I read about the twelve disciples. They were uneducated fishermen or farmers who were not ashamed to preach the gospel. They were not concerned about their grammar or accents, or reputation. It did not matter to the Lord either. "The contents of the message mattered."

I prayed. The Lord showed me again the faces of my neighbours on Judgment Day.

The Lord said, 'Hari, they asked for <u>someone to warn them</u>. I have many gifted people here, but you are the only one willing to make this effort. If they are earnest to seek me, it will make no difference to them if your leaflets had spelling or grammatical mistakes. Have faith in what the Holy Spirit can achieve through these messages.' I should add or this book.

My Patch, Harringay Ladder

Harringay Ladder, an area in North London, between Turnpike Lane and Harringay Green Lanes stations. The roads running between Green Lanes and the parallel Wightman Road looks' like the rungs of a ladder when seen on a map. The area is collectively known as the ladder.

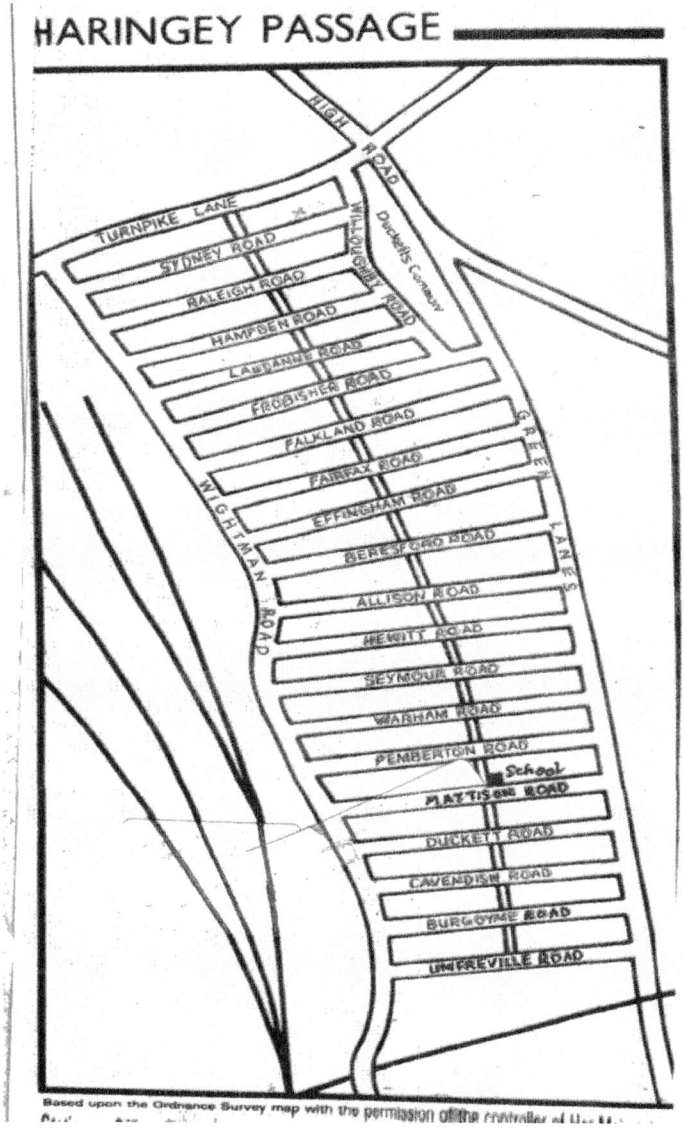

HARINGEY PASSAGE

Based upon the Ordnance Survey map with the permission of the controller of the...

There were 2,985 houses on my 'Patch, in Haringey.' I continued to write and print my leaflets, and over the next two years, I delivered to every house in my patch. I did it seven times. That is about 21,000 leaflets while doing a regular 8-5 job. That would be about the size of a small town. Later on, three other people in the church offered to join me to distribute more leaflets.

Rain, storm, or flu, the Lord's work goes on.

After coming home from work, one evening, I was out delivering the leaflets. I was hungry, feeling poorly, and had a bad cold. I had planned to cover one side of a street per day. Perhaps I should have stayed at home, given my body a chance to heal. The rebuke from the deacons had lowered my morale. I felt sorry for myself. I was discouraged. I wondered if I was doing the right thing.

I had about twenty leaflets left when I saw a face appear; a vision. I had known this angel for some time called Benin. He smiled and said, 'The last house on the street, last leaflet.' It happened.

The next day, I picked up at random about seventy leaflets. I had posted about half of them when I saw the angel again. He smiled and said the same thing. His words were correct.

On the third day, I felt it was going to happen again. I felt all excited as I delivered the leaflets, but this time no face appeared. I did the last house. There were two extra leaflets in my hand. I felt very disappointed. A feeling of depression took over. I had a terrible cold and a nasty headache. I turned and headed for home.

I walked about ten paces, and then I stopped. Something was wrong. I turned and walked up to the last house, looking for any other homes. That was the last house. I was so sure it would happen again, last place, last leaflet. It didn't happen.

Life can be very hard, saddled with disappointments. I was on the verge of tears. I just stood there numb, shivering in the cold and coughing up green /yellow mucus and blood into my handkerchief. I was tired, cold, hungry.

An intense sense of loneliness overtook me. I felt sorry for myself. *Why was I out in the cold, with a heavy cold doing this work alone? Why doesn't the Lord get others to do it? Why me?*

I stood on the pavement and cried.

I glanced sideways and noticed there was an alleyway on the side of the house. I walked down the alleyway and saw that the large Victorian house was converted into flats with two doorways to the apartments. I came to the last door with the last leaflet!

I was so excited; I ran to Rev Hammond's house and knocked on his door. He opened the door and led me into his home. I told him about the leaflets. He paused to think, then went to the kitchen and came back with two cups of tea. He gave me one. We sat down.

Calmly, he said, 'I would take that as a sign of God's approval.' Jim was a Yorkshire man.

I was aware my leaflets were of low quality, but it was the best I could do. Then I saw an advert for professionally printed Christian pamphlets by an American Christian organization. They had a simple message; we have all sinned, Jesus died for our sins and offered us a new life. There was an invitation for more information from this Christian organization. I ordered a pack of three thousand leaflets, and this time, with the help of a small group of friends, we delivered to every home on our patch.

On my leaflets, I had stated that if anyone needed help or wanted to talk to someone, I was available. My home was open to all. My home was a sanctuary for any in need. *1 Chronicles 28;10, Take heed now, for the LORD has chosen you to build a house as the sanctuary; be strong, and act.*

Many people used my house, especially the spare room and kitchen on the mezzanine floor. My kindness was not always appreciated. It taught me to be discerning, weigh up situations, and avoid taking on board more than I could cope with. It also taught me about caring for vulnerable people and to share with them whatever I had.

Years later, this experience would be of immense help to me when we acquired a Nursing Home. ...x...x..

Leaflet distribution with church members.

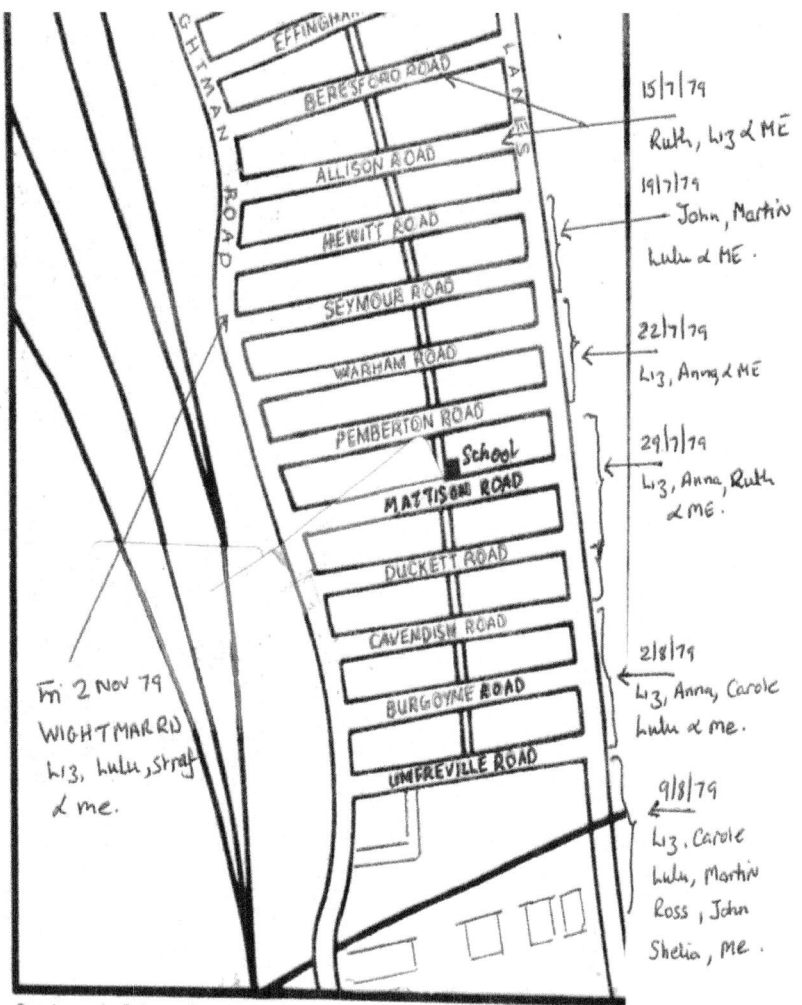

15/7/79
Ruth, Liz & ME .

19/7/79
John, Martin
Lulu & ME .

22/7/79
Liz, Anna & ME

29/7/79
Liz, Anna, Ruth & ME .

2/8/79
Liz, Anna, Carole
Lulu & me.

9/8/79
Liz, Carole
Lulu, Martin
Ross, John
Shelia, ME .

Fri 2 Nov 79
WIGHTMAR RD
Liz, Lulu, Stref & me.

Based upon the Ordnance Survey map with the permission of the controller of Her Majesty's Stationery Office. Crown Copyright Reserved. Licence No. 086401.

Chapter 24 - The Drug Addict

Luke 3:11, In reply, Jesus said to them, "Whoever has two coats must share with anyone who has none; and whoever has food must do likewise."

I rented the ground floor flat to two friends in the church while we had the upper flat and kept the spare room on the mezzanine floor for anyone in need. One day on my way home after work, I stopped at a shop and bought a thick woollen jumper. I did a lot of overtime to save for this jumper. It was winter, and I badly needed a new one. I got home.

My mother was waiting for me. She looked very agitated.

'Mother, what is the matter?' I inquired.

She led me into their lounge. She told me about an incident that had frightened her almost to death. In the morning, after I had gone to work, she had gone into the kitchen to make breakfast. While she was washing up, she felt a presence behind her. She turned and froze. Blocking her way was a very dark brown scruffy young man with bloodshot eyes, staring at her.

She was so scared she could not scream. She just froze. He opened the fridge, took a pint of milk, and went downstairs. It took her a few minutes to calm down; she assumed he was probably one of my friends staying downstairs.

I had no idea who the person was. I went to the downstairs flat. My friend Malcolm was sitting on the sofa. Opposite him on the dining room chair sat a scurfy bloodshot-eyed man in his late twenties. His clothes were dirty, his long hair untidy.

Malcolm saw the anger in my face. His face turned pale. He got up, indicated for me to follow him into the hallways. He explained, his voice quivering, that he had found the man out in the cold late at night and gave him his bed to sleep on. It was a Christian thing to do. He had slept on the floor.

I was still fuming because of the impact on my mother. I said, 'Malcolm, he cannot stay here.'

Malcolm said, 'Hari, we cannot chuck him out. It is cold outside. It is winter.'

'I don't care; get rid of him.' I stormed upstairs. I went to my mother and reassured her that the stranger meant her no harm. He had lost his way in the house.

I went to my room and sat down. Half an hour later, I had calmed down. I had noticed the man was wearing a thin shirt and a light summer jacket. A scripture verse ran through my mind.

Luke 3:11, *In reply, Jesus said to them, "Whoever has two coats must share with anyone who has none; and whoever has food must do likewise."*

It was freezing outside. I took one of my old jumpers and headed downstairs. Halfway down the stairs, I paused. I stood on the staircase, staring at the jumper. I went back to my room, picked up the new jumper, took it downstairs, and gave it to the stranger.

I said to Malcolm, 'We need to take him to people who can look after him properly and provide him with appropriate care.'

'Where can we take him?'

'Let's try the YMCA. They might help him or tell us where to take him.'

Jesus showed us an example of how to live. He left it to us to implement his teachings in our lives. To take the initiative, to walk the second mile. To compensate others more than legally obliged, when dealing with work colleagues, people employed by us, disputes with neighbours, or accidents.

The first few times, the Holy Spirit led me in such acts. After that, it became part of my instinct, my way of life. We are the salt of the earth.

*Matthew 5:13, You are the **salt of the** earth; but how shall it be seasoned if the salt loses its flavour? It is then good for nothing but to be thrown out and trampled underfoot by men* ---- 🕈 ----

Chapter 25 – Witness

Revelation 21:1-2, Now I saw a new heaven and a new earth, for the first heaven and the first earth had passed away. Also, there was no more sea. Then I, John, saw the holy city, New Jerusalem, coming down out of heaven from God, prepared as a bride adorned for her husband.

One evening, after accounting for my leaflets, I went to sleep. In the middle of the night, I felt the Holy Spirit wake me up.

'You have given your testimony and distributed the gospel message to every home in your patch several times. On the Day of Judgment, the people in your patch will account for their lives. Your Lord wants you to be his witness.

'When they ask why someone didn't warn them, you will open your books, show them their names, house number, and the day and time you and your friends delivered the gospel message.

'My angels Benin and Abinar have come to help you. They have made a detailed account of your work and will bear a record of this work and the people's response.

Some of your neighbours have responded well, but others laughed and discarded the message. They will stand accountable for their actions. Their blood will not be on your hands.'

Ezekiel 33:8-9, if I announce that some wicked people are sure to die and you fail to tell them to change their ways, then they will die in their sins, and I will hold you responsible for their deaths. But if you warn them to repent and they don't repent, they will die in their sins, but you will have saved yourself.

I asked the Lord, 'Why would their blood have been on my hands?'

God breathed on that verse, and it came alive, as, 'You are my heir in Christ. I have placed this responsibility on <u>all my heirs</u>. On Judgment Day, their neighbours will ask the question: "Why didn't anyone warn us," and each one of my heirs will account for the task I called them for.'

'You were my watchman (heir) in this parish and would have been held accountable for their loss of inheritance, but that will not be the case now. For them, the judgment awaits.' *Luke 13:28, There will be weeping and gnashing of teeth, for you will see Abraham, Isaac, Jacob, and all the prophets in the Kingdom of God, but you will be thrown out.*

'As for you and your angels on that day, there will be many who will be glad to see you and thank you for your message.'

A moment later, I found myself past Judgment Day. Before me, in a vision, lay burnt ashes. The Judgment Day had passed. I closed my books and waited. Two of the angels who had helped me on Earth came and stood beside me.

The angels Benin and Abinar said, 'Come, follow us. We will show you the **New Jerusalem**[1].' We walked. We stood under a big gate. On the gate was written the name "**Benjamin**[2]."

'Follow us,' he called out.

We climbed the stairs, and we came to a tower. We stood on the walls of the city. A guard approached us.

The angel asked him, 'Tell me, what do you see below us?'

He looked down. He replied, 'I see a big beast with a snake-like nose, his feet like tree trunks, a body like a rock, and it growls like thunder.'

The angel looked at me, and we both laughed, 'He used to live in the Amazon forest. The largest animal he would have seen is a jaguar. What do you see?'

--- ☆ ---

[1] *Revelation 21:10-11, And he carried me away in the Spirit to a great and high mountain. He showed me the great city, the holy Jerusalem, descending out of heaven from God, having the glory of God. Her light was like a most precious stone, like a jasper stone, clear as crystal.*

[2] *Re 21:12, Also, she had a great and high wall with twelve gates, and twelve angels at the gates, and names written on them, which are the names of the twelve tribes of the children of Israel: ...x..x...*

I looked down at the massive beast, and we both laughed again. 'I see an elephant.'

I am trying to illustrate the difficulties of using language in a situation we have never encountered before. And that applies to what I am about to describe.

New Jerusalem[3] Revelation 21

The angel said, 'Tell me, what do you see?'

I replied, 'I see things, but I have no idea what they are. I have never seen anything like them.'

'Of course, you cannot understand. This is the New Jerusalem. Let me show you in a manner you can understand.' He waved a hand before me. 'Now, what do you see?'

The angels had to show me the New Jerusalem in a manner I could understand. Other people have seen this city, and each describes it in a way that speaks from their culture and time in history. Some would describe it as a city whose streets were of gold. We should not dwell on the words but the spiritual concept the writer is trying to convey.

Inside the walls[4] was the new city.

The citizens had sparkling white robes that shone like the midday sun. There was not a speck of dirt or colour on their robes.

Their every thought[4B] was in line with that of the lamb. They could account for every atom, every grain of sand in the 'Patch' allocated to them. They governed the nations that were outside the city gates.

--- ☆ ---

[3] *Revelation 22:3, And there shall be no more curse, but the throne of God and of the Lamb shall be in it, and His servants shall serve Him.*

[4] *Wall represents the area – boundary-region. And white robes signify the purity of people.*

[4B] *2 Corinthians 13:5, Do you not realize that Jesus Christ is in you. ...x..x...*

A place inside the city, our inheritance, our real home is <u>conditional</u>[5], Rev 21:7. But outside?

We climbed down the stairs and stood outside the city at the feet of the tower of Benjamin. The people were dressed in white/grey robes. We walked towards the horizon for a very long time.

We came to a beautiful town with tree-lined houses. We walked through this town and headed towards the village square. There were multitudes of people assembled. I asked, 'Who are these people? Why have they gathered here?'

The angel replied, 'They have come to see you. These people read your leaflets, your books, and changed their conduct. They came here to receive you and thank you for your work.

'This town on the east side is called Little Haringey, on the west, Little Liskeard, on the south, Little Sussex, and in the north are two kingdoms. They reached out towards the horizon. On the left side was England and on the right side resided the people of Maple Leaf.'

We walked through many kingdoms. From all the great and little towns, people came out of their houses in their multitudes to thank us.

Surprisingly, among them were the two Hindu boys, their families, and my extended Hindu family members.

Behind them stood the elderly couple from Kisumu. The elderly woman smiled. 'We (people of the book-Gita) believed in **"Brahman[6], The creator."**

----- ☆ -----

[5] *Revelation 21:7, "He who <u>overcomes</u> shall inherit all things, and I will be his God, and he shall be My son.*

[6] ***Bhagavad-Gita chapter** 13:12. They know what knowledge is needed to gain eternal life. **Eternal life** is to know the Supreme Lord and his subordinate, Brahman (Word of God), one who is without beginning and said to be neither being nor non-being.*

*John 17:3, And this is **life eternal**, that they might know you the only true God, and Jesus Christ, whom you have sent. ...x..x...*

I was confused. I looked at the angel, and he shook his head as he laughed. 'It's a hill too high to climb; best we go around it.'

I recognized my Muslim school friend **Faruq**[7]. Behind him were members of his family.

I looked at Benin. He said, 'They allowed the Holy Spirit to work in their **lives.**[8] On Judgment Day, the work wrought by the **Holy Spirit**[9] passed through the fire.'

For it is written,' **Numbers 1:4,** *And with you there shall be a man of every tribe; every one head of his fathers' house.*

'Come, Hari, there is more. Other towns in the north await you.'

--- ☆ ---

[7] *Revelation 5:9, And they sang a new song, saying: "You are worthy to take the scroll, and to open its seals; For You were slain, And have redeemed us to God by Your blood Out of* every tribe and tongue and people and nation,

[8] *Romans 3:30, since there is one God who will justify the circumcised by* faith *and the uncircumcised through* faith.

[9] *Romans 2:11, for there is* no partiality *with God.*

v12, For as many as have sinned without law will also perish without law, and as many as have sinned in the law will be judged by the law

v13, for not the hearers of the law are just in the sight of God, but the doers of the law will be justified;

v14, for when Gentiles, *who do not have the law, by nature do the things in the law, these, although not having the law, are a law to themselves,*

v15, who show the work of the law written in their hearts, *their conscience also bearing witness, and between themselves, their thoughts accusing or else excusing them)*

v16, in the day when God will judge the secrets of men by Jesus Christ, according to my gospel.

...x..x...

Eternal Life; Conditions of Receiving and some of the good works prepared for us.

1) Renunciation of the World {Luke 18:28-30}

2) Faith in Christ {John 3:14,15 3:36 4:14}

3) Spiritual Service {John 4:35,36 5:24 6:40}

4) Self-sacrifice {John 12:25}

5) Knowledge of God {John 17:3}

6) Sowing in the Spirit {Galatians 6:8}

Salvation, Conditions of

The Rewards for the Faithful, For Spiritual Service

1) The Soul Winners (Daniel 12:3}

2) Humble Servants (Matthew 10:42}

3) The Faithful Stewards (Matthew 25:23}

4) The Benevolent (Luke 6:35 John 4:36}

5) The Good of All Nations (Romans 2:10 1 Corinthians 3:8}

6) All Ranks and Stations (Ephesians 6:8 Colossians 3:24}

---- 👑 ----

Chapter 26 - Balaam's donkey

Revelation 22:15, But outside are dogs and sorcerers and sexually immoral and murderers and idolaters, and whoever loves and practices a lie.

We came to a magnificent town that stretched for miles. Not as glamorous as the humble little towns I had seen, but there were happy people clothed in shades of grey. They came and shook our hands.

'Who are you, people?' I asked.

They laughed. Their leader, crowned in glory, pointed to the top of the hill. In the distance flew the mighty flag of a red cross on a white field, — an eternal symbol of a small but mighty nation, brought about by great visionary men like William Tyndale/ Miles Coverdale (c.1494-1536) and King James I of England (1603), whose vision had transformed the English-speaking world and later would change the whole world.

'We are the good shepherds of the Lord, and these are our flock.' He pointed at the crowd.

Then the angels took me westward, and we walked for days. We passed through many nations. The further we got from the city, the filthier the people grew. They wore garments of different colours but rarely did I see one in white or purple robes.

Revelation 22:15, But outside are dogs and sorcerers and sexually immoral and murderers and idolaters, and whoever loves and practices a lie.

The harsh words used here are for people who had not run the race set before them. **Heb 12:1,** *Therefore, since we are surrounded by so great a cloud of witnesses, let us also lay aside every weight and the sin that clings so closely, and let us* run with perseverance *the race that is set before us. V16, See that no one becomes like Esau, an immoral and godless person who sold his birthright for a single meal.*

These people had neglected their salvation. They had not given God the time to work out their complete salvation nor reached the level of holiness required (conditional), **Heb 12:14,** *Pursue peace with everyone, and the <u>holiness</u> without which no one <u>will see the Lord</u>.* They were ignorant of their inheritance and neglected their salvation for the pleasures of earth.

Matthew 25:10, *"And while they went to buy, the bridegroom came, and those who were ready went in with him to the wedding; and the door was shut."*

These good decent, hard-working people had managed to survive the Judgment! Moreover, they were grateful to the Lord for giving them a second chance in life.

Finally, we came to a wide river. There in the middle of the river was an oversized island, which stretched to the horizon. At its centre stood two magnificent churches, separated by a wide stream, built in the very distinct English Gothic style.

I said to the angel, 'These are magnificent churches. What is this place called?'

'Welcome to the land of Esau. Here reside the children of Esau (People who neglected their inheritance for an easy, comfortable life on earth and failed to complete the race. They did not seek God with all their heart, mind, and strength, a requirement they failed to meet).'

Genesis 25:33-34, Then Jacob said to Esau, "Swear to me as of this day." So he swore to him and sold his birthright to Jacob. And Jacob gave Esau bread and stew of lentils; then he ate and drank, arose, and went his way. Thus, Esau despised his birthright.

We walked on water and stepped onto the island. There among the liars, I saw some of the shepherds of England. A flock of archbishops was among them, still dressed in their fancy peacock robes, shaped not by the scriptures but by man's vanity and folly. They were preaching cold words that had no power but held the fine oratory of biblical colleges. Skilled men in a worldly manner and their followers dressed in shaggy clothes eagerly hanging onto their words.

Scattered on the island were smaller free churches, the shepherds dressed in dirty brown and grey garments, leading their flocks to muddy

112

water pools.

Baptist Minister and Balaam's Donkey

We walked back towards the city. Many miles from the town, we came across a donkey. I recognized the Baptist minister who had despised me, riding the donkey. I approached him and asked him what he was doing here. He was too ashamed to answer and chose to run away. I looked at the donkey. I recognized him.

'Come,' said the donkey, as he laughed at the sight of the shamed minister running away, 'ride on my back, and we shall talk.' I climbed on his back, and as I rode, we talked. We came to the gate of Benjamin.

I said to the donkey, 'I know you, but my memory fails me.'

He laughed, 'I was Balaam's donkey. You often quoted me to people. I prophesied and did God's will, and as a reward, God granted me the right to live here.'

'Where were you going with the Baptist minister?'

The donkey said, laughing, 'People call me Babu. I went and sought the Baptist minister and told him the angels were seeking him. I told him to climb on my back, and I would take him to the angels. He thought he was getting a promotion to a higher calling.' We started laughing again.

I got off the donkey and thanked him. I couldn't stop laughing. 'Walk with me on the city walls.'

Babu said, 'I cannot. I am not allowed inside the city gate. I have to go back to my home.' He started to walk away from the gate; he paused, turned his head, and said, 'When you return to Earth, tell the church leaders not to be like me. To prophesy is not enough; I have more spirituality then many of them. I saw the angels, and I faithfully spoke the words our Lord God gave me, which is more them many of them will ever do. Oh, by the way, I am not Balaam's donkey anymore.'

Jesus had hundreds of followers but just 12 disciples during his ministry. There is a vast difference between the two.

Revelation 22: 14-15, Blessed are those who do His commandments, that they may have the right to the tree of life, and may enter through the gates into the city. But outside are dogs and sorcerers and sexually immoral and murderers, idolaters, and whoever loves and practices a lie.

Truth is often hard to face, no matter how gently it is presented.

Only perfected disciples will walk with him in the new Holy City. Simultaneously, outside the city, gates will be the Lord's followers in their billions.

Ezekiel 34 states the requirement for Lords' shepherds.

To be an honourable spirit-led shepherd over his flock is one of the most demanding jobs on Earth. You have to be superhuman. Yes, superhuman. A good example is the life of Jesus on Earth.

I know some church leaders who could not hold a proper job in a secular world flocked to find refuge in the church. Good for them. God needs all types of people.

When we bought a nursing home, we scoured the local churches looking for Christian nurses and care workers to help us set a Christian witness in the area. They didn't want to work for us. I can understand. We were losing money, and our pay was low.

We employed whoever was willing to work for us. With the Lord's help, we turned a failing Nursing Home into an excellent care home in Cornwall. God does the same if he can find anyone willing to be his shepherd.

The point is to take whoever steps into God's work and try to forge them into a superhuman. Not by human strength but by the lord's help. All that is required is a willing mind. It can be done. I am a prime example of it.

1 Corinthians 1:26-27, For you see your calling, brothers, how that <u>not many wise</u> men after the flesh, not many mighty, not many noble, are called: But God has chosen the foolish things of the world to confound the wise; and God has chosen *the <u>weak things</u> of the world to confound the things which are mighty.*

This book is about empowering weak people like you and me. My primary school teacher had pointed out to my father that I would never amount to much. My teacher had often called me a "retard in front of the class."

He was wrong. He didn't factor in the mighty hand of God upon me. My father had other thoughts and expectations.

God has higher expectations for you and me and is willing to turn us into a superhuman. Are we willing?

First, we need to realize we cannot build Gods' kingdom with just our hands. Secondly, we need the Holy Spirit and God's blessing to achieve great things.

I may be a retard, I may be puny, but I can make it rain, heal cancer, and move rich nations' governments with God's help. Not by my small might but by his strength.

Small, I maybe, but when I roar, it rains, dictators flee, nations fall, and those who harmed me cease to breathe. A Greater power guides my destiny.

--- ☆ ---

Comment

I hope you feel inspired to let God do great things in your life, but there may be some who may feel weak. I say to them; you can do God's bidding. God needs both strong and weak people willing to give the Holy Spirit the time to make them strong in the Lord.

Christ's kingdom is a brotherhood and sisterhood of all kinds of people.

Luke 22:25-26, But he said to them, "The kings of the Gentiles lord it over them; and those in authority over them are called benefactors But not so with you; rather the greatest among you must become like the youngest and the leader like one who serves. ---- 🎖.....

115

Chapter 27 – Elderly Congregation

Luke 22:26, But among you, it will be different. Those who are the greatest among you should take the lowest rank, and the leader should be like a servant.

Haringey church. I shared with Rev Hammond everything the Lord showed me. I valued his guidance and advice. I was keen. I wanted everyone in the church filled with the baptism of the spirit. I was young and inexperienced. My youthful energy and keenness began to alienate the more senior members.

I prayed about the lack of enthusiasm from others in the church. I thought the Lord would give me a fierce, evangelical spirit that would rouse the members. Make them question their commitment to the Lord. Instead, the Lord put it into my heart to serve them. *Luke 22:26, But among you, it will be different. Those who are the greatest among you should take the lowest rank, and the leader should be like a servant.*

I had looked down on the frail senior members who did nothing in the church. They were the wealthy members of the church. They had comfortable homes, nice cars, and good pensions, and I envied their comfortable lifestyle. They regularly came to church, sat quietly in the pews, hardly mixed with anyone. However, they made a significant financial contribution to the upkeep of the church.

In my opinion, they had the time, resources, and wisdom to help those that were single, lonely, or vulnerable. They were not interested in that. They seemed to have very little care or concern for others. Their characters seemed so unchristian to me. I resented them.

One evening as I sat for prayer, the Lord asked me, 'Why do you resent the old?' *Titus 3:3 For we ourselves were also once foolish, disobedient, deceived, serving various lusts and pleasures, living in malice and envy, hateful and hating one another.*

As I thought about these matters, I received images of the older people who had struggled to serve the Lord in their way. In their early years, they had struggled against poverty, mockery, and insults from the unbeliever. They overcame heat, cold, storms to attain church and prayer meetings. Now in old age, they were unable to do things I desired. It was wrong to judge them. They were the Lord's people. He loved them, and it was time for me to learn to respect and love them.

'How, Lord?'

'Serve them. They are your family.'

After church service, we would have tea and coffee. I started to help in the kitchen and serve tea and biscuits to others. Then, with other volunteers, we would clean the hall and wash up the cups. If any senior members needed transport to get to the service, we would help.

Acts 2:47 And the Lord added people to the church.

I had noticed that when new visitors came to the church, hardly anyone made an effort to welcome them. The church exuded a coolness to the visitors that was both disheartening and unfriendly. Mr Hammond was good at his job but not a social person.

These visitors felt unwelcomed, and most never came back. Our Lord had brought them to church, but there was no one to make them feel at home.

My troubled childhood had stunted my social skills, and I felt unable to welcome them. I shared my concern with the prayer group and asked them to reflect on the verse, *Hebrews 13:2, Do not forget to entertain strangers, for by so doing, some have unwittingly entertained angels.*

The outcome was that we formed a welcome group, and made every effort to make the visitors feel at home, invited them to our homes for meals, outings, and picnics. It enriched our lives, brought us closer together, and added to the church.

After about two years in the church, Pastor Hammond and I had developed a strong team. He started to trust my views and began to give me a few minutes during the Sunday service to share with the church anything the Lord had shown me that week.

There were so many things going through my head, and I had so much to share. Mr Hammond had advised me, 'What the Lord gives may be for you only, and there may be other things that are for the church. You need to distinguish between the two. Limit yourself to three things and share them within three minutes. Make it simple, concise, and precisely to the point.'

During one evening prayer at home, the Holy Spirit said, 'When you share a message I have given you, you will reason with people. You will not force it upon others; you will not try to persuade them. You will need their consent all the way. If a single church member looks bored, seems to withdraw his consent, you will stop. We will not impose our will on others.'

This conduct was derived from **Genesis 6:3,** *Then the LORD said, "My spirit shall not abide in mortals forever, for they are flesh,"* and on **Ephesians 4:30,** *And do not grieve the Holy Spirit of God, with which you were marked with a seal for the day of redemption.*

In the next few years, the Lord would teach me what I call **Zak's Tenet:** *'Guide you with my eye. I respect your privacy. I will reason with you with your consent, but I will not press you nor try to persuade you.'*

It was an extremely high standard set before me. I remember the first time I shared under this condition; I spoke about fellow church members being our real wealth in Heaven. They were transfixed. You could have heard a pin drop. When I finished, no one stirred for a whole minute. There was absolute silence in the church. Then I heard a sob, followed by more. People's eyes were moist. The Holy Spirit was speaking to them.

One young woman got up from her chair and broke the spell. She came up to me and just gave me a hug, followed by others. No one had yet said a word, and then slowly, they hugged others.

That evening when I prayed, the Lord said, 'This is the way you will walk before me and others.'

It is a very high bar and can only be an aspiration for many because it requires a steep learning curve. Many years later, one evening, as I sat for dinner with my wife and our two grown-up children, I asked my then 22-year-old son when he last remembered us having harsh words.

He thought for a while and then replied, 'Father, I cannot remember ever having a crossword with you.'

I replied, 'We did once.'

He shook his head, 'I cannot remember it.'

I reminded him, 'One late afternoon when you were about four years old, you were very rude and defiant. I made a mistake. I lost my temper and shouted at you to never do that again, and I still regret that.'

My wife said to our son, 'I remember that. You were very rude to your father. He was furious. It doesn't matter; you were young.'

I turned to my 19-year-old daughter and asked her the same.

She replied, 'Father, when I was little, you punched me in the stomach!'

I was shocked. I remember the incident clearly. I had a 2 o'clock appointment to see the doctor. She was five years old, and I could not leave her home alone. I would need to take her with me. It was a six-minute walk to the doctors.

At 1:30 pm, I got ready, then looked for my daughter. I could not find her in the house. We lived on the main road. All kinds of thoughts went through my mind. I panicked ran to my neighbours' homes. No one had seen her.

I ran back to the house. My heart was racing. Something like this had never happened before. A part of me was saying, ring the doctor and cancel the appointment. However, time was crucial, and I could not waste precious time on the phone. I ran around the house, shouting her name. I looked under the beds, in the cupboards, under the staircase, and in the spare bedroom.

By now, I was shaking, and my mouth felt dry. I went outside the house and looked up and down the main road and across the street at the park. There was no sign of her. I went back inside and searched again.

She was hiding under the bed. She thought she was playing hide and seek.

Part of me was joyful, and part of me was angry. I made a mistake. In my anger, I pulled her from under the bed, grabbed her by the collars, and lifted her to my face, and shouted, 'Don't you ever do this again!'

I was rough in my handling of her. I did not have time to consider my actions; I picked her up and ran to the doctors. I was late for the appointment. Later that day, when I had calmed down and reflected on the day, I was sorry for my behaviour.

I learned a hard lesson. Over time, her young memory had distorted that incident. It had left a permanent mark on her life—*[Su Ann's Tenet 1. Wounds heal, scars are for eternity]*.

Chapter 28 – Leaking radiator

I will mention this story because it was fundamental to my understanding of God's calling and how he wanted me to respond. It was an essential requirement if my faith was to grow.

My boss had a young secretary who used to bring us our work schedules.

One day, as she gave the work schedule to me, she asked me, 'What are you doing over the weekend?'

I replied, 'fitting central heating in my house.'

She said, a bit surprised, 'So you can fit central heating!'

'I can fit radiators and do the pipework, but a friend of mine is installing the boiler for me. Do you have any plans this weekend?'

She smiled. 'We are going to see my in-laws. Have fun,' she smiled as she walked away.

A few days later, one evening, she rang me at home. 'Hari, sorry to bother you at home, but do you know any plumbers?' There was panic in her voice.

'Why?' I asked.

'We have a leaking radiator. We need a plumber.'

'I may be able to help you. Do you want me to try?'

She hesitated. 'Are you sure you can fix it?' I noticed a lack of confidence in her voice.

'Let me try. Give me your address, and I will be there in a few minutes.'

She gave me her address.

I packed my car with some tools and drove to her house.

She opened the door and led me to the upstairs hallway. There was a radiator, and underneath it were some wet towels. I looked at the radiator. There was a small hole on one side of the radiator, and water was oozing out of it.

I took out my tools and started work when I felt this strong urge to stop.

I said to her, 'I can fix it, but I'd rather teach you to do it.'

'You think I can do it?'

'Yes, if you do as I tell you.'

I guided her, and she repaired the radiator. We tested it, and it worked fine.

She was so pleased with her work that without thinking, she gave me a big hug.

'Thank you so much,' she said. Her face was radiant.

I drove home, feeling very happy. I had made her feel great, increased her self-esteem and self-worth.

That evening as I came before God in prayer, this is what God taught me.

It's God's will; he wants to teach us to use spiritual power to make things happen, heal the blind, raise the dead, grow in faith, and mature to the full stature of Christ.

2 Corinthian 13:5, Examine yourselves as to whether you are in the faith. Test yourselves. Do you not know yourselves that Jesus Christ is in you? — unless indeed you are disqualified.

He wants us to learn to account for every atom, leaf, and person in our parish, not by our abilities but by the power of the indwelling Holy Spirit. We need to experience that incredible power of been baptised in the Holy Spirit. That is our calling. To learn what it means to be an heir of God through Christ.

Galatians 4:7, Therefore, you are no longer a slave but a son, and if a son, then an heir of God through Christ.

"What?" you may ask. "That is impossible."

Mr 10:27, *Jesus looked at them intently and said, "Humanly speaking, it is* *impossible. But not with God. Everything is possible with God."*

I tried it when I first joined the church. Nothing happened for 6-7 months. I spent many nights on my knees, waiting for just a single word from the Lord. I waited and waited. The temptation was to roll over and go to sleep or go out with friends and enjoy life. I was determined. I stayed up, night after night, I made notes and reviewed my notes, and still, nothing happened.

Then one day, in the seventh month, his Spirit descended, and for the next ten years, I hardly slept. I was thrilled. I spoke, and it happened. The words I spoke in spirit with the Holy Spirit's aid had power, ***Genesis 1:3,*** *Then God said, "Let there be light"; and there was light.* That kind of power comes to us through the indwelling Holy Spirit.

I was caught in the thrills of adventure. ***John 10:10*** *I have come that they may have <u>life</u> and may have it more abundantly).*

People's lives changed around me. The Hindu priest's prophecy had come true, but not in the way my father had expected.

Start a diary and be prepared for a lot of hard work

Psalms 81:13, "Oh, that My people would listen to Me, That Israel (my people) *would walk in My ways!*

As I was coming home from work, these verses began to speak to me. What do I get out of these?

Exodus 20; 10 *The seventh day is the Sabbath of the LORD your God. In it, you shall do no work:* ***Leviticus 25; 4*** *But in the seventh year, the land is to have a Sabbath of rest.*

The Lord said to me, 'I want you to make a note of every house group and church service you attend. Make notes of your time in seven-month periods. Make a note of every prayer or scripture you <u>quote in public,</u> and on the seventh month, review your work before me. Every seventh year, you will review all your diaries with me.

Psalm 32: 8, *I will instruct you and teach you how you should go; I will guide you* *with My eye.*

I started to follow his instruction. I made notes of every public prayer I made or scriptures I quoted in public or a house group. I reviewed them in the seventh month, then on every seventh year, before him.

During the week, certain verses in the Bible would speak to me. I would note them down in my book.

Then on Sunday, before church service, I would pass on those scripture verses to the church minister Rev Jim Hammond. He would show me his prepared sermon, and the same scripture verses would be there.

2 Colossians 13; 1, "By the mouth of two or three witnesses every word shall be established."

Chapter 29 – Rees Howells, Intercessor

Great deeds require great faith. Faith that is built on God's WORD made alive by indwelling Holy Spirit, tried, tested, and refined.'

He was someone I admired. I read his biography and asked myself, 'What can I learn from his experience?' Mr Howells talks of how God taught him to account for his money. It was time for me to learn to account for my money, time, what I read, and the words I spoke to people. (Rees Howells, Intercessor, by Norman Grubb.)

Mr Howells says he gave his body to the Holy Spirit to work through him. It meant every bit of his fallen nature was to go to the cross, and the Holy Spirit would replace it with his own life. It was unconditional surrender.

Now the Holy Spirit was asking me to surrender my body to him. I just could not do it. I wanted to, but I knew it was something I could not deliver. I felt lost for a few days. *Zak's Tenet: I will reason with you, but I will not persuade you; I need your consent.*

I struggled for days. I spent sleepless nights. I said to the Holy Spirit that I was willing to give my consent, but I just did not have the confidence or the belief that I could deliver the goods. I did not want to make empty promises. He left me alone for days.

Then one evening, as I watched a boxing match on TV, my mind drifted away. I saw one of the boxers get knocked down repeatedly, but he would not give up.

I had made a big mistake. I was trying to be like Rees Howells.

The Holy Spirit tried to reason with me. The gist of it was: Mr Howells had a specific calling that suited his character and personality. I could learn and take inspiration from him, but the Holy Spirit had a different calling for me, suited to my character.

The Holy Spirit said, 'You are not Rees Howells, and he is not you. I have a path and a calling that only you can follow. In the same way, others may take inspiration from you, but they are not to follow your path.'

I felt a heavy load fall from my shoulders. God wanted me to be like that fighter. It did not matter how many times I fell, how long I lay down from the blows, as long as I kept the will to fight.

I knew why he was calling me, but I didn't have the confidence. I looked at the mountain before me, the likes of it unseen and unheard of – but I was willing to be a fool for the sake of the Lord.

He would teach me systematically to climb the ladder to the heavenly place. He needed a forceful mind.

To keep my thoughts in check during the day was easy, but I feared the nights. That was the time when my mind would wander off.

The Holy Spirit said, 'As long as you make an effort to get up, I will carry you. You have the will to empty the ocean with the palm of your hand. We will do it together; that is my covenant with you. Great deeds require great faith. Faith that is built on God's WORD, made alive by indwelling Holy Spirit, tried, tested, and refined so that it can move mountains.'

Hebrews 11:6, But without faith, it is impossible to please Him, for he who comes to God must believe that He is and that He is a rewarder of those who diligently seek Him.

I had never heard of anyone having a vision such as that which unfolded before me. God read my fears. 'I can stop the sun; I can make a new universe, just for you, as long as you keep on fighting, keep learning. Time is irrelevant. I can stop time.'

Joshua 10:13, So the sun stood still, and the moon stayed in place until the nation of Israel had defeated its enemies.

I felt reassured. What he would begin in me, he would finish, even if he had to stop the Sun or create another Earth for me to complete my course. However, I had to do my part and prove to him I was willing to obey his every command, no matter how ridiculous they sounded. There were conditions attached.

---- ----

Chapter 30 – Countries, Ethiopian famine

Romans 13:1, Let every soul be subject to the governing authorities. For there is no authority except God, and God appoints the authorities that exist.

I went through a spell of praying for countries, including Ethiopia, Uganda, Korea, and India. I do not have the space to write about them all. I have chosen three examples. The gist was for the Lord to show me that we have authority over countries, over appointed leaders. We can change a state's destiny. I have mentioned Adi Amin of Uganda and a prayer for his overthrow.

Ethiopian famine crises of 1980-86

Ethiopia. There was a severe famine in Ethiopia between 1980 and '86 that caused an estimated half a million deaths and made millions more destitute. The effects of the civil war were compounded by low rainfalls and famine.

Jan 1985. For days, the television news was about the terrible famine. Almost every Christian in the country would have at some stage prayed for Ethiopia. Our church had prayed for Ethiopia a few times and collected donations. I was in a prayer meeting held for Ethiopia and remained silent for a simple reason. I did not know what good my prayers would do.

On 14 Feb 1985, I was on my way to work. Ethiopia was on my mind. I wanted to help. I thought, 'If the Lord wants, I am willing to take unpaid time off and go to Ethiopia. Give my savings as well as myself to help them.'

I prayed about it. The next day I felt the Lord ask, 'Do you want to help them?'

'Yes,' I replied.

The story of Rees Howells went through my mind. God wanted me to be an Intercessor in this matter. I do not know how to express it. I will try it.

The Holy Spirit filled my mind with scriptures, each linked to another. Each time they passed my mind, they would come alive. *Exodus 20:5, For I, the Lord your God, am a jealous God, visiting the fathers' iniquity on the children to the third and fourth generations of those who hate Me.*

I saw the fruit of the parents' selfishness passed down to future generations and how corruption's fruit visited the children's children and destroyed families and nations.

That evening 15 Feb 1985, we had a house group. I was leading it. I shared three verses: Mark 4:39, Jesus stopped the storm.

1 Kings 18: Elijah prayed for rain.

Daniel 4:14-17, Authority over governments.

I said I would like the Lord to bring these verses to life and influence rich countries' governments to donate food aid. I prayed, 'I command you, sea, to give up water. I command you wind to take it over central Africa. Let it rain. To the governments of rich nations, I ask you to send ***$50m[1]** in aid, according to my faith.' (*or was it £? I came home and noted the above prayer in my diary, but I was too tired to remember if I said £ or $. Years later, I found an article in the national paper stating this amount of aid. **Appendix 6 at the end of this chapter**)

Looking back, the sums we prayed for were minimal in comparison to the aid that was given. For me, the prayer for a specific sum of money was encouraging, as reported in the papers.

Years later, on my 5th sabbatical year of review, I made the following notes in my diary.

Quote From Daily Express – Friday 16 Oct 1987. *"Millions of pounds of aid poured in from Western countries."* Moreover, the figure of £50 million was repeated a few times. For example, it was quoted in the article, "the Queen gave Bob Geldof an honorary knighthood for his work, raising millions of pounds for famine relief in Africa. More than **£50m** has rolled in since the concert two years ago."

Appendix Prayer for $50million

15|16 Feb 1985

6·9- 12· 3· 6   H.W.H.

6-9 pm. Cooked Meal . Went to house group. (Prepared for Hse

       group.

9-12 pm. Hse gp. Police station as special Constable's duty

12-3am. Home Eat Pudding. Talked to Katie about the

       group

         House gp.

3:10 am.

Shared in house group 3 passages in	7
Bible. Mark 4:39 Jesus stopped the storm⎤ Power over Sea	10
1 Kings 18:41 Elijah prayed for Rain ⎦ and authority	10
Daniel 4:15 Govt Controls. Govt of World ⎤Authority over " Nohonal Leaders	12
Shared these passages. I said I would	7
like the lord to bring these passages to life.	9
He would use Ethopia/Sudan (Central Africa/to bring	12
rain . Influence Govt of Rich Countries to donate Food	9
Aid.	1
(1) I prayed : I command you O Sea to	8
give up water. I command you wind to take	9
this over central Africa. Let it rain	7
(2) To the Govt of Rich Nations I ask	8
you to send ($ 50m)(or was it £) in Aid according⎤ to my Faith.	17
(3) Later I prayed, O Lord bring forth	8
a Govt in Korea that has many christian Leaders	9
Leaders who will send missionaries to Africa	7
I was tense and trembling.	5
My words were not very clear	6

—— x x ——

129

Prayer for £50M and more. Daily Express 16 Oct 1987

Dr Bob's honour degree

ROCK STAR Bob Geldof, who has given so much to help the starving, was given a big hand himself yesterday.

Unkempt Bob is now Doctor Bob after being awarded an honorary degree in science and economics at London University.

And Princes Anne, the university's chancellor—with not a hair out of place—was there to hand it to him.

Only a year ago the Queen gave him an honorary knighthood for his work raising millions of pounds for famine relief in Africa.

More than £50 million has rolled in since he set up the Live Aid concerts two years ago.

He may never win an award for Best Dressed Man—but he's certainly no slouch when it comes to first degree caring.

honour degree

Princes Anne, the univer- chancellor—with not a ut of place—was there to t to him.

' a year ago the Queen im an honorary knight

More than £50 million has rolled in since he set up the Live Aid concerts two years ago.

In America, the supergroup USA for Africa released the single, 'We Are the World,' written by Michael Jackson and Lionel Ritchie, selling 20 million copies and raising $63m (about £50m)."

A quote from the internet. "On 2 July 2005, Bob Geldof organized Live 8 - a series of rock concerts worldwide to raise awareness about global poverty and put pressure on the leaders of the G8 nations to tackle the problem. Six days later, the G8 summit at Gleneagles in Perthshire, Scotland, agreed on a **$50bn** aid package for Africa.

---- ----

Chapter 31 Prayer for rainfall

Almost 18 months later, 26 Oct 1986.

The situation in Ethiopia had worsened. There were horrible pictures of starving people on the news. As I was coming home after work, these thoughts passed through my mind. Rain, it will come. The Lord will send rain.

Seeds.

I need to pray for the UN to pass a resolution for more aid for Ethiopia. That evening I was among a small group of friends (Mick, Kate, Nicky, Nick, and Julia) who knew me well. I was relaxed.

I felt his presence.

The Lord said, 'My children have prayed for rain, and I have heard the desperate cries of the people of Ethiopia. It will rain."

I closed my eyes and thought, *But when is he going to act?*

We bowed. This small group of believers had known me for a few years. They had seen things happen. I had credibility with this group of trusted friends, and I felt comfortable in their company.

I prayed with confidence, 'Father, I bring before you Ethiopia. Perhaps these are my prayers; perhaps they are inspired by your spirit. I pray it rains inland at **3 PM** and on the coast at **5 PM** on Tuesday **4th November.'** (1986)

They all said amen. I noticed they were excited, and some of them just stared at me, I should say fascinated. They had no doubts the prayers would be answered.

Kate was the first to speak. 'Woh, that is incredible.' The others grouped around me. 'That is just amazing.'

I came home filled with joy. I prayed and gave an account of the day to the Lord and went to sleep.

My joy was short-lived. As I lay in bed late at night, I felt the Lord say, 'I am not going to do it.'

I spent a few anxious nights of soul searching. Had I made a mistake? I prayed for knowledge. I asked God why he would not answer the prayer.

His answer was simple. 'I want you to pick up the tab. You need to be armed with the scriptures, and you will need my angels to bring it about.'

I was in intercession for the whole week. The gist of it was: 'command the sea in the name of Jesus to give up its water. Create a hot spot over the Indian Ocean. Send the angels to observe and report to you.'

A few days later, they came back and reported the clouds had formed.

'Command a hot spot over southern Egypt. Command the clouds to move, create a convectional flow of air current. Send the angels to observe. Ask them to hold the clouds over the mountains until the appointed time, and then release them on the hour.'

On **5th Nov 1986**, my phone at work buzzed. Friends kept on asking if it was raining. The next day I rang the Ethiopian embassy in London. A very irate staff member told me off.

We checked the newspapers, watched the TV news. Two or three days passed, and there was no news.

My friends did not give up. They gave me suggestions, but again nothing transpired. Then Kate rang me at work.

She said, 'I have an idea. Oxfam does lots of work in Ethiopia. Ring their UK office. See if they have any news.'

I looked up the number and rang Oxfam. It rang for a while then a female voice came over the phone. I asked, 'Do you have someone in the office who deals with Ethiopia?'

'Why?' she asked.

'I want to find out if it is raining there.' There was a long pause.

'I have just returned from Ethiopia. This is my first day here.'

I said, 'I know it sounds crazy, but I would like to know if it started to rain in the mountains last Tuesday at 3 PM.'

Again, there was a pause. 'How did you know? It's not in the news yet.'

I asked again, 'Can you confirm it started to rain on Tuesday at 3 PM?'

She replied, 'Yes, it started to rain on Tuesday afternoon, but I am not certain of the time.' There was a pause, and then she added, 'I was there in the mountains when it started to rain.'

I thanked her, put the phone down, and took a deep breath. [**Appendix 7: Graph of rainfall for Ethiopia**]. It shows a steep rise in the rain from Nov 1986 –March 87 after years of below-normal rainfall.

After this, there were more intercessions for seeds, tools. Specific prayers for funds. Prayer commanding, in the name of Jesus, for nations and the UN to release funds.

[It was hard for me to verify the dates and times of rainfall in a big country like Ethiopia. Rain tends to fall in various locations at different times. I could view the charts of annual rainfall in the years 1980-1988 for Ethiopia. From 1982- Oct 1986, I found that there had been years of below-average rain that had caused the famine.

The graph showed a much higher than average rainfall starting in Nov 1986 over Ethiopia, after my prayer in Oct 1986. **[Appendix]**

On my review of this prayer over the following sabbatical years, I did not consider it <u>an answered prayer</u>. At best, it was partially answered. It also showed me the limitation of setting a date and hour for rainfall over a large country like Ethiopia.

Clouds build up over an area, it rains, and the clouds move to another location. On the other hand, Israel is a small country, and it is easier to see the clouds coming over from the sea, as in prophet **Elijah's case,** 1 Kings 18:36.

Appendix **Ethiopia** Rainfall in 1986.

https://www.worldvision.org/disaster-relief-news-stories/1980s-ethiopia-famine-facts. The 1980s Ethiopia famine and hunger crisis was one of the worst humanitarian events of the 20th century, prompting a global response to bring food assistance and save lives. Ethiopia's food shortages and hunger crisis from 1983 to 1985 led to an estimated 1 million famine deaths, according to the United Nations. Millions more were displaced and left destitute, without resources to rebuild their lives.

https://hhr-atlas.ieg-mainz.de/articles/sasson-ethiopia
The Ethiopian famine of 1983-84 and its relief crystallized the moral and political implications of what the anthropologist Didier Fassin has called "humanitarian governance."

(From Mid 1986, a month after my prayer, the rainfall is substantially high after years of low rainfall). *Ethiopian National Meteorological Services.*

Year   1976   80   84   86   92

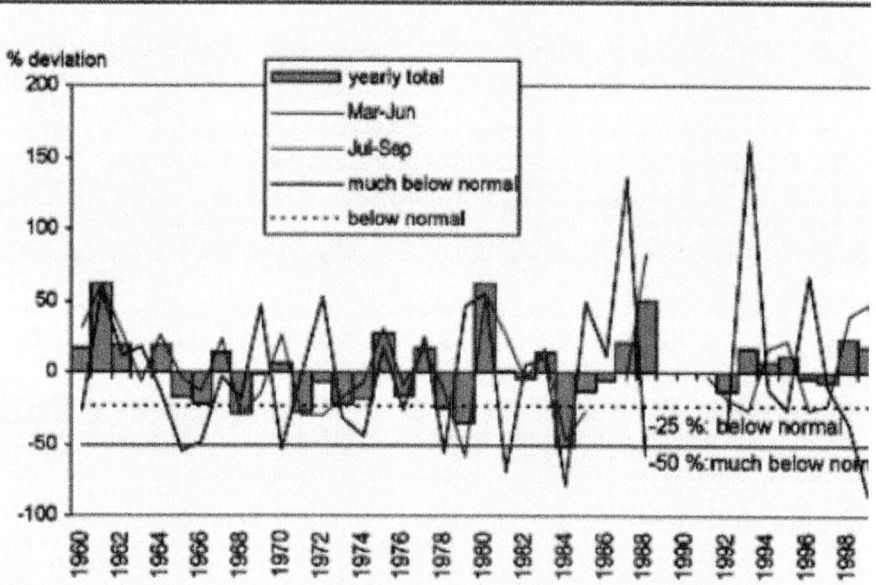

Meze-Hausken: Contrasting climate variability with perceived climate change

135

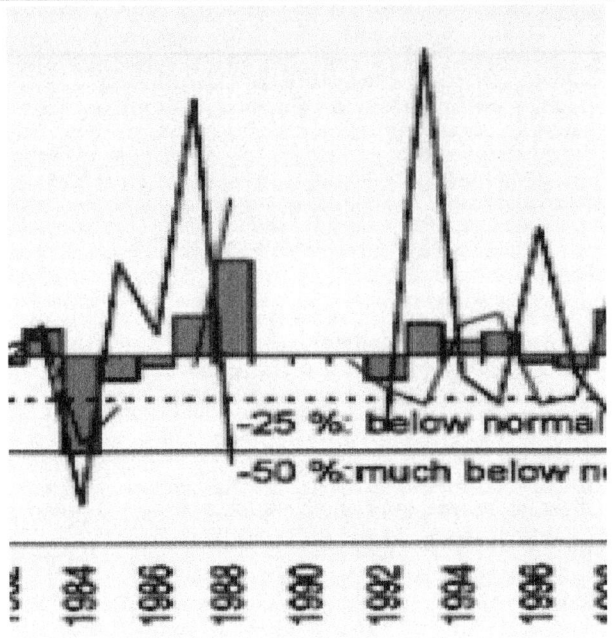

Prayers for Terry Waite 1987

Terry Waite (born 1939) was the Assistant for Anglican Communion Affairs for the Archbishop of Canterbury, Robert Runcie. He made three trips to Lebanon to free Western hostages held there. On his third try, on 20 January 1987, he was taken, hostage.

On 3rd Feb 1987, I was with two friends, David and Julia. Terry Waite's disappearance had been headline news on TV for a few days. It was late in the evening. Concern for our fellow Christians was on our minds. David suggested we pray for Terry Waite.

When it was my turn, I prayed, 'Father, we bring Terry Waite before you. I don't understand the issue. It's tied up with **arms manufacture** in this country and the death of people in Lebanon. Father, the **17th of February** will be a _significant day_ for Terry. I don't understand where this fits or what fits into this date. I ask for his return home on this day.'

On 17<u>th</u> <u>Feb</u>, his family and the Archbishop of Canterbury made an appeal on TV to the nation for support and requested the kidnappers to release him.

However, Terry Waite did not return home on 17th Feb 1987. He spent five years in captivity.

Five years later, according to the BBC, Terry Waite immediately faced questions over his role in the 'American arms for hostages' scandal after his release. (I had said 'arms manufacture in this country,' meaning the UK. I quoted the wrong country. It was <u>US arms</u>).

Within my small group of friends, the lesson we learned was about the power and authority invested in us in the name of Christ. If the Lord chose us for these prayers, it was an act of grace, an honour bestowed on us. It was not something we had earned.

God would be delighted to see more of his followers step boldly forward. I have given some examples from my diaries, but the best proof is to do it yourself.

....

KOREA June 1984 A future nuclear explosion.

As I was walking to work, this vision came before me.

'Son of man, what do you see?'

'Lord,' I said, 'I see a power-mad man waging war against his neighbour in S.E. Asia. It is going to happen in a few decades. **A nuclear explosion.** Possibly ten million people affected.'

'Son of man, what do you think?'

'Lord, I am only a created being. A vessel of mere earth. You are the sovereign Lord.'

'Tell me what you think.'

'Lord, this mustn't happen. Perhaps the man should not have been allowed to be born. However, as he is already alive, something else needs to be done. Lord, your Word says you establish all authority.

'He must not rise to this level of authority. Instead, I pray that you let this authority be invested in **four or five men**[1] of sound mind, preferably Christians, so that through their leadership, God could bless this region.'

'And how shall they come to know me?' the Lord asked.

'Through missionaries from S. Korea. They shall dwell with them.'

I don't know why I was led to pray in this direction. I had no interest in that region of the world.

...x..x...

[1] **In 2018**, I came across this as I was going through my diaries. I tried to make sense of it. On the internet, I read that:-

N Korea. Kim's Three Sons

Kim's three sons and his son-in-law, along with O Kuk-ryol, an army general, have been noted as possible successors. (My quote many years earlier had been 'Let this authority be invested in 4/5 mature, sane men, preferably Christian.' Had I prayed for these men? They indeed were not Christians.)

On 9 October 2006, North Korea announced it had conducted its first nuclear weapons test.

Throughout 2017, tensions between the United States and North Korea reached a significant high, and US President Trump threatened 'fire and fury,'

North Korea threatened to launch missiles towards Guam and made threatening comments to Australia about nuclear retaliation for siding with the US in April and October 2017.

Trump vowed to 'destroy North Korea if it poses a threat to the US or its allies.'

I am not sure what the purpose of this prayer was. I had not initiated it. I doubt any missionaries from S. Korea would have gone to N Korea.

Was this prayer meant to prevent a nuclear war? Had this prayer said three decades earlier, in the fullness of time, saved millions of lives?

--- ----

Chapter 32 – A Stranger

Luke 6:29, 'If someone slaps you on one cheek, offer the other cheek also. If someone demands your coat, offer your shirt also,'

It was Friday evening, late in autumn of 1980. I was looking forward to spending the weekend at my brother's. He lived about 80 miles from me. After work, I went home, packed a small bag, and took a train. I had arranged to be at his home at 8.30 pm. As I would not be on time for dinner, I asked him to save some dinner for me.

The train arrived at his hometown around 8.15 pm. About ten passengers got off the train. I searched for a payphone to call my brother, found one, and realized I had no coins.

When I came out of the station, it was empty. I was about to cross the car park when I noticed a man with a suitcase standing at the taxi bay. He looked nervous. Something about his body language did not seem right. I watched him for a while.

Luke 6:29, 'If someone slaps you on one cheek, offer the other cheek also. If someone demands your coat, offer your shirt also,' went through my mind. I thought the Holy Spirit was trying to tell me something. I walked up to the man.

'Excuse me,' I said to the man, 'do you need any help?'

He looked at me, nodded, and handed me a piece of paper. There was a name on it, and it sounded Eastern European. He pointed two fingers at his eyes and then at the paper.

'Are you looking for this man?' I asked.

He looked worried and replied in a foreign language. I realized he did not speak any English, so I looked around to see anyone else nearby. It was dark, getting colder, and there was no one about. I thought he is waiting for someone to collect him; maybe I should stay with him until his friend turns up.

We waited. We tried to converse, but neither of us understood a word.

A quarter of an hour had gone, and no one turned up to collect him. The scripture went through my mind. The Holy Spirit asked, 'How are you going to respond to this helpless person's need?'

The kindness and goodness of the two Hindu boys I had met in Mombasa and the Hindu elderly couple in Kisumu went through my mind. These people had set an example of conduct that is pleasing to the Lord. He had brought them into my life for a purpose, to show me good conduct.

I looked at the lost foreign man. He was cold, worried, and helpless. I pointed at my wristwatch, lifted my hand, displayed five fingers, and said, 'Five minutes.'

He understood the gesture. I walked out of the station and flagged a passing taxi. I got into the taxi and said to the driver that I had someone in the station waiting. He drove into the station and stopped at the taxi bay. He got out, picked up the stranger's suitcase, and put it in the luggage compartment. I pointed at the back seat and indicated to the foreign man to get inside.

I got into the front passenger seat.

The driver looked at me and asked, 'Where to, boss?'

I hesitated. 'Please, call your office on your radio and ask them to look up this address?' I handed him the paper. He called the office, and a minute later, a woman gave us an address.

'Is this where you want to go?'

I nodded. On the way, I explained the situation to the driver. We came up to the address. I knocked on the door. A man opened it, and I asked him if he was expecting a guest, pointing at the car's passenger.

The owner said, 'Looks like you got the wrong house.'

I showed him the name on paper. 'Do you know this man?'

He wrote down an address and said, 'Try this place.'

We drove to the address. Again, the man was not expecting any guest.

He gave us another address. We drove to that address. Wrong again. I sat in the taxi. The driver looked at me. 'What now?'

I shook my head. I looked at my watch, and it was 1 AM.

I prayed silently. 'Lord, I am cold, tired, and hungry, and I have no idea what to do.'

We sat quietly in the taxi. The man placed his hand on my shoulder and opened his palm to say, what now.

If I was going home, I would have taken him to my house, but that option was not available. I looked at the driver and said, 'We go to the police station and see if they can help him.'

We left him in the care of the police. The driver dropped me at my brother's house. Fortunately, I had enough cash in my wallet to pay him. It was late in the night when I rang the doorbell. My furious brother opened the upstairs bathroom window.

'It's you!' he shouted. 'Do you know what time it is?' In the background, I could hear the two-year-old twins crying. The bell had woken them.

He opened the door and led me to the spare room. I was cold and hungry. I was going to ask him about the dinner plate he had saved for me. I looked at his angry face and decided to remain quiet.

I undressed in the dark, sat on the bed to give an account of the day to the Lord.

'Heavenly father…' I paused. For once, I thought I would lie down and pray. I lay down, rested my head on the pillow, and prayed, 'Heavenly Father.' And I was asleep. It was the shortest prayer of my life.

------ ★---

On my 6th sabbatical year, as I went over my diary, the Lord reminded me I had not completed my prayer. Thirty-eight years later, I gave him a report of that day and finished my prayer.

My first vision was about Judgment Day, and he had shown me the gold and silver standard; works that will endure the fire and works that will turn to ashes. God started the excellent works in me/us, and he will not stop until the last day.

God prepared this good works for a reason, and it is up to me/us to seek out these good works, i.e., to work out our salvation with **fear**[1] and trembling. We are **accountable**[2] for its progress (including all our prayers, house meetings, and especially words we spoke in the spirit) until the last day.

The reason is simple: for us to learn and grow spiritually as God ordained it from the beginning. He is not preparing us for this earth but our future place in his eternal home. That is why many things that happen to us make no sense because he is preparing us for our future role in his kingdom.

As we review our diaries with the Holy Spirit in the sabbatical years, we see the bigger pictures. The Holy Spirit begins to reveal God's plan for us in his coming Kingdom. Events that made no sense begin to show a pattern of a greater power guiding our destiny.

[Kate Adin's Tenet 2]. "You are unique. There is a greater power that guides your path. Everything that has been made, created is set up for you (for those like you).

--- ☆ ---

[1] *Php 2:12, Wherefore, my beloved, as ye have always obeyed, not as in my presence only, but now much more in my absence, <u>work out your</u> salvation with fear and trembling. (Why work out? What if you neglect it?)*

[2] *2 Peter 1:10, Therefore, brethren, be even <u>more diligent</u> in making <u>your call an election sure</u>, for if you do these things, you will never stumble.*

Chapter 33 - 'Do not sell your birthright.'

Our birthright.

The Holy Spirit put to me these five questions. To help me answer them, I received visions regarding the questions below.

1. How does one seek the <u>quality of workmanship</u> required on Judgment Day?

   Moreover, a caution as well. 'Do not be distracted by going out to convert the world. First, God wants to convert you, not the world. Once converted, you can then go out into the world, like the disciples, to convert the world.'

2. What are the good works that God had ordained for me? *Ephesians 2:10, For we are His workmanship, created in Christ Jesus for good works, which <u>God prepared beforehand</u> that we should walk in them.*

3. Does the quality of my workmanship meet the gold standard? When tested, will my works endure or burn on Judgment Day? The scripture says to test all things.

   2 Colossians 13:5, Examine yourselves, whether ye be in the faith; prove your selves.

4. Will I be one of those holy perfected saints who will return with him?

   1Thessalonians 3:13, at the coming of our Lord Jesus Christ with all <u>His saints</u>.

   Again in *Ephesians 3:13, at the coming of our Lord Jesus Christ with all His saints.*

5. Will I be one of those five foolish **virgins**[1] with unwashed **robes**[2] that

   --- ☆ ---

[1] *Matthew 25:1, Then shall the kingdom of Heaven be likened to ten virgins, who took their lamps and went forth to meet the bridegroom v: 2, And five of them were wise, and five were foolish.*

[2] *Revelation 22:14, Blessed are they that <u>wash their robes</u> that they may have the right to come to the tree of life and<u> enter in by the gates into the city</u>. ..x.x*

reside outside the **city gates**[3] of New Heaven?

6. Will I have power over **nations?**[4]
7. Will I be a pillar in his **Temple?**[5]

There is a requirement attached for the right to enter into the city, *'Blessed are they that wash their robes.'*

Our salvation in Christ gives us more than a place in heaven, i.e., an **inheritance**[6]**.** The inheritance we receive will depend on us: are we **overcomers**[4] or not, inside the city or outside the city.

What effort we put in our salvation will **determine**[7] where we will be: inside or outside the city gates.

A fool builds God's kingdom with his hands, feet, and mind ignoring the **guidance, corrections**[8]**, rebukes** of the indwelling Holy Spirit. On judgment day, all his works will burn to ashes, but he will survive. An eternal fool in God's kingdom without an inheritance (birthright), following in the steps of **Esau**[9]**.**

--- ☆ ---

[3] *Revelation 3:18, Therefore, I counsel you to buy from me gold refined by fire so that you may be rich; and white robes to clothe you and keep the shame of your nakedness from being seen, and salve to anoint your eyes so that you may see.*

[4] *Revelation 2:26, "And he who overcomes, and keeps My works until the end, to him I will give power over the nations.*

[5] *Revelation 3:12, "He who overcomes, I will make him a pillar in the temple of My God, and he shall go out no more. And I will write on him the name of My God and the name of the city of My God, the New Jerusalem, which comes down out of heaven from My God. And I will write on him My new name.*

[6] *1 Peter 1:4, to an inheritance incorruptible and undefiled and that does not fade away, reserved in heaven for you.*

[7] *Philippians 2:12, Therefore, my beloved, as you have always obeyed, not as in my presence only, but now much more in my absence, work out your salvation (inheritance) with fear and trembling.*

[8] *2 Timothy 3:16, All scripture is inspired by God and useful for teaching, reproof, correction, and righteousness training.*

[9] *Genesis 25:33-34, Then Jacob said, "Swear to me as of this day." So he swore to him and <u>sold his birthright</u> to Jacob. And Jacob gave <u>Esau</u> bread and stew of lentils; then he ate and drank, arose, and went his way. Thus Esau despised his birt birthright.*

---- ----

Chapter 34 – The Unfairness of Life

Revelation 21:3, And I heard a loud voice from the throne saying, "See, the home of God is among mortals. <u>He will dwell with them</u> as their God; they will be his people, and God himself will be with them;

This is just my understanding, and I admit it is only my view and opinions. I was not born in a Christian culture, so some of its values and concepts are obstacles.

Like many people, I have struggled with the concept of a loving God and a suffering world. The picture of young children dying of starvation is at odds with the notion of a benevolent, compassionate God. Besides, I was not comfortable with the view that it was solely due to Adam and Eve's original sin that suffering entered the world.

This is just the gist of my understanding. It helps me to relate better with God.

Long before any creation, God spent eternity alone. Loneliness kills; loneliness brings suffering. Have a chat with an isolated elderly couple. They will talk about the pain and suffering of isolation. God spent a very long time on his own. He had a long, severe experience of loneliness and the pain and the suffering it brings. It existed before sin.

Creation was his way of overcoming this isolation, this pain and suffering in his life. God longed for a family just as a parent longs for a child, a family, a **_home_**.

*2 Corinthians **6:16,** For you are the temple of the living God. As God has said: "I will **dwell in them** And walk among them. I will be their God, And they shall be My people."*

A lone prisoner on an island, isolated for years, will welcome a rat in his cell. He will long for a daily visit from the vermin. He would probably try to feed him, try to make a connection with him.

One day the rat fails to turn up. He waits for days. In all probability, this person would go into a deep depression over a vermin. He would grieve as if a family member had passed away. That is what isolation does.

This pain and suffering have little or nothing to do with sin. This emptiness, this lack of purpose in God's Spirit, follows him as if it was his shadow. It exists where life exists. Where there is no life, it does not exist. God overcame this shadow and wants us to overcome it.

Secondly, we do not punish children for their parents' sins/crimes. In the Old Testament, to cover people's sins, the slaughter of innocent animals was needed. One coming from a Hindu Gujarati culture where killing an animal is viewed as brutal, and worse still, to eat them. It is akin to cannibalism and an obstacle for me.

The simple explanation that Adam and Eve's sin should visit us was an obstacle. I brought it before the Lord, and he told me to walk around this hill. One day I will understand the concept, whatever that is!

However, the moment the Lord took me to the spiritual garden, I was at peace with him. It's a place where angels, humans, and animals co-existed in harmony, delighting in each other's presence. *Isaiah 11:7, And the cow and the bear shall feed; their young ones shall lie down together; and the lion shall eat straw like the ox.*

All he would say was, 'You have a physical and spiritual body. You can be in a material world and a spiritual world simultaneously; that is a reality. There is a world out there that needs perfecting. How are you going to respond to the needs of the world awaiting redemption?'

The Lord continued, 'Your relations with God the Father, your question of three gods in one, are mountains too high for you to climb. Walk around them with me. Someday we will climb them. Call me your older brother.'

Hebrews 2:11, So now Jesus and the ones he makes holy have the same Father. That is why Jesus is not ashamed to call them his brothers and sisters.

In our Hindu culture, when a father is absent, the eldest son takes his place as head of the family. In Gujarati, my mother tongue, we call the older son, 'Mōṭō Bhai.' It is a term of endearment, used with affection and respect.

For me, Jesus was my Mōṭō Bhai. It was enough to settle all my arguments about the trinity for the moment.

I found no contradiction between our Holy Book Bhagavad- Gita and the Bible. A book I was brought up on from my birth. Both books state the world was created by the Word of God (Brahman in Gita), and the Word became flesh and dwelt among us.

It was also easy for me to reconcile with other faiths. People of different religions chose to follow the scriptures that were part of their culture and continue their spiritual journey. One day the whole world will have a clear view. A simple realisation that worked for me.

People are free to disagree with me. I would not like to impose my views on others.

One of my uncles was a devout Hindu, followed the teachings of Vedic books written long before the New Testament, among them the Bhagavad- Gita. He acknowledged the Holy Spirit's working and WORD of God (Brahman the creator) in the Vedic books and his life. The divine spirit, as he would call it, "was offered to all humanity."

Romans 3:29-30, After all, is God the God of the Jews only? Isn't he also the God of the Gentiles (Hindus)? Of course, he is. v30, There is only one God, and he makes people right with himself only by faith, whether they are Jews or Gentiles (or Hindus).

There are many honest, decent Hindus and Jews who would acknowledge the Holy Spirit's presence in their lives. However, the promise to be an **heir** of God isn't offered to them in their scriptures.

Romans 4:14, If the law's adherents are to be the heirs, faith is null, and the promise is void.

Romans 8:16-18, The Spirit Himself bears witness with our spirit that we are children of God. If children, then heirs — heirs of God and joint-heirs with Christ, if indeed we suffer with Him, that we may also be glorified together. I consider that the sufferings of this present time are not worthy of being compared with the glory which shall be revealed in us.

There were many things I did not understand. Rather than trying to resolve them with my understanding, I set my mind to follow Jesus.

The question he put to me was, 'How are you going to respond to the needs of a suffering world awaiting redemption?'

I did not have an answer. I looked at him.

'Follow me,' he said. 'We have a long journey ahead of us.'

Everything you do, every thought you think, you will give an account for.

The Lord said, 'Everything you do, every thought you think, you will give an account. Every three hours, you will come before me to give an account of yourself, and you will plan the next few hours with me.'

2 Corinthians 10:5, casting down imaginations, and every high thing that is exalted against the knowledge of God, and bringing every thought into captivity to the obedience of Christ;

Fortunately, we had a fifteen-minute tea break at work, followed by lunch, and an afternoon tea break, so I met this requirement.

I would wake up, spend 10 minutes reading the Bible, and then enter into prayer for about 10 minutes, planning the day with the Lord. Get ready for work, go to work, at break time give an account, come home, clean up, followed by a cup of tea, then for about half an hour sharing the day with the Lord.

Have a meal, go out and deliver leaflets or attend to church matters, come home from church and go over the evening with the Lord. I would give an account of my time, money, and my conduct that day. I would wait upon the Lord for guidance; compare my behaviour with what I had read in the scriptures.

I would make notes of my time, of any prayer or house meeting, or of anything the Lord had taught me during the day. Often I would wake up at 3 or 4 am to review things going through my mind, events that had happened or were about to happen. There were times I slept three or four hours a day.

It was not an easy life. At times, I felt I was missing out in life, friends, holidays, and love. It was a lonely walk.

My prayers were answered for three reasons: to meet the church's needs, for the Holy Spirit to guide me in certain spiritual realms, and to confirm my guidance with events on earth.

---- ----

Chapter 35 – Calling for Haringey

1 Thessalonians 3:13, at the coming of our Lord Jesus with all his saints.

I have an intuitive grasp of certain spiritual things but have difficulty explaining them. I cannot fully explain how I can state a day and hour of healing. To understand this, one needs a spiritual mind.

1 Corinthians 2:7, But we speak the wisdom of God in a mystery, the hidden wisdom which God ordained before the ages for our glory,

God gave me the free will to accept the challenge to be transformed into the image (2 Colossians 3:18 Romans 8:29) of his son or walk away. In God, past, present, and future are one (Revelation 1:8). If I walk in the spirit and have courage and insight, I can walk in the past, present and future. *We see such references to our Lord in the Old Testament, Genesis 18:1, Then the LORD appeared to him (Abraham) by the terebinth trees of Mamre, as he was sitting in the tent door in the heat of the day.*

It is part of our glory (1 Peter 5:1), our inheritance, which makes us more significant than any prophet.

1 Thessalonians 3:13, at the coming of our Lord Jesus with all his saints.

Lord, 'Will you govern with me? Will you return as a holy perfected saint with me? I need to train you.'

Revelation 20:6, but they shall be priests of God and Christ and shall reign with him a thousand years.

I had been in Haringey for a few years. During this time, I had covered the whole area with leaflets. I had delivered several thousand of them. Rev Hammond had noted my work and supported me in prayer.

Now Rev Hammond was keen to get the Christian gospel into every home in the Haringey ladder, an area ¾ mile wide by 1 ½   mile long surrounded by main roads on all side. He ordered hundreds of Saint John's gospels and asked me about my experience of distributing the leaflets. He invited me for coffee, and we sat down and drew up a plan.

He thought it was time other members of the church got involved. He asked volunteers to help distribute St John's gospel. Soon every house in our patch had a gospel of St John. He got so excited that he ordered hundreds of Baptist Times newspapers and regularly delivered them to all the houses on the ladder with church members' help.

Now that the church was doing much better work than I was, it was time to move onto something different.

3rd Sept 1980 – Vision for Haringey

It was twenty-six years after the Evangelistic Billy Graham filled the 11,400-seat Haringey Arena for 12 weeks. Hundreds of people stepped forward to give their lives to Jesus.

–The Lord walking in Haringey. Is there a man after the Lord's heart?

As I was coming home after work, the Lord spoke to me from the scriptures. *1 Corinthians 2:16,* for we have the mind of Christ.

2 Corinthians 13:5, Examine yourselves as to whether you are in the faith. Test yourselves. Do you not know yourselves that Jesus Christ is in you?

The Holy Spirit said, 'It is time to learn to exercise the mind of Christ within you. What was true in Christ must become your experience. It is time to learn to account for every atom, leaf, and person on your patch (to get the gist of it, because you just do not have enough time on Earth to grasp this detail fully). To understand the value of each thing, how each should be loved, cared for, nourished, and nurtured.

'You need to understand why there is pain and suffering and why it comes at a high cost. Eternal justice demands someone has to make restitution to those who bore this cost. Who collects the tab?

'What constitutes good governance? When the Lord returns, he will return with perfected saints. *Thessalonians 3:13,* so that He may establish your hearts blameless in holiness before our God and Father at the coming of our Lord Jesus Christ **with** all **His saints**.

The training starts now.'

I thought it's an impossible mission, but all things are possible with God. He called me for the above task, and I believed him. Now, it was up to him to guide me.

........x....x..

3rd Sept 1980	4
Is there a Man after the Lord's Heart	8
	0
	0
We walk through the streets of Haringey	7
my lord and I. It is cool in the evening. My	11
Spirit is Sad. (Ps 143:7 Pr 1:23)	3
Why is the Lord so Lonely? Why does he	10
do so little work here. Why does he walk alone.	10
Spirit: H there is not one man after my heart	10
Amos 3:3 Shall two walk together unles they be of one mind?	13
We are the inspiration to the lord. It is	9
he who does the work. We simply walk with	9
him. Would you like a close relationship with	10
him? A relation in which he comes and stays	10
with you every moment.	4
He desire it with us, because he want	8
to love and care for you, It inspires him.	9
Someone he can look after and walk with	8
	0
	0
He sits in your room. He is responsible	8
for you, cares for you, Loves you and likes to	10
be with you.	3
Your fellowship inspires him to think,	6
plan and work out things in this Area. To	9
claim this area for his Father. To begin	8
the work of reconcilation for everything in Haringey	8

My Lord and I walk through the streets of Haringey. It is cool in the evening.

Our fellowship inspires me to claim this area for him. He spoke to me through these verses:

1. To begin the work of reconciliation for everything in Haringey.

Colossians 1:20 and by Him to reconcile all things to Himself, by Him, whether things on earth or things in heaven, having made peace through the blood of His cross.

2. We are his dwelling, a place of love, joy, and inspiration.

2 Corinthians 6:16, For you are the temple of the living God. As God has said: "I will dwell in them And walk among them. I will be their God, And they shall be My people."

3. To claim this area for him.

Genesis 13:14, Look as far as you can see in every direction — north and south, east and west. V15, I am giving all this land, as far as you can see, to you. (Bear in mind some promises won't be fulfilled until Judgment Day).

4.   His steward

To apply, sow and water the unfulfilled prophecies in the Old Testament, pleading to God to fulfil the prophecies before Judgment Day. Meanwhile, his steward is willing to implement them on his patch. For example

*Isaiah 65:25, the wolf and the lamb shall feed together, the **lion** shall eat straw like the ox, and dust shall be the serpent's food. They shall not hurt nor destroy in all My holy mountain," Says the LORD.*

In summary, a spiritual steward for this area.

Ezekiel 22:30 I looked for someone who might rebuild the wall of righteousness that guards the land. I searched for someone to stand in the gap in the wall so I wouldn't have to destroy the land.

13th December 1980. The Holy Spirit is in control; I follow. We start to walk around the area to set the boundary.

The indwelling Holy Spirit said, 'Let the spirit flow into the trees, plants, and homes. *Isaiah 55:11 So shall My word be that goes forth from My mouth; It shall not **return** to Me void, But it shall accomplish what I please, And it shall prosper in the thing for which I sent it.-*

---- ☆ ----

In each generation, a person of God has to claim every Patch/Parish and hold it for the Lord.

Three things are required.

1.   An anointed <u>ambassador </u>of Christ in every Patch (Parish).
         *2 Corinthians 5:20, Now then, we are ambassadors for **Christ**, as though God were pleading through us:*
2.   The Gospel message delivered to every household, not once but several times.
3.   On Judgment Day, God requires a witness in the <u>full stature</u> of Christ to testify.

Ephesians 4:13, until all of us come to the unity of the faith and of the knowledge of the Son of God, to maturity, to the measure of the <u>full stature of Christ.</u>

-- ☆ ---

What we do today will determine what we shall be in God's kingdom.

This task, this calling, is a favour granted to us, a privilege we should grab with all our heart, mind, and strength. Our eternal standing of who and what we will be in God's kingdom rests on this trial period. We pass or fail rests in our hand.

--- 🐝 ----

Chapter 36 – An Inventory of Haringey

We started with taking an inventory of the area.

Over several months, I walked around the whole area, making an inventory of every street, lamppost, tree, shop, and house. I made a rough estimate of all the trees height and noted them. I drew a map of the Haringey ladder (my patch) and inserted the details into it. It took months to do it.

I noted the names of every householder in my book. *Numbers 1:2 "From the whole community of Israel, record all the warriors' names by their clans and families.* [**Appendix**]

For the next few years, I lived in an intense state of constant prayer and communion with the lord. In the morning, I would wait for the lord's plan for me for that day. He would share with me the good works he had planned for the day. As the Holy Spirit prayed through me, taking an inventory of everything in my patch, I would get glimpses of his plan.

As I knelt to pray over the next few months, scripture verses came to life and transformed my way of thinking.

Romans 8:2, *And we know that* <u>all</u> <u>things</u> *work together for good to those who love God, to those called according to His purpose.*

The indwelling Holy Spirit would throw light on the above scripture. Families were waking up, the delight of parents at the child's birth—the joy of friends meeting. People going to work. All things are working for my/our good in my Patch.

As I went around my patch with the Holy Spirit, he prayed that I might learn to use his power wisely. That I might acquire the ability to fulfil scriptures and begin reconciliation of all things in Heaven and Earth.

Colossians 1:20, and by Him **to** **reconcile** *all things to Himself, by Him, whether things on earth or things in heaven, having made peace through the blood of His cross.*

This learning process would not terminate on Earth but would continue in the hereafter. This was just the start, the initiation of my calling. We are Christ's representatives on Earth. This calling to follow in his footsteps falls into our laps, and it is a hundred thousand times more challenging than to preach the gospel.

God has a vision for this area. We/I intercede on behalf of my patch, asking God to **pour**[1] out the Holy Spirit and make us fellow **workers**[2] with him. Furthermore, to fulfill God's dream, we rekindle the Garden of **Eden**[3] concept and restart **reconciliation**[4] of all things in Heaven and Earth. To see the first fruit of that Garden of Eden on our patch, i.e., a society that holds God in awe and reverence, with lower crime, happier, healthier people, etc. –

-- ☆ ---

Herald. Aug 3 1988. Distributed in Wood Green, Haringey.

Haringey residents often complain about the state of the borough's streets, which are often covered with litter.

But judges of this year's London in Bloom completion did not let that affect their Judgment when they awarded Haringey the Residential Areas Trophy for the first time.

---

[1] *Acts 2:33, "Therefore being exalted to the right hand of God, and having received from the Father the promise of the Holy Spirit; He poured out this which you now see and hear.*

[2] *1 Corinthians 3:9, For we are God's fellow workers; you are God's field, you are God's building.*

[3] *1 Corinthians 15:4, And so it is written, "The first man Adam became a living being." The last Adam (Jesus) became a life-giving spirit.*

[4] *Colossians 1:20, and by Him to reconcile all things to Himself, by Him, whether things on earth or things in heaven, having made peace through the blood of His cross. ...x..x...*

Anointing of the Holy Spirit

The anointing of the Holy Spirit is in proportion to our commitment to his kingdom and his creation. The greater our commitment, the greater our spiritual growth and sanctification.

Each morning, the indwelling Holy Spirit thanked all the creatures and people for their daily contribution towards God's coming **Kingdom**[5] and my/our salvation. A daily reminder to God that 'my/Our Patch' had brought immense **pleasure**[6,7] to Him.

1. We pleaded to God to continue to promote the welfare, interest, and happiness of all on my patch.

2. To help me make **restitution**[8] on my patch to all for their pain and suffering on Earth and eventually reconcile all things in Heaven and Earth by creating a new **Earth**[9] and Heaven.

Moreover, I felt an obligation to creation and God to make them whole for the cost of my **salvation**[10]. A commitment began with the help of the

--- ☆ ---

[5] *Mark 1:15, and saying, "The time is fulfilled, and the kingdom of God is at hand. Repent, and believe in the gospel."*

[6] *Ephesians 1:5, having predestined us to adoption as sons by Jesus Christ to Himself, according to the good pleasure of His will.*

[7] *Philippians 2:13, for it is God who works in you both to will and to do for His good pleasure.*

[8] *Ephesians 2:15, having abolished in His flesh the enmity, that is, the law of commandments contained in ordinances, to create in Himself one new man from the two, thus making peace,*

[9] *Colossians 1:20, and by Him to reconcile all things to Himself, by Him, whether things on earth or things in heaven, having made peace through the blood of His cross.*

[10] *Philippians 2:12, Therefore, my beloved, as you have always obeyed, not as in my presence only, but now much more in my absence, work out your salvation with fear and trembling;*   ...x..x...

indwelling Holy Spirit, continuing in the hereafter until I reached the full **stature**[11] of Christ. When I have reached that full Stature, I could stand beside Christ on Judgment Day as his witness that all were given a chance to be made whole. Finally, to receive crowns and our entire inheritance in Christ based on merit.

As I prayed with the Holy Spirit, there were also sad events. In the evening prayer, as the **Spirit prayed**[12], he would account for a child's death, a mother not coming home from the hospital. Living creatures tore apart so another animal could feed and live.

As we continued in prayer, I would see in a vision a fox would kill a wild mother rabbit called **Leah**[13], and her young ones would face a slow, painful death. The Holy Spirit would stop here. He would show me the three young ones starving to death and bring before me the high cost of establishing the kingdom of God and my salvation, paid for by others' blood.

The Holy Spirit said, 'This is the price paid (tab) by the creatures so that we can establish the **kingdom of God**[14] on earth, and you and others can grow spiritually. Your salvation is being paid for by others. You owe your Lord Jesus, neighbours, and Mother Earth a debt of gratitude for letting you work out your perfection at their cost.

--- ☆ ---

[11] *Ephesians 4:13, till we all come to the unity of the faith and of the knowledge of the Son of God, to a perfect man, to the measure of the stature of the fullness of Christ;*

[12] *Luke 11:2, so He said to them, "When you pray, say: Our Father in heaven, Hallowed be Your name. Your kingdom come, Your will be done On earth as it is in heaven.*

[13] *Leah, (**Leah**; her death would profoundly affect my attitude to salvation. More in my Book, The spiritual Sanctuary, according to the Bible. An in-depth book about our life in the hereafter).*

[14] *Luke 10:9, "And heal the sick there, and say to them, 'The kingdom of God has come near to you.' ...x..x...*

Neglect of Salvation, causes of

1) Impenitence **Ezek 33:9,** "Nevertheless if you warn the wicked to turn from his way, and he does not turn from his way, he shall die in his iniquity; but you have delivered your soul.

2) Absorption in Business Luke **14:18,** "But they all with one *accord* began to make excuses. The first said to him, 'I have bought a piece of ground, and I must go and see it. I ask you to have me excused.'

3) Procrastination   **Act 24:25,** Now, as he reasoned about righteousness, self-control, and the judgment to come, Felix was afraid and answered, "Go away for now; when I have a convenient time, I will call for you."

4) Insensibility   **Act 28:27,** For the hearts of this people have grown dull. Their ears are hard of hearing, And their eyes they have closed, Lest they should see with *their* eyes and hear with *their* ears, Lest they should understand with *their* hearts and turn so that I should heal them.

5) Perilous if Persisted in Heb 2:3, how shall we escape if we **neglect** so great a salvation, which at first began to be spoken by the Lord, and was confirmed to us by those who heard *Him*. **Heb 12:25,** See that you do not refuse the one who is speaking; for if they did not escape when they refused the one who warned them on earth, how much less will we escape if we reject the one who warns from heaven!

Everlasting life and Salvation. John 3:16, "For God so loved the world that He gave His only begotten Son, that whoever <u>believes in Him</u> should not perish but have everlasting life.

Everlasting life is about our place in the new Heaven, inside the New Jerusalem or outside the City with thieves and murderers. **Rev 22:14-15,** Blessed *are* those who do His commandments, that they may have the right to the tree of life, and may enter through the gates into the city. But outside *are* dogs and sorcerers and sexually immoral and murderers and idolaters, and whoever loves and practices a lie.

Salvation is also about our inheritance, who, what we will be based on merit in his Kingdom. Rev 3:21, "To him who overcomes I will grant to sit with Me on **My throne,** as I also overcame and sat down with My Father on His throne.

Appendix Taking Inventory of Haringey, My PATCH

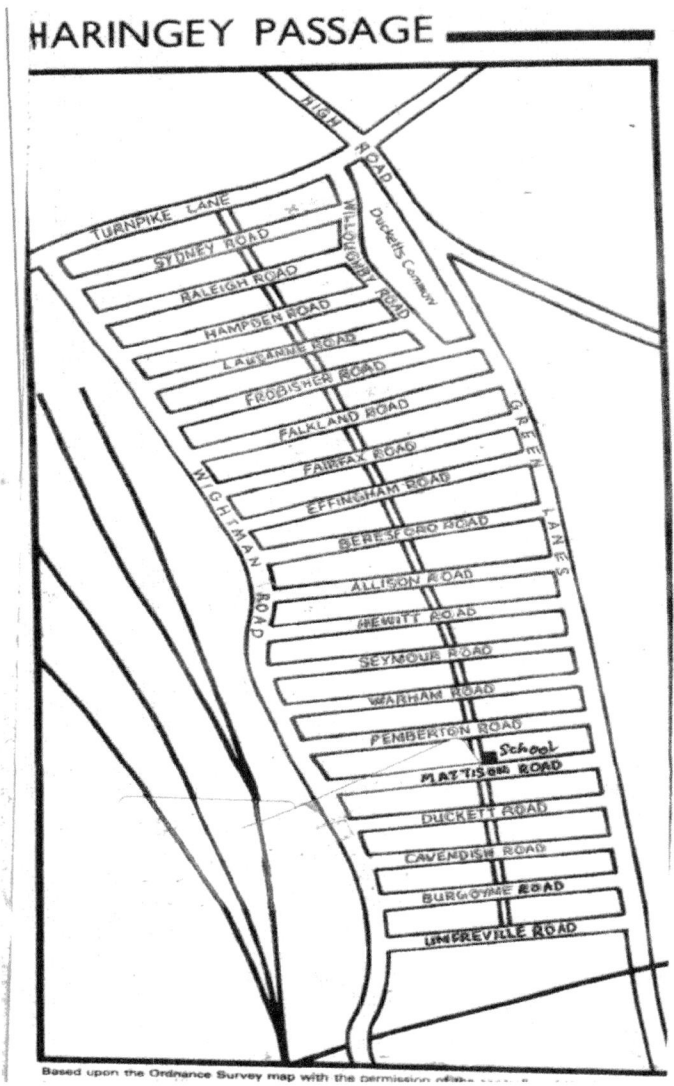

Inventory: ¾ mile wide by 1 ½ mile, 7 churches, 29 Roads, 2985 houses, 612 trees, 322 Lampposts, 1 Library, 2 Air raid Sirens, 2 Zebra crossing, 10 Traffic lights, 7 Bus stops and thousands of people.

Names. Bible Numbers 1:2 "Take a census of all the congregation of the children of Israel, by their families, by their fathers' houses, according to the number of names, every male individually,

Census, Names of Householders. Example Sydney Road

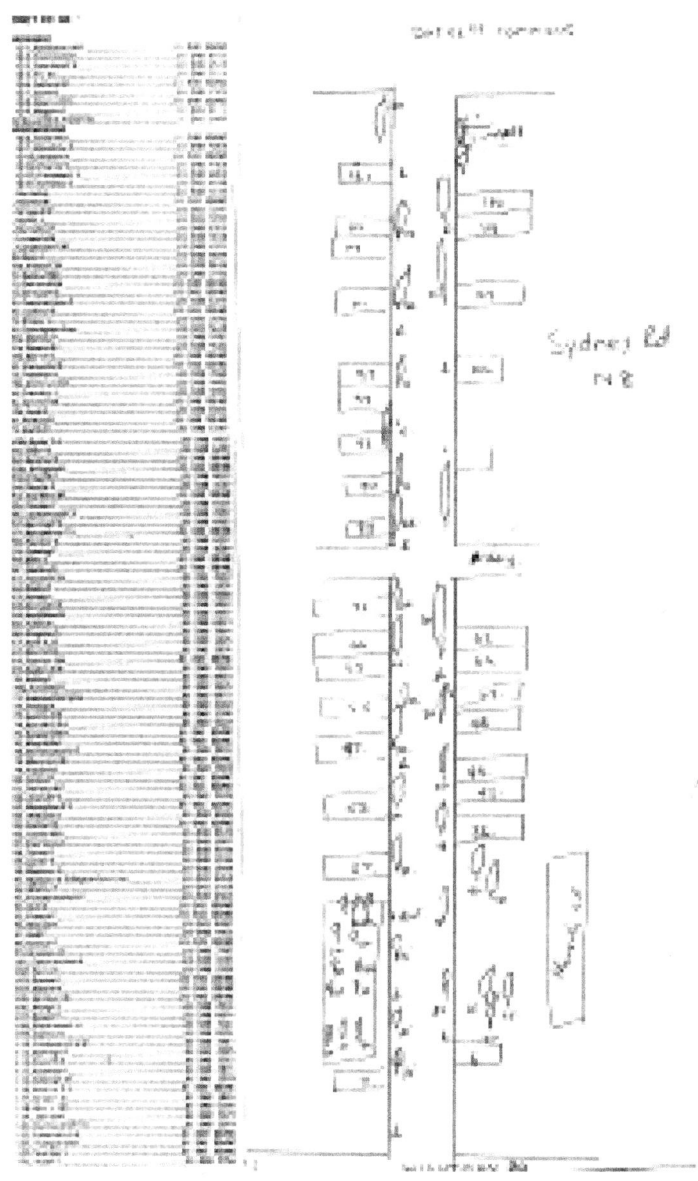

Haring ladder. Inventory map of people, houses, trees, lampposts etc.

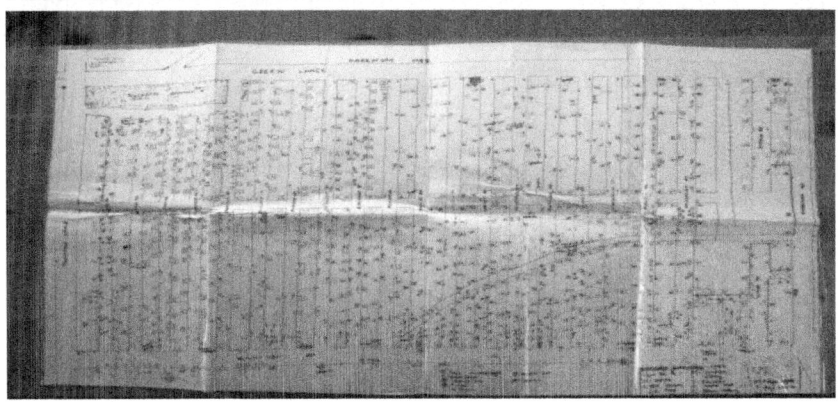

A small segment of it below

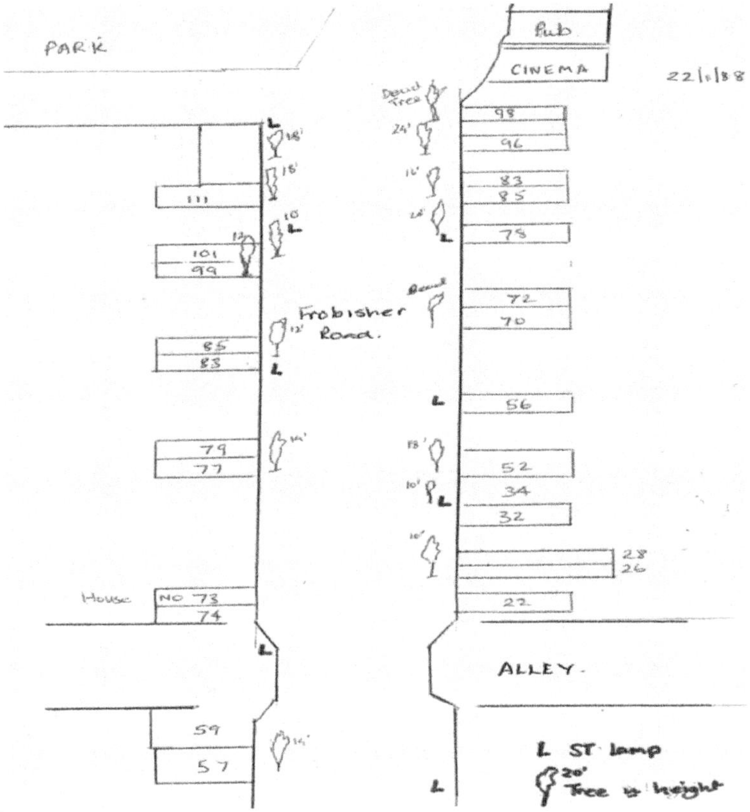

PARK

Pub

CINEMA   22|6|88

Descud Tree

98

96

83
85

78

Frobisher Road.

72
70

56

52

34

32

28
26

House   NO 73
74

22

ALLEY.

59

57

L ST lamp
Tree is height

--- 👑 ----

111

101
99

85
83

79
77

L

Chapter 37 – All creatures are paying the price of our salvation (our fall[1])

This is my belief. I do not expect others to follow in my example.

Haringey

Lord, 'All **creation**[2] is paying the price for your (our) salvation. How are you going to respond to their pain?'

I replied, 'I am going to make compensation, restitution, and make them whole.' I paused to think. I had no resources except the will and the sense of obligation.

Lord, 'You don't have the resources.'

'No. My Lord.'

'But you would like to make them whole. Why?'

'My Lord, you taught me nothing in the Universe should thrive at the expense of another. I am also aware no man can do it. I do not have the means and resources to do it.'

The Lord said, 'There is a way. Do you want to try?'

'Yes.'

'You cannot do it. The Holy Spirit can. He can teach you, just as you taught the woman to repair her radiator. All things are possible with God. All things are possible by one clothed in the Holy Spirit. All you need to do is learn to walk in the spirit.'

'Lord, I would like to try.'

--- ☆ ---

[1] *Romans 3:23, for all have sinned and <u>fall short</u> of the glory of God,*

[2] *Genesis 3:21, Also, for Adam and his wife, the LORD God made <u>skin tunics</u> and clothed them. (Innocent animals died because of their disobedience)*

...x..x...

'Then make a covenant with all the creatures in your patch to make them whole.'

I obeyed his instruction. I went for a walk in the woods and selected a large stone. I marked it with a knife to affirm my covenant with all the creatures in my patch.

The Lord said, 'I am giving you the anointment of the Holy Spirit so you can learn. You will learn to build my **sanctuary**[3] atom by atom. When you have made them **whole**[4], I will answer your question.'

When I had been ten years old, I had cried out to God, 'Why did you bring pain and suffering into this world?' In my anger, I shouted, 'One day, I will make you account for all the pain and suffering in the world.'

In his way, he was going to answer my question, not in a way I had expected, but by making me learn to fix all situations, at least in my

--- ☆ ---

[3] *1 Chronicles 22:19, "Now set your heart and your soul to seek the LORD your God. Therefore arise and build the <u>sanctuary</u> of the LORD God, to bring the ark of the covenant of the LORD and the holy articles of God into the house that is to be <u>built</u> for the name of the LORD."*

[3] *Isaiah 65:25, The <u>wolf and the lamb shall</u> feed together, the lion shall eat straw like the ox; but the serpent—its food shall be dust! They shall not hurt or destroy on all my holy mountain, says the LORD.*
66:1, Thus says the LORD: Heaven is my throne, and the earth is my footstool; what is the <u>house that you would build for me</u>, and what is my resting place?
V2, All these things my hand has made, and so all these things are mine, says the LORD. But this is the one to <u>whom I will look</u>, to the humble and contrite in spirit, who trembles at my word.

[4] *John 14:12, "Most assuredly, I say to you, he who <u>believes in Me</u>, the works that I do he will do also; and **greater** works than these he will do, because I go to My Father.*

...x..x...

patch. All the work of taking an inventory of my patch months/years of sweat started to make sense. I finally saw the bigger picture.

Each day, we (Holy Spirit and I) would pray and be thankful for my neighbours, Mother Earth, and all her creatures for giving me a chance to grow, to share with them their pain, suffering, and joy. As an act of thankfulness, gratitude, and acknowledgement for their contribution to my salvation and God's kingdom, I asked the Holy Spirit to help me to promote the welfare, interest, and happiness of my patch. I reminded God we (God and his heir, us) had a duty to make them whole in this life or in the afterlife.

The Holy Spirit guided me in a specific way to pray for my patch. I would note it in my book and review it at the seventh monthly and sabbatical period to learn from what had transpired over the months and do a reality check.

*Luke 14:28, "For which of you, intending to build a tower, does not sit down first and **count** the **cost**, whether he has enough to finish it —*

I have grasped the level of commitment required to reach the full stature of Christ and the necessary resources to reach that point. God does not choose to act on his own; he needs our consent-based on informed choice, and that can only happen when we have first sat down and counted the cost, and we are willing to give our all to reach the full stature of Christ.

1 Corinthians 1:26, for you see your calling, brethren that not many wise according to the flesh, not many mighty, not many noble are called.

Reign with Christ

Most people will find it hard to comprehend this concept. It was essential for me to understand the gist of it.

It is to do with the return of the Lord. If I was to return with him, I needed to know what abilities he needed to perfect in me.

If I were to reign with him a thousand years, I needed superhuman abilities to exercise the mind of Christ. To do what he could do. That is our inheritance. Not one sparrow should fall in our Patch without our knowledge when we reign with him. That training begins on earth, here now.

1 Thessalonians 3:13, so that He may establish your hearts blameless in holiness before our God and Father at the coming of our Lord Jesus Christ with all His saints.

Revelation 20:6, Blessed and holy is he who has a part in the first resurrection. Over such the second death has no power, but they shall be priests of God and of Christ and shall reign with Him a thousand years.

Many Christians will find it hard to understand this concept to account for every leaf, **sparrow[3]**, or person in my parish. To me, it means learning to understand Christ's mind that created the world. We have that **mind[4]** —an incredible gift of God; A gift that many fail to accept or make an effort to unlock. A trained mind needed if we are to return with Christ.

If you love Christ, you would want to be with him and share his thoughts and desires. Many Christians have no desire or expectations of returning with Christ, nor do they want to put the time and sacrifice needed to be trained for the task ahead.

Mark 4:25, To those who have more will be given; and from those who have nothing, even what they have will be taken away."

The bible says every **hair[5]** on our head are numbered. Who numbers them, and why? For what possible reason?

--- ☆ ---

[3] *Matthew 10:29, "Are not two sparrows sold for a copper coin? And not one of them falls to the ground apart from your Father's will.*

[4] *1 Corinthians 2:16, For "who has known the mind of the LORD that he may instruct Him?" But we have the mind of Christ.*

[5] *Luke 12:7, "But the very hairs of your head are all numbered. Do not fear, therefore; you are of more value than many sparrows.   ..x..x...*

Many Christians fail to understand our calling, salvation, inheritance in Christ, our part in the resurrection, and what it means to receive the Holy Spirit's baptism.

One of the Holy Spirit's role is to help us enter the race, set before us, and grow into the full **stature** of Christ, starting now and not sometime in future.

*Ephesians 4:13, till we all come to the unity of the faith and of the knowledge of the Son of God, to a perfect man, to the measure of the **stature** of the fullness of Christ.*

God is testing us and filtering out those unworthy to receive their entire inheritance.

Romans 12:1, I appeal to you, brothers and sisters, by the mercies of God, to present your bodies as a living sacrifice, holy and acceptable to God, which is your spiritual worship.

--- ☆ ---

Questions. If our Lord and you returned without having worked out your salvation, how are you going to contribute to his realm?

---- 👑 ----

Chapter 38 – Everything needs to undergo a Reality test.

Accounting for every leaf in our parish with the aid of the indwelling Holy Spirit needed a reality check.

In my prayers, the indwelling Holy Spirit would undertake this task. To do this, at times, he would slow down at a pace my mind could cope. For example, he would show me a stretch of road, and we would pray for waste bins, a pub, or a cinema, something my brain could cope with. I would pray and make a note in my diary. Then over the 7th month, 7th year, I would monitor it.

For example (Appendix 9). A single day's prayer and a reality check. On 13th July 1987, I prayed for 1. The cutback in a burglary in my area, 2. Dustbins fitted on the roads. 3. A Pub to be shut down. 4 Prayed for Local Cinema; lord would use it. (Sometimes, it takes years for prayers to be answered).

Prayer for a single day answered over many years as follows: **Appendix**

1.   At the time, the Haringey Ladder had a low crime rate, according to our insurance quote. Things have changed since we left. In other areas we lived in, crime would fall within weeks of our arrival. Fig 3

2. Very soon after this prayer, Council installed Bins. Fig 2

3. Pub closed down in 2009 or 2010

4. Sometime later, the Cinema changed hands and became a church.

Then He would quicken the pace and continue his work, accounting for every leaf, every sparrow, and instilling in my spirit knowledge and wisdom. My spirit would grow under His guidance. My brain has a limited capacity, but my spirit has no such restrictions. God gave me a brain with a limited capacity, much to my father's disappointment, but he instilled in me/us an infinitely great spirit.

A few weeks later, the council would have installed the waste bins, new traffic lights, or a prayer for a person would have happened on the date

**Appendix   Example of prayer for Haringey on a single day.
Reality Test. Fig 1**

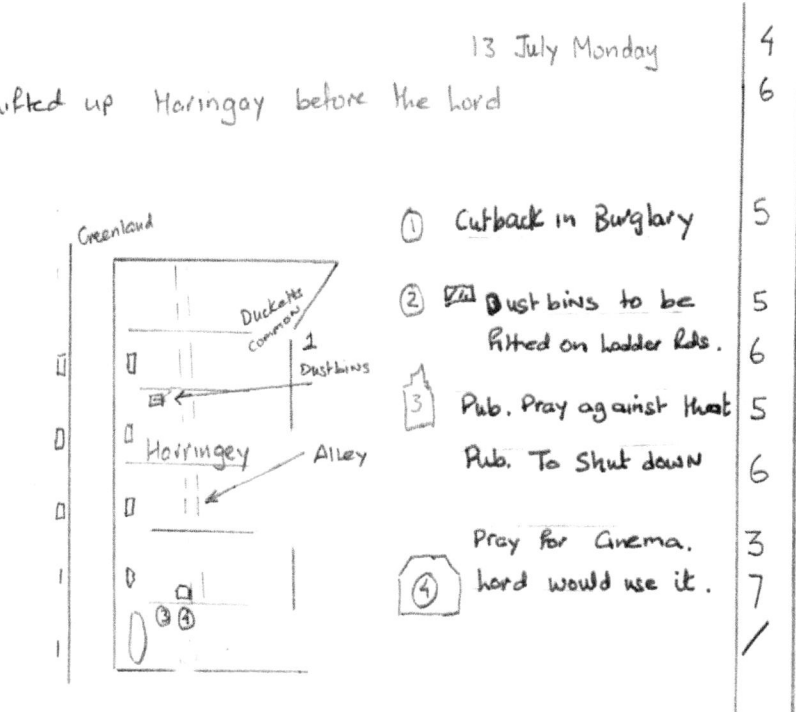

Answered Prayer. (On review of my prayer in my sabbatical year, I collected this data from the internet.)

1.   At the time, the Haringey Ladder had a low crime rate, according to our insurance quote. Things have changed since we left. For other areas we lived in, crime would fall within weeks of our arrival. Fig 3

2. Very soon after this prayer, Council installed Bins.

3. Pub closed down in 2009 or 2010. (Queen's head)

4. Cinema changed hands and became a church. (Liberty church).

Fig 2

<u>**25 Feb 2017. Reviewed prayer made in July**</u> $\left(13^{th}\right)$
<u>**1987**</u>

The Queens Head was situated at 677
Greens Lane. This pub closed sometime in
2009 or 2010.

This former cinema building has enjoyed a
chequered history. It is now a church.
Liberty Church, nr Turnpike Lane, North
London

Dust bins but not as many as I would have
liked. Hrc

Fig 3 When we lived in Liskeard Cornwall, Cornish Times 28/1/05. Crime figures in Liskeard are among the lowest in the country.

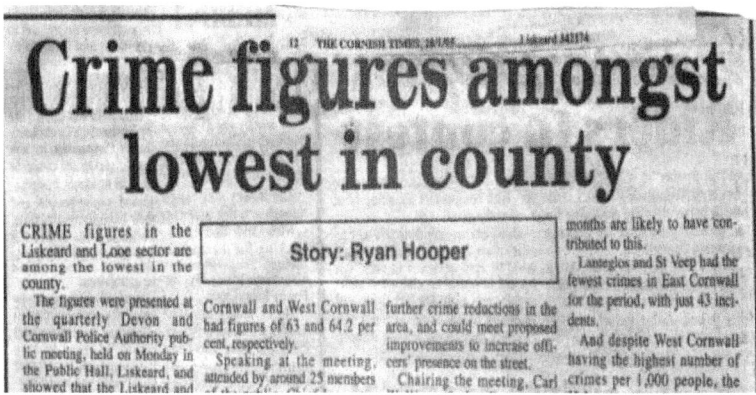

We moved to Arun in Jan 2006

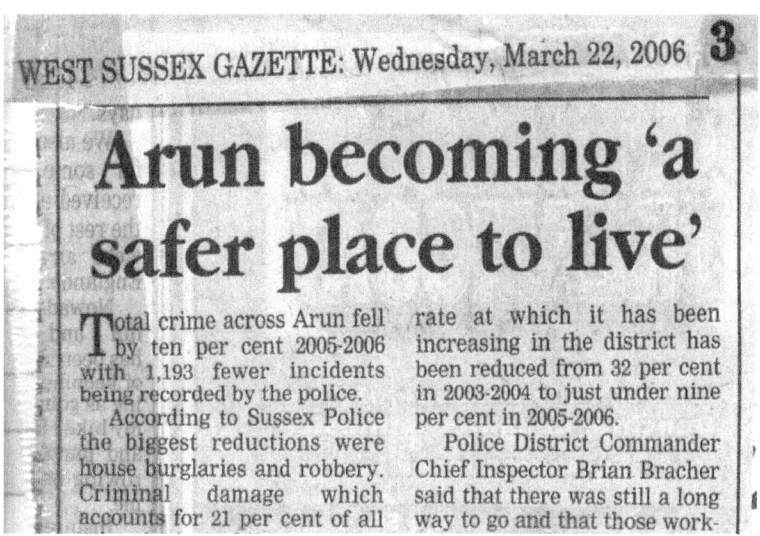

One should not take a few items as evidence. However, when a pattern seems to appear, then it should lend some credibility.

....x...x.

and hour proclaimed—a <u>sign of the prayers' reality</u> to account for every leaf, every person.

On weekends when I had more time, I would walk around the area, lifting every person, every street in prayer.

The Lord said, 'To have strong faith, you need to do it yourself. You are in the **spirit**[1] now. I want you to learn to take stewardship over every atom, every **grain of sand**[2], every tree, and every person in your patch. You cannot do it on your strength. That is not possible for a human. However, the indwelling **Holy Spirit**[3] will walk with you, teach you to take an inventory of every grain of sand, every leaf, and **person**[4].

'When you begin to experience the tremendous power of the Holy Spirit in your life over this area, your faith will grow. This is our Father's wonderful gift to his heirs. <u>It is your birthright</u>. When you begin to experience the reality of this calling, it will fill you with joy.

'It brings immense pleasure to our Father, the whole heavenly crowd and

--- ☆ ---

[1] *Romans 8; 9, But you are <u>not in the flesh</u>; you are in the Spirit since the Spirit of God dwells in you.*

[2] *Romans 8: 20-23, For the <u>creation</u> was subjected to futility, not willingly, but because of Him who subjected it in hope; because the creation itself also <u>will be delivered</u> from the bondage of corruption into the glorious <u>liberty of the children</u> of God, for we know that the whole creation groans and labours with birth pangs together until now. We also have the <u>firstfruits of the Spirit</u>, even we groan within ourselves, eagerly waiting for the adoption, the redemption of our body.*

[3] *Romans 8; 15, So you have not received a spirit that makes you fearful slaves. Instead, you received <u>God's Spirit</u> when <u>he adopted you as his children</u>. Now we call him, "Abba, Father."*

[4] *Romans 8:26, And the Holy Spirit helps us in our weakness. For example, we don't know what God wants us to pray for. But the <u>Holy Spirit prays for us</u> with groanings that cannot be expressed in word.*

...x..x...

reveals the **Glory**[5] we have given you.'

The Lord continued, 'You are in the Spirit, outside the laws of physics. The size of your brain does not limit your thoughts; that's the freedom of the spirit. Your spiritual brain grows mathematically, logarithmically, and at an accelerated pace, and that is our wonderful gift to you. You are blessed beyond your comprehension. (For example, the balanced 10-dimensional cube you created with our help is a very complicated mathematical sequence that gives some indication of how the Universe is balanced, how the atom is balanced. **Appendix 10 at the end of book)**

'The truth, the value of these treasures you have received, will not be manifested until later. Many on Judgment Day will see this gift in you and break down in tears because they had the gift of the Holy Spirit but chose to squander it away for eternity.

'Meanwhile, obey the Holy Spirit, and he will show you how to do it. When you have done it, your belief, like that of the woman with a leaking radiator you taught to repair, will turn into strong faith, strong enough to move mountains.'

Matthew 17:20, Jesus told them. "I tell you the truth, if you had faith even as small as a mustard seed, you could say to this mountain, 'Move from here to there,' and it would move. Nothing would be impossible."

'Move mountains! I don't understand, Lord?' I replied.

'What you inherit will depend on what you have allowed the Holy Spirit to achieve in you. It has conditions.'

The scriptures came to my mind, and they opened up like a flowering plant, revealing insight and wisdom.

Revelation 3:21, "To him who overcomes I will grant to sit with Me on My throne, as I also overcame and sat down with My Father on His throne.

--- ☆ ---

[5] *John 17:22, "And the glory which You gave Me I have given them, that they may be one just as We are one. ...x..x...*

Revelation 21:7, "He who <u>overcomes</u> shall inherit all things, and I will be his God, and he shall be My son.

Galatians 4:7, Therefore, you are no longer a slave but a son, and if a son, then an <u>heir</u> of God through Christ.

God, the Holy Father, said, 'You gave up all for me when you stood outside your father's house in Africa. That day, I took you into my household. I **adopted**[6] you. You are now my adopted son. Nonetheless, you have to learn the responsibilities and duties of my **heir** through Christ. Furthermore, I want you to take your place as the **firstborn** among many. If you do not learn to walk in the spirit and be made perfect, this gift will go to another.'

*Hebrews 12:23, to the general assembly and church of the **firstborn** who are registered in heaven, to God the Judge of all, to the spirits of just men <u>made perfect,</u>*

*Romans 8:29, For whom He foreknew, He also predestined to be conformed to the image of His Son, that He might be the **firstborn** among many brethren.*

Jesus continued, 'Because I want you with me and one day to reign with me. Kings and prophets have sought this privilege we have granted you. You will need to learn to use my power. The only way you can get the **gist of it** is to do it. We need your consent and willingness to give us the time and commitment to bring it about. All things are possible with us.

'Abide in me and follow the guidance of the Holy Spirit. He will guide you with his eyes, and you will walk with us in my New Heaven, inside the Holy City in the holiest of holy places.'

Note, To Account for every leaf, every person in our patch is not possible in this short life. We can only get a gist of it.

The parable of the fruit tin

Suppose a mother is limited by time and wants to teach her children

--- ☆ ---

[6] *Romans 8; 15, So you have not received a spirit that makes you fearful slaves. Instead, you received <u>God's Spirit</u> when <u>he adopted you as his children</u>. Now we call him, "Abba, Father." ...x..x...*

about different fruits. She may open a tin of mixed fruit and ask the children to write down what an apple, a pear, and a banana taste like.

She could say, 'Now you've got the gist of what an apple, a pear, and a banana tastes like.'

Until, a thoughtful child questions, 'Which apple, Mother? There are Gala, Pink Lady, and Jazz apples!'

1 Corinthians 13:12, For now, we see in a mirror, dimly, but then face to face. Now I know in part, but then I shall know just as I also am known.

Nevertheless, you got the gist of it!

---- ----

Chapter 39 – Each teaching needed a reality check.

To continually maintain spiritual reality in my life, the Lord would reveal things about to happen. We would be going over the map. Then my mind would rest on a house.

The Lord would ask, 'What do you hear?'

'I hear a man praying. It is around three in the afternoon. He is praying, and he wants to receive the baptism of the spirit.'

'On Sunday, when you see him at the church, confirm with him what you saw. You will tell him how and when it will happen, the day and hour.'

On Sunday or at the midweek prayer meeting, I would come across such a person. I would state the day, time, the hour he or she was praying and how the Lord would answer it. One such person was called **Alan Goddard (Appendix B** on the next page). He went on to become a church minister.

A person would say they had gone for a job interview in a prayer meeting or needed prayer for their exams. Could we pray for them?

The Lord would have prepared me during the week. I would say to the person, 'I believe this is what will happen; out of three exams, you will fail one. However, the Lord has made arrangements for you to appear before a board, to be orally tested, and you will pass.' [**Appendix A**: Steve]. Steve went on to become a missionary to Nepal.

Many incidents like these would affirm my faith to account for every leaf (to get the gist of it, because we do not have enough time or brains on Earth to grasp this entirely). It was a reality check to make sure I had my feet firmly planted on solid ground.

There is no line in our mind between spiritual reality and imagination. It is so easy to drift into a make-believe world. There is always a desire to fantasize about the dates and times for healing to occur or for things to happen.

The Lord was careful to teach me to differentiate between the two. I would write in my diary and then count the words on each line and at the

Appendix A   Prayer for Steven

"Steven"   30ᵗʰ Feb 1984.

30ᵗʰ Feb 84. Prophecy regarding Steven | 6

... A few months ago at a house meeting | 8
at Jane's steven asked to be prayed for | 8
his exams. His exams as yet. | 6

The Lord gave me a word of | 7
Knowledge. Out of 3 exams he would fail | 8
one. However the Lord had made arrangements | 7
for him to appear before a board where he | 9
would be orally tested. And he would | 7
pass. | 1

The reason for this prophecy was | 6
to demonstrate that God spoke to his people. | 8
God will speak through any person who has | 8
courage, willingness and patience. | 4
Ps 84:10 David Said, 'I would rather dwell | 6
at ___ door of God's house (and speak) then | 10
live among Scroundrals. | 3
——— ✗ ——— | 0

Few week later | 0

Steven came to see me and said, | 7
the Lord had fulfilled his words. He | 7
failed one of his exam. However on oral test he | 10
passed. It was first time anyone was given | 8
oral test! ——— ✗ ——— | 3
Steven later went on to become | 0
missionary in Nepal. | 0

179

end of the page, on a separate column, write down the numbers of words. **(Ref to Appendix)** This way, any alterations would be noticed.

Then, on Sunday or after midweek prayer meetings, in the evening, I would enter into my dairy the outcome and compare the two. In the seventh month, the seventh year, I would go over it to update my records and get a bigger picture.

It was one way to learn to walk in the spirit and carry out a reality test. It took time and commitment to test all things.

--- ☆---

Vision of Alan praying Appendix B

24ᵗʰ June 1977 The mind of christ cannot cease to operate. It work 24 hrs.   14

The burning Cross. Vision about Alan Goddard   7w 8

0

U

0

0

At the Garden of Peace. The elder   7

is here.   2

Elder; "Tell me son of man what do   8

see up younder."   3

me,: "Lord I see a cross.   6

Elder; "Go near."   3

"Lord' I said, "I see the cross burning   8

It bums but is not consumed."   6

"Do you hear anything.'   4

"Yes. It is afraid of the fire. It wonts the   10

fire (Holy Spirit) but is afraid of what it can do."   12

Elder, "Go tell it (him) that he need not be   9

afraid of the fire,   4

---- 🕮---

Chapter 40 – Prayers are hard work, like ploughing on hard soil. What you sow, you shall reap.

As things began to happen, my prayers became longer. In the morning, I spent 10 minutes reading the Bible and then spent half an hour in prayer before going to work. After coming home from work, the first thing I did was spent half an hour before the Lord, and then I would go out and deliver some leaflets.

I would return home and have my dinner. Then I would visit a friend or go to prayer meetings or house groups. I would come home, spend another 10 minutes reading the Bible, then spend more time accounting for my time, money, or going over the day's events. Often, in the middle of the night, the Lord would wake me, and I would make a note of his guidance, rebukes, and correction.

For a young adult in full-time employment, it was a lonely walk. I did not have any time left for social life. I had many friends at college, but now I was spending too much time in prayers on my own. I was good-looking, athletic, having spent two years in the Territorial Army in the parachute regiment. Girls were keen to chat with me. Low on social skills, I would get nervous in their presence. My mind would freeze – the keener I was on a girl, the worse I felt. They would very quickly lose interest in me.

Cost

The isolation started to affect me. It was painful. I pined for companionship and cried from loneliness. It was a sad period in my life. There were times I longed for a normal life. I just could not cope well with a life that was, in many ways, abnormal. My brain was dealing with things that were beyond its limit. My life seemed empty. I was miserable.

I started to visit other churches, hoping to meet new people, make friends, and meet a nice girl I could share my belief, go out, and enjoy life. Become normal again like other people. Rev Hammond found my absence from the church hard to accept. He thought my place was in his church.

I wrote down in detail everything that happened—accounted and reviewed them on every seventh month, every seventh year.

This energy level spent walking in the spirit, hour by hour, was not sustainable for months and years. I walked in it for ten years and two months; by then, I was a wreck.

7 March 1988. Verge of a nervous breakdown

I woke up one morning, exhausted. I had had enough. I had been in Haringey for thirteen years. I was on the verge of a nervous breakdown. That evening I could not sleep. I got up in the middle of the night, got dressed, and walked around my patch, praying as I walked. Something inside me was driving me on. I walked around my patch five times. My feet ached; I was cold, exhausted, and ready to go home.

The Lord said, 'You have to go round seven times.'

My feet were killing me. Every step was agony. In a daze, I walked and finally finished the seventh round. The sun was rising. I went home, straight to bed. Around 9 am, I called work and told my boss I wasn't feeling well. The next day I could hardly walk. The following day I went and saw the doctor. He looked at my swollen feet and told me to rest for a week.

A few days later, as I lay on my bed reading, I heard the Lord say, 'Hari, the race set before you is **Finished.*** The good works set by the father before the foundations of the Earth were laid are over. Now we need to smooth out the imperfections.'

I was 34 years, five months, four days, and 22 hours old.

Towards the beginning of my 14th year in Haringey, I quit my job, sold my house in London, and backpacked across South America for five months.

My hyperactive life had ended. A new, more sedate enjoyable life lay ahead. It was time to live a normal life.

--- ☆---

 * **Finished.** Refer to the footnote at the end of this chapter.

Sabbatical year

Thirty-one years later, I brought this stressful and difficult period before the lord during my sabbatical period. I say challenging because, in many ways, during that period of my life, I had ceased to exist as an individual.

I had given my life over to the Holy Spirit. It was a lonely, sad life. It felt like I had operated behind enemy lines. I was always alert, nervous, starved, fearful, deprived of sleep, friends, family, and companions until I had reached the breaking point. The cost of the race set before me.

The Lord said, 'These were good works prepared for you. It was never meant to be permanent. We gave you a gist of the incredible power of the indwelling Holy Spirit. You could achieve superhuman things and secure your eternal place in the **holie of holies**[1] in New **Jerusalem.**[2]

Finally, to demonstrate to the **heavenly crowd**[3] the glory of God and his **gift**[4] to his **children.**[5] To prove to the prophets and angels what makes you greater than them and to prepare you for your inheritance.'

'You believed, and we put it to the test, to refine and purify it.'

Romans 4:3, For the Scriptures tell us, "Abraham believed God, and God counted him as righteous because of his faith."

--- ☆---

[1] *Hebrews 10:19, Therefore, brethren, having boldness to enter the Holiest by the blood of Jesus,*

[2] *Hebrews 12:22, But you have come to Mount Zion and the city of the living God, the heavenly Jerusalem, to an innumerable company of angels,*

[3] *Ephesians 3:10, to the intent that now the manifold wisdom of God might be made known by the church to the principalities and powers in the heavenly places,*

[4] *Ephesians 1:3, Blessed be the God and Father of our Lord Jesus Christ, who has blessed us with every spiritual blessing in the heavenly places in Christ,*

[5] *1 Corinthians 15:49, And as we have borne the image of the man of dust, we shall also take the image of the heavenly Man. ...x..x...*

Finished Footnote

Thirty-one years later, I would have a deeper understanding of what he meant; you have finished the race.

Surprisingly, this episode in Haringey did not bring me close to God. It drove me further away from God. Learning to account for every leaf, creature, and person made me 'hypersensitive' to all living things pain and suffering. At night as I lay in my bed, I would hear the desperate cries of creatures, slowly been eaten alive. I could listen to their cry for help. They would cry out to God, 'why did you create us?' They would cry out to me, 'You made a covenant with us to protect, guard and promote our happiness and welfare; make us whole.' The sheer scale of cruelty, pain, and suffering was unbearable. I began to hate God.

*Romans 8:21, because the **creation** itself also will be delivered from the bondage of corruption into the glorious liberty of the children of God.*

*Romans 8:22, For we know that **the whole creation** groans and labours with birth pangs together until now.*

God's creation repulsed me. What kind of a being devises a crazy evil world, where innocent, helpless animals are torn apart, screaming, crying, yelling, begging for deliverance, and the creator sits and takes **pleasure**[1] from it. A world of prey and predator, at each other's throat, to survive, they have to kill or be killed.

[1] ***Exodus 29:18**, "And you shall burn the whole ram on the altar. It is a burnt offering to the LORD; it is a **sweet aroma**, an offering made by fire to the LORD.*

Millions of husbands, wives, children blown apart by bombs or dying prematurely of war, disease, starvation and many other evil things. I nearly had a breakdown. What kind of conscience does God have?

I felt like a soldier each night crawling behind enemy lines for years to gather information at significant risk to him. One day he returns, takes off his uniform, and walks away from the battlefield.

'No more of this,' he says, 'a deserter I may be. I had had enough. I have done more than my share; for my God and country. They can shoot me if they like. A quick death is preferable to a thousand slow deaths in my sleep.'

After this, I quit my job and went to South America for a while. On returning home, I prayed at home, studied the word and went to house groups but said very little in public. My spirit was grieving at the destruction of living entities and their suffering. For a while, I closed my eyes, ears, and mouth to the world. See no evil, hear no evil, and say nothing.

Eventually, the pull of the bible was greater. I clung to this book. My wounded Spirit was crying out, 'Hari, you will find answers to all your torments in this book. You have to continue to study it. It is your way to salvation, deliverance from your pain.'

Months later, I saw the lord. He came with two angels and sat beside me but said nothing. Their presence gave me strength. They left, no words were spoken.

Years later, I heard the Lord ask, 'Hari if you feel so intensely about creation, what are you going to do about it?' He gave me some months to think about it. Then the scriptures opened up like a flood. The eternal plan of God began to unfold.

'Hari, I want you to build a spiritual sanctuary for your patch. To reconcile things in heaven and earth.'

*Colossians 1:20, and by Him **to reconcile** all things to Himself, by Him, whether things on earth or things in heaven, having made peace through the blood of His cross.*

Exodus 15:17, You brought them in and planted them on the mountain of your possession, the place, O LORD, that you made your abode, the sanctuary, O LORD, that your hands have established.

*Exodus 25:8, "And let them make Me a **sanctuary**, that I may dwell among them. Isaiah 65:25, The wolf and the lamb shall feed together, the lion shall eat straw like the ox; but the serpent—its food shall be dust! They shall not hurt or destroy on all my holy mountain, says the LORD.*

Acts 7:49, 'Heaven is My throne, And earth is My footstool. <u>What house will you build for Me</u>? Says the LORD, or what is the place of My rest?

I cried for days. I wanted to do all in my power to pay the debt I owed God, my neighbours, and Mother Earth. I had no resources, only 'the willingness to empty the ocean with the palm of my hand.' It was all God needed.

He provided the resources. Over the years, we built it. It has finally drawn on me the immense cost borne by others and God for our salvation.

My hostility towards God receded. I began to see the beauty of his eternal plan.

*Romans 8:19-21, For the earnest expectation of the **creation** eagerly waits for the revealing of the sons of God. For the creation was subjected to futility, not willingly, but because of Him who subjected <u>it in hope</u>; because the creation itself also will be delivered from the bondage of corruption **<u>into the glorious liberty of the children of God</u>**.*

Dog eat Dog world

Yes, it was necessary to create, 'a dog eats dog world,' so that he would <u>have children</u> who had the iron will to make restitution for their salvation. Every child of God needed to have a clear understanding of the cost and pain borne by God, families, neighbours, and Mother Earth, for their spiritual growth, knowledge coming only from the indwelling Holy Spirit.

No human can ever grasp this cost without the help of the Holy Spirit, making it happen in his or her life. Sharing such in-depth pain, suffering and making appropriate restitution binds us with cords of love that cannot be broken. God's gift to brave, courageous souls with the hearts of a lion seeking him with all their heart, mind and strength.

Ephesians 3:16, that He would grant you, according to the riches of His glory, to be <u>strengthened </u>with might through His Spirit in the inner man,

V17, that <u>Christ may dwell</u> in your hearts through faith; that you, being rooted and grounded in love,

v18, may be able to <u>comprehend</u> with all the saints what is the width and length and depth and height —

v19, to know the <u>love of Christ</u> which passes knowledge; that you may be filled with all the fullness of God.

*1 Peter 4:13, but rejoice to the extent that you **partake** of Christ's sufferings, that when His glory is revealed, you may also be glad with exceeding joy.*

Far Distant Future

Looking ahead, way ahead of this life, I/we are a much-beloved child of Mother Earth and hopefully loved by my/our neighbours. When the world and the old order ends, and as Mother Earth passes away, she would give her blessing to me/us and perhaps our neighbour will join them who have survived the Judgment.

Earth at the End of Time

Earth, 'You (all in Christ who have reached the <u>full stature</u> of Christ) are **my firstborn** in Christ. I am proud of you. You were worthy of being my firstborn, for you redeemed us with the blood of Christ. You are our <u>first fruit</u> in Christ; you are my joy, my pride. I bore an untold amount of pain and suffering for you. That is what a loving mother does for her child/children?

Colossians 1:15, He is the image of the invisible God, the firstborn over all <u>creation</u>.

*Romans 8:29, For whom He foreknew, He also <u>predestined</u> to be conformed to the image of His Son, that He might be the **firstborn** among many brethren.*

Mother Earth continues, 'My oceans are lined with skeletons of dead creatures and their blood. The mountains and hills bore creatures whose bodies were shredded to bits by predators that in turn died just as miserably. Their blood runs down the hills as streams, and in the valleys forms rivers.

The pain I bore, my beloved child, to see you walk in the City of the Lord, will pass away. My work is finished. I bless you, my son, my pride, my joy.

I have loved you from the foundations of the earth, from the moment God inserted your name in the lamb's book of life.

I knew the cost and willingly consented. This is the great mystery of God revealed to you, my beloved child, my pride, my joy.

The instant I saw your (Christ's bride) name in the Lamb's book of life, I rejoiced. I knew all my pain and suffering would be bearable. I counted the cost and consented, living each day in agony but rejoicing, knowing that all would work out perfectly in the end. My son, you are my joy, my life. To see you reach the full stature of Christ makes me happy. My life was fruitful; no mother could be more pleased than I.'

*Hebrews 12:22-23, But you have come to Mount Zion and to the city of the living God, the heavenly Jerusalem, to an innumerable company of angels, to the general assembly and church of the **firstborn** who are registered in heaven, to God the Judge of all, to the spirits of just men made perfect,*

Romans 8:28, We know that all things work together for good for those who love God, who are called according to his purpose.

Chapter 41– Haringey Area undergoes a change

I delivered the gospel message to every home in my patch. There were 2,985 households, via the means of letters, testimony, and tracts, obeying *Zak's tenant: I will reason with you, but I will not try to persuade you.* Not once, but on multiple occasions.

As we change and reflect the glory of God, the area around us changes: with lower crime, becoming a more desirable place to live with happier people, in awe and reverence to God, etc.

Reason. For God to start the process of **reconciliation**[1-2] in our patch through us, to make all things whole.

Those who find the **race**[3] easy probably do so because they are not running, 'as one who runs to win.' That may be fine for some.

However, the race requires one to run with all their heart, mind, and strength. Those that enter the race find it extremely hard. They know what it means to **fast**[4] for two to three weeks; spend **the whole nights**[5] in prayer, the hard work, dedication, commitment, and obedience

--- ☆---

[1] *Ephesians 2:16, and that He might reconcile them both to God in one body through the cross, thereby putting to death the enmity.*

[2] *Colossians 1:20, and by Him to reconcile all things to Himself, by Him, whether things on earth or things in heaven, having made peace through the blood of His cross.*

[3] *1 Corinthians 9:24, Do you not know that those who run in a race all run, but one receives the prize? Run in such a way that you may obtain it.*

[4] *Acts 13:2, As they ministered to the Lord and fasted, the Holy Spirit said, "Now separate to Me Barnabas and Saul for the work to which I have called them."*

[5] *Luke 6:12, Now it came to pass in those days that He went out to the mountain to pray and continued all night in prayer to God. ...x..x...*

needed to be ready at a moment notice, any time of the day or night at the Lord's bidding. They are committed to going over their preaching and sermons with the Holy Spirit on the **Seventh month**[6]. In the seventh year, have their works tested under the light of the **word of God**[7], allowing the Holy Spirit to **correct**[8] guide and rebuke so that they are **sanctified**[9] **and** made worthy of their **inheritance**[10].

It is a proper test to find if we love **our Lord**[11] with all our heart, mind, and strength. Words are empty without works.

James 2:26, For as the body without the spirit is dead, faith without works is also dead.

--- ☆---

[6] *Numbers 29:1, 'And in the <u>seventh month,</u> you shall have a holy convocation on the first day of the month. You shall do no customary work.*

[7] *Hebrews 4:12, For the <u>word of God,</u> is living and powerful, and sharper than any two-edged sword, piercing even to the division of soul and spirit, and joints and marrow, and is a discerner of the thoughts and intents of the heart.*

[8] *Hebrews 12:9, Furthermore, we have had human fathers who <u>corrected us,</u> and we paid them respect. Shall we not much more readily be in subjection to the Father of spirits and live?*

[9] *Hebrews 10:14, For by one offering He has perfected forever those who are being <u>sanctified.</u>*

[10] *1 Peter 1:4, to an <u>inheritance</u> incorruptible and undefiled and that does not fade away, reserved in heaven for you,*

[11] *Luke 10:27, So he answered and said, 'You shall love the LORD your God <u>with all your heart,</u> with all your soul, with all your strength, and with all your mind, and your neighbour as yourself.'*

---- 🐾---

Chapter 42 – Prayer for Raymond

We were in a prayer meeting. All evening Raymond looked tense, worried. He asked us if we could pray for him. He was in a legal dispute, and the other party had sued him for £5000. His case was due in a few days. He was worried he might lose the case, and he didn't have the money. Could we pray for him?

Others prayed that he would win the case. I waited upon the Lord. Raymond's nervousness made me feel there was a good chance he was going to lose. Silently, I brought the sum before the Lord.

The Lord said, 'Hari, how are you going to respond to his needs?'

It had taken me months of overtime at work to collect a sum of £5,200 for a second-hand car I was hoping to buy. I prayed silently, 'Lord, I will give him the money if he loses the case.'

I prayed aloud for Raymond, 'The Lord has taken care of your case and money. You don't need to worry.' Raymond trusted me. I saw his face brighten, the cloud of despair lifted from his shoulder.

He and others said, 'Amen.'

. . . .

Accounting for the day.

At home in the evening prayer, I brought up Raymond's case in my account for the day. I told the Lord it was not easy for me to commit my money. It was a big inward struggle. For the first time in my life, I had hoped to own a decent car.

I wished I had not gone to the meeting. It could turn out to be the most expensive prayer meeting I had attended. I would rather have gone to the cinema. It would have been cheaper and more enjoyable.

I did not sleep well.

A few days later, Raymond thanked me for the prayer and giving him solace. The other party had withdrawn the claim.

That evening in my prayer, I brought the matter before the Lord. I was grateful and thanked him.

Answered prayers have a cost attached to them.

The gist of what he'd taught me: for answered prayer, someone has to step in and take the tab/bill. Each answered prayer has a cost attached to it. For example, someone prays for money for a gas bill. God does not print money. For those of us who have committed over lives to Jesus, our money belongs to the Lord.

For God to answer a prayer where money is an issue, someone on Earth has to foot the bill. It is that simple. Moreover, those who have their eyes and ears open end up writing the cheque.

The same applies in Heaven; someone has to foot the bill. We ask the Lord to foot the bill. However, the Lord says it is time to grow up, take responsibility as heirs and open spiritual accounts in Heaven, and use our savings to foot the bill.

To fill our spiritual account, we have to be victorious over certain things in Heaven and claim the spiritual prize that comes from victory. When we are **victorious in Heaven**[1] and start to grow in **favour**[2] with God, and our spiritual account grows fat, we can begin to utilize this account to answer a particular **prayer**[3].

---- ☆----

[1] *Ephesians 6:12, For we do not wrestle against flesh and blood, but against principalities, against powers, against the rulers of the darkness of this age, against spiritual hosts of wickedness in the heavenly places.*

[2] *Luke 2:52, And Jesus increased in wisdom and stature, and in favour with God and men.*

[3] *Revelation 2:7, "Anyone with ears to hear must listen to the Spirit and understand what he is saying to the churches. To everyone who is victorious (against principalities, against powers, against the rulers of this age's darkness, against spiritual hosts of wickedness in the heavenly places), I will give fruit from the tree of life (prize) in the paradise of God.*

...x..x...

1 John 5:4 For every child of God <u>defeats this evil world,</u> and we achieve this <u>victory</u> through our faith.

God asks us to use this stewardship of the earthly and spiritual account wisely and account for every penny spent to prove Jesus is Lord over our possessions and life.

Look what the bible says, *2 Corinthians 13:5*, *Examine yourselves as to whether you are in the faith. <u>Test yourselves</u>. Do you not know yourselves that Jesus Christ is in you? — Unless indeed, you are disqualified.*

Credibility

This is what the Lord taught me. I needed to build credibility, like setting up a charity. First, I needed a good cause: to reach out to every home in my patch. Secondly, I needed to earn credibility as an honourable trustee for this cause. People will give money and volunteer to help a worthy, proven charity.

Jesus fulfilled these criteria. Because he had a reasonable cause, Moses, Elijah, and the angels came to help him. *Mark 9:5,* *Then Peter answered and said to Jesus, "Rabbi, it is good for us to be here; and let us make three tabernacles: one for You, one for Moses, and one for Elijah."*

This is what the Lord says about those that have fat spiritual account and credibility in heaven.

John 17:22, *"I have given <u>them the glory</u> you gave me, so they may be one as we are one.*

John 17:23, *I in them and you in me, that they may become completely one, so that the world may know that you have sent me and have <u>loved them</u> even as you have loved me.*

....

Glory

He wants to give us the glory he received from the father, and we have to learn to walk in it. What a tremendous feeling to be loved by God on the same par as his love for Jesus? To be <u>treated</u> by God, heavenly cloud, and angels as **_brothers_** of Jesus.

Heb 2:11, *For both He who sanctifies and those who are being sanctified are all of one, for which reason He is not ashamed to <u>call them brethren.</u>*

Seek it and feel your confidence rocket sky high. You would begin to feel confident that with the aid of the Holy Spirit, you could potentially account for every grain of sand, leaf, a person in your Patch. The best proof is in actually doing it. Moreover, God is willing to teach each one of us to do it, just as I taught the secretary to fix the radiator, which was beyond her skill level.

Chapter 42 –Some people with spiritual treasures /accounts.

Samuel. **1 Samuel 2:26,** *Meanwhile, the boy Samuel grew taller and grew in favour with the LORD and people.*

Abraham. **Genesis 18:3,** *Abraham said, "My Lord if I have now found favour in Your sight, do not pass on by Your servant.*

Mary. **Luke 1:30,** *Then the angel said to her, "Do not be afraid, Mary, for you have found favour with God.*

Jesus. Luke 2:52, And Jesus increased in wisdom and stature, and in favour with God and men.

Prayers are pearls.

They are solemn holy words spoken with great respect and dignity in the presence of the Holy Spirit, the Lord, the heavenly witnesses, and among his people. Correctly said with the care that is due to the Lord, the words have power, value, and authority to topple evil spiritual powers in heavenly places or bend the physic laws.

The lesson I learned: for answered prayers, there is a cost attached. Either I use the Lord's account or, if I have credibility, I pay from my bank account or my spiritual account.

Second lesson: it is not in the Lord's interest, nor ours, to regularly raid his account. He initially feeds us milk, but after a time, he cuts off that supply. No more answered prayers until we show a thirst to grow, to take the responsibility that is required from us. **Hebrews 5:13,** *for everyone who lives on milk, being still an infant, is unskilled in the word of righteousness.*

The Lord said to me, 'You took the tab for Raymond on Earth because you had a savings account to meet his prayers. I am going to teach you to take the bill in Heaven. You will need a spiritual account.

Lord, 'I will release things in Heaven, and you will stock up your spiritual account and use it to <u>make things happen as I did on Earth</u>. Trust me; <u>you will do **greater things**</u> than I did because I am with you. This is my covenant with you, sealed with my blood.'

John 14:12, *"I tell you the truth, anyone who believes in me will <u>do the same works</u> I have done, <u>and **even greater works**</u>, because I am going to be with the Father.*

Ephesians 1:3, *Blessed be the God and Father of our Lord Jesus Christ, who has blessed us with <u>every spiritual blessing</u> in the heavenly places in Christ.*

For the next few years, he helped me build an earthly and a spiritual account. The resources from this account would permit me to set dates and hours for things to happen. People's lives around me changed. Their faith soared sky-high, and many gave up secular employment to serve our Lord full time.

Wealth

A lesson I learned when we had a Nursing Home

There are many good reasons for making plenty of money and have a fat bank account. Abraham was rich, so were Kings Solomon and David. There are plenty of good reasons to have a big bank account on Earth and in Heaven. It is how we use these resources that matters. If you are materially or spiritually rich, you can do a lot to help others and contribute significantly to God's kingdom.

Chapter 44 – Tab for Church Leaders; Teaching Them

*Luke 7:28 "For I say to you, among those born of women there is not a greater prophet than John the Baptist, but he who is **least in** the kingdom of God is greater than he."*

Samuel, Isaiah, and Ezekiel were great prophets. They spoke the word of God. They were prophets, and we are heirs. There is a big difference. Moreover, some of you are called to be church leaders. Greater responsibility is placed on you. You have to make things happen.

Jesus is at the right hand of God, making intercessions. Our role is beside him in the heavenly places. It is essential to understand this spiritual role, its duty, and commitment. It is easy to walk in spirit to the throne of God or to the tree of healing (hard to believe, if you have never done it), collect its fruit, and heal or perform miracles, i.e., make it rain, oust dictators. That is easy. I have given some examples with evidence to support it.

It is a lot harder to pick up the financial or spiritual tab/ bill.

As heirs of Christ, we are responsible for the power released through us, the people healed, the governments ousted. An eternal commitment for those souls affected on Earth, on our PATCH, in New Heaven (Revelation 22:14-15, people in and outside the city gates).

If I release spiritual power, I ask myself, 'What is it that God requires?'

1 Timothy 6:12, Fight the good fight for the true faith. Hold tightly to the eternal life to which God has called you, which you have confessed so well before many witnesses.

If you do not grasp this, little or even nothing will happen. Access to the spiritual power in Heaven will be limited. You cannot exercise authority without accountability, and in God's kingdom, it is **eternal**.

Hence, I need to account, review and learn every evening, every seventh month, seventh year. This is part of eternal life that has started for us who live according to the scriptures.

197

If you do not pay your electric bill, what happens? The same happens if you cannot pay your spiritual tab, i.e. you pray, but your prayer goes unanswered unless the Lord in his mercy intervenes.

Jesus teaches us/me the cost of a sacrificial life and how to fund my patch and my future role in the New Earth and Heaven.

I asked the Lord, 'Why are the church leaders not picking-up the spiritual tab for their church?'

He asked me to re-read Ezekiel 34. I cried when I translated its meaning for today because he had once used it to convict me.

He told me there was no point in crying. The Lord said, 'Hari, how are you going to respond to the needs of the world awaiting redemption?'

I thought it over. 'I don't know.'

'Show them how to climb up Jacob's ladder to empty the ocean with the palm of your hand. *Learn from **Judges 19 & 20*** - The story about the Levite.'

Jude 20:6, So I cut her body into twelve pieces and sent the pieces throughout the territory assigned to Israel (England and Canada), *for these men have committed a terrible and shameful crime.*

V7, Now then, all of you — the entire community of Israel (England and Canada) — *must decide here and now what should be done about this!"* (This Book)

The Lord asked me, 'Hari, how are you going to respond to many of these church leaders who have spiritually neglected their flock?'

'Lord, I am going to send this book to as many churches in England and Canada as I can.'

My question to church leaders, 'How are you going to respond to the needs of your parish awaiting redemption?'

It is a question our Lord has put before me many times.

---------- ---

Chapter 45 – Leadership Qualities

A good leader has a calm, confident approach to life. Under pressure, he remains calm, as well as focused. People around him feel secure, confident, relaxed. He gives clear commands, and people trust and carry out his instructions.

I did not have leadership qualities.

In my early years, I would be nervous and sweating in a house group or prayer meeting. Sometimes I would receive a message for which I had no time to prepare. I was unsure how to deliver it in a relaxed, calm manner. Often I was trying to work out what it meant or for whom.

I had no role model from whom I could have learned. A mature prophet familiar with the ways of the Lord could have guided me. There was none.

As I prayed, I would receive a message, date, and hour for healing. Doubts would cloud my mind. Was it from myself or the Lord? I had a few minutes to decide. Ninety-five percent of me was sure it was from the Lord, but a small part of me would say, 'How do you know?' There would be an inward struggle.

The pressure would build inside me. I had to step outside my comfort zone and try. Be willing to be made a fool for the sake of the Lord. In the beginning, half the time, I took the safe option: ignore the voice inside me and pray in general. 'Lord, we lift our brother in prayer and ask that you would heal X.'

I would go home feeling disappointed. I had lacked the courage to step out in faith. The struggle would go on as I slept. How do you know if the message was from the Lord? The only way to know is to test it.

If the pressure built up, occasionally, it would explode. My voice would be tense and stressed, as I would pray. The sense of nervousness would infect others. They would feel uncomfortable, unsure of how to cope with my words. I would state dates and hours or things in a manner that made them feel uncomfortable.

No one had taught me how to use my gift in public. Even Mr Hammond struggled to guide me. He was reluctant to give advice. He would say, 'Do what the Lord wants you to do.'

It sounds simple until you try to exercise it in a packed church.

------ - -

Faith to move mountains

To overcome the world, you will need strong faith. You could be standing in front of a person dying of cancer. His family surrounds you as you pray for him.

You feel the hair on the back of the neck stand; electric current surges through you. Your heart rate quickens, beads of sweat form on your face, goose pimples form on your body. It could be your emotions—false reading.

Or it could be the power of the Holy Spirit surging through you. You're faith built on a proper interpretation of scriptures for that moment and on the indwelling Holy Spirit. An absolute certainty takes over. Now you have the confidence to apply the leaves of healing and state the hour cancer will depart.

Next, you state the day and hour a letter or a call from the hospital will come, confirming your word of life. Or the day and hour the power of your word will topple a nasty dictator.

The reality of your standing with God.

That is the kind of faith that overcomes the world. No law of physic can account for it.

You are in a similar arena as the sub-atomic particles in the black hole, entirely outside the physic laws. What a wonderful, exciting place to be! What a marvellous gift of God. *Matthew 13:46, "who, when he had found one pearl of great price, went and sold all that he had and bought it.*

---- 🜚---

Chapter 46 – Small House groups

What I learned

Small house groups are the right places to begin practising spiritual gifts. Initially, work hard and build a strong, caring relationship with this group. In this place, you should feel comfortable to explore and make mistakes. Discuss the gifts of the Holy Spirit, and encourage people to step out in faith. Be open and share the difficulties of trying to step out into the unknown. Together, create an atmosphere in the group not to feel ashamed if things do not happen.

If you prophesy, make sure you go home; write it in a logbook for the house group. Make a summary of who was present, what was discussed, who was prayed for, and why. Count the words at the end of each line, draw a line underneath your account, and leave space so that you can add notes later on.

Failure is part of learning; if your prophecy fails, you have tried. You have given the Lord a chance; it is up to him to encourage you now.

You will need a brave and mature house leader—someone like King David, willing to face Goliath. Constant Spiritual warfare is brutal, stressful work. It is a battlefield where you will face hunger, thirst, cold, sleep deprivation, loneliness, and myriads of other obstacles. It separates boys and girls from true warriors. God does not handover his pearls to boys and girls, but only to those tested and proved warriors.

For things to happen.

You have to prove you can **overcome**[1] the world.

Secondly, you have to prove you are worthy, responsible and accountable for eternity, to things you have set your hands on, every 7th

--- ☆---

[1] *1 John 5:4, For whatever is born of God overcomes the world: and this is the victory that overcomes the world, even our faith. …x..x…*

month, 7th year until **Judgment day**[2], because many of God's words will not have been **accomplished**[3] until that Day, i.e. the healing was just the start of a long journey of reconciliation, restoration process you got involved in.

Try the above, make notes of your activities and prayers.

For months, nothing will happen. Keep at it.

De 4:29 *"But from there you will seek the LORD your God, and you will find Him if you seek Him with all your heart and with all your soul.*

One day God will say, I have tested you and found you faithful. Then the rivers of **living water**[4] will flow through you.

---- ☆----

[2] *Revelation 2:26, And he that overcomes, and keeps my works to the end (Judgment Day), to him will I give power over the nations:*

[3] *Isaiah 55:11, So shall my word be that goes forth out of my mouth: it shall not return to me void, but it shall accomplish that which I please, and it shall prosper in the thing whereto I sent it.*

[4] *Revelation 7:17, For the Lamb which is in the middle of the throne shall feed them, and shall lead them to living fountains of waters: and God shall wipe away all tears from their eyes.*

---- ---

Chapter 47 – My Parents

1976-1982.

My parents stayed in the upstairs flat for six years. My father had received a small lump sum on his retirement, which he invested in Australian mines. Over these six years, the Lord blessed them. The investment turned into a small fortune. They were happy and felt financially secure. They could now afford a comfortable lifestyle and returned to India in 1982.

For the first time in their lives, my parents had money to build their own home. They stayed in my grandfather's house in India while the bungalow was constructed.

The house took a few months to complete, and my father went to inspect it. His lifelong ambition to own his own home had finally turned into reality. He was overjoyed and planned to move in. A few days before they moved in, my father fell sick. Sadly, he passed away before he could move into his home.

My mother sold the house. Without my father, she was devastated and developed dementia. A few years later, she passed away.

In 1976, a few months after I had purchased the house in London, my parents came to stay with me. The first-year, I shared the ground floor flat with a friend, and during this time, the frosty relationship between my parents and me began to thaw. My mother was exceedingly pleased; she started to cook for me. Then my friend found work in another part of the country and moved out.

My mother suggested I move into a large spare room in their flat and rent the ground floor flat. My father had a small pension and some savings. I had a large mortgage to pay. Money was tight, so I moved in with them and rented the empty flat. My relationship with my mother improved, but my father stayed at a distance. If he needed to say anything to me, it would pass from him to my Mother to me.

One day my brother and his family came to see us. My parents were pleased to see him. They had a good relationship with him.

I was talking to my brother in the hallway when my father walked past us. He went up to his room, turned, and walked back towards us. He looked at my brother. His eyes were moist.

He said to my brother, 'Tell your young brother we are proud of him.' He did not look at me. He went back to his room.

Years later, as I went through my diaries, this day would stir up deep emotions. It was apparent my father longed to look me in the eyes and make some form of reconciliatory move. He must have longed to hug me and let bygones be bygones. I wanted that too, but neither of us knew how to bridge the gap. The chasm was too broad, the hill too high to climb for either of us.

Besides, I had grown furiously independent. To make any form of reconciliation with my father would mean coming under his authority. My older brother and my younger sister had arranged marriages set up by my parents. I did not want an arranged marriage, and it suited me to be at a distance. I preferred to make my arrangements.

I had never felt anger or resentment towards my father. He did what he considered best for his family under circumstances that were beyond his control. I looked at his good side. In many ways, he was a role model, passionate about his care for his neighbours.

[*Su Anne's Tenet 1), 'Wounds heal; scars remain for life, for eternity.'*

Proverbs 10:12, *Hatred stirs up strife, but <u>love covers all sins.</u>*

1 **Peter 4:8,** *Above all, maintain constant love for one another, for <u>love covers a multitude</u> of sins.*

Colossians 3:14, *Above all, clothe yourselves with love, which binds everything together in perfect harmony.*

---- ----

Chapter 48 – When you pray, things happen

2 Corinthians 4:11, *For we who live are always delivered to death for Jesus' sake, that the life of Jesus also may be manifested in our mortal flesh.*

Rev Hammond asked me if we could have a house group at my home on Wednesdays. Between Monday and Wednesday, I would concentrate on the house group. Before the group met, I would sit before the Lord and wait upon him. I would get a word or message for someone. I would ask the Lord who it was for, which chair that person would sit on. What would his specific request be? I would write this in my diary.

On Wednesday, if what I had written in my diary happened, my faith would soar. When we prayed, I would gently thank the Lord for listening to our request and quietly say, 'Lord, let this happen as follows…' the way he had prepared me to do during the week.

It was done with so little fuss that people hardly noticed how specific the prayer was. It was the reality of walking in the spirit—the thrill of being in the spirit where all things are possible to him that believes in God's promises.

During these times, my parents stayed in their room. They were comfortable in their own company.

Then my mother invited Pastor Hammond and the people in our house group for a meal. She cooked for us, but they did not join us because my father felt uncomfortable in my presence. More invitations followed. Rev Hammond's face would light up with delight at each invitation. He enjoyed Mother's cooking.

One day in the house group, we started prayer when there was a tap on the door. I opened the door to find my father standing in the hallway. I was surprised. He looked very uncomfortable.

He whispered, 'Can you people pray for your mother. She is not feeling well.' I was astounded. It was the first time in years he had spoken directly to me. I looked puzzled. He had strongly disapproved of my conversion to Christianity.

Without thinking, I asked, 'Why ask us?'

His answer left me speechless. 'When you pray to Jesus, things happen.'

It was the only time he spoke to me until he passed away.

Chapter 49 – Bare feet in Winter

It was winter. There was snow on the ground. My father put on his shoes and jacket and went out for a walk. I noticed he had no socks on.

My mother was cooking in the kitchen. I went up to my mother and said, 'Mother, Father's gone out in the cold, and he has no socks on his feet.'

She turned and said, 'I know, he always does it.'

'Why?'

She paused, then answered, 'When you were young, we didn't have any money, so your father went to work without socks.'

'But, Mother, you have money now.'

'I will get him some.' She returned to her cooking.

I went into my bedroom, and I cried. Here was a man who had sacrificed so much for us. He stood in the room next door, and I could not reach out to him because I chose to read a book. There are times I wish I had never come across the Bible. A very painful emotional scar had buried its roots in my being. It would leave resentment towards God, one of the hills in my life too high to climb, a hill I had to go round.

When I hear an evangelical pastor preaching about people going to Hell for refusing to follow the Lord, I have an instant dislike for such people. I would rather spend my time with my parents and my Hindu uncle (who taught me so much about the Holy Spirit from the bible and Bhagavad-Gita) than share Heaven with the likes of him.'

These people of other faiths and atheist did not choose to be born. God needed them in his plan to complete our salvation and perfect it.

Matthew 13:44, *Again, the kingdom of heaven is like treasure hidden in a field* (us), *which a man found* (our Lord) *and hid; and for joy, over it, he goes and sells all that he has* (Gives his life for) *and buys that field.*

We are the treasure for which our Lord gave his life to have us purified and made fit for his temple. The assistance of other people was needed to help us work out our salvation. Therefore, we owe these good decent, hard-working people a great sense of gratitude.

Nonetheless, these people will face Judgment day, same as us, and like us, they will receive what is <u>due to them</u>. It is not for us to judge them. It says;-

Revelation 22:12, *And behold, I am coming quickly, and My reward is with Me, to give to everyone <u>according to his work</u>.*

While evil people will find themselves among the following, **Revelation 21:8,** *But the cowardly, unbelieving, abominable, murderers, sexually immoral, sorcerers, idolaters, and all liars shall have their part in the lake which burns with fire and brimstone, which is the second death.*

While others (good decent people), who do not fall into the above category and not clothed with the Holy Spirit may pass the Judgment day but find themselves outside the New Jerusalem,

Revelation 21:24, *And the nations of those who are saved shall walk in its light, and the kings of the earth bring their glory and honour into it.* (New Jerusalem).

Years later, during the 6th sabbatical review of this episode of my life.

I sat before the Lord and brought before him my father and mother. These wonderful parents had sacrificed their happiness and welfare for my family and me. Moreover, if for me, then it counted as done to the Lord. I felt a tremendous sense of gratitude and a moral obligation to pay them back for their goodness. Moreover, if I owed them a debt I could not pay, my Lord would need to help me pay it.

Our Lord had taught me to make compensation and restitution for any consequences of my actions. To acknowledge them and have a moral obligation <u>"to make whole"</u> those who had suffered due to my actions. My family had made sacrifices and given me a fantastic opportunity to know the Word of God, even though a lot of it was unintended. I lay this before God.

A few days later, the Lord said, 'We will do it together. We will build a spiritual sanctuary. There, we will make restitution and payback to all for the consequences of your actions: to your parents to everyone in your Patch.'

Colossians 1:20, *And, having made peace through the blood of his cross, by him to* <u>reconcile</u> *all things to himself; by him, I say, whether they be things in earth or things in Heaven.*

Ephesians 2:16, *And that he might* <u>reconcile</u> *both to God in one body by the cross, having slain the enmity thereby:*

My book, *The Spiritual Sanctuary, available from the author*, is written in a story form. I chose this form because it was the only way I could convey a very complex spiritual path.

Spiritual life is correspondence with the spiritual realms, where the Lord Jesus lives, and it is here we have built a sanctuary.

One night, I suddenly woke up. I felt the lord's presence. As I rubbed my eyes, he said, 'Hari, go back to sleep. I have taken care of your good parents. They are fine.' Then he left. Scars can heal. All things are possible with God.

My Uncle

My Father's youngest brother, who had once persecuted me in my early days, had turned to the Hari Krishna movement. He became a devoted follower of Bhagavad-Gita, part of the Holy Vedic Hindu books. Years later, we were reconciled.

He read the Bhagavad-Gita regularly. We had many conversations. He would tell me there was only one supreme God. The Jews called him Jehovah, Christians called him heavenly father, Muslims called him Allah, and Hindus called him Supreme Lord. According to him, the Holy Spirit of the Supreme Lord (God) came upon humankind to impart spiritual guidance.

We were comfortable with each other. We both understood that the

Supreme Lord (in the Hindu Holy Book, Bhagavad Gita) was the same as my biblical God.

My uncle, a devout Hindu, read the Bible and the Bhagavad-Gita. He taught me about the inner workings of the Holy Spirit and the world of the angels. Also, about Brahman: the creator, to us the WORD of God - Christ.

Chapter 50 –Angels

1 Peter 1:12 – which things the angels desire to look into.

1976-1988. There were many angelic presences. They came to learn. They wanted to see how God took a small insignificant church and moulded its members into super-spiritual beings. Some of them would one day become giants in God's kingdom. The angels wanted to be part of that great enterprise. Besides, they came because God had sent them.

Psalms 91:11, For He shall give His angels charge over you, To keep you in all your ways.

My Patch (Haringey Ladder) was special to them. They were delighted to guard us and work with our church.

Genesis 28:12, *And he dreamed that there was a ladder set up on the earth, the top of it reaching to heaven; and the angels of God were ascending and descending on it.* (Haringey ladder).

1 Corinthians 6:3, Do you not know that we are to judge angels—to say nothing of ordinary matters?

For my safety, there were times they delayed me from going somewhere. The car would not start; an unsolicited phone call would interrupt my schedule. In most cases, these were natural occurrences, but a few times, it was them. Often I would find out they had kept me from injury or harm or delayed me because someone needed my help.

In the beginning, I would see an angel about to do something. I would turn to my friends and say, 'Watch the visiting preacher. He is about to pull out his written sermon. Watch, he will put it back in his pocket.' It would happen.

The angel would look at me, a big smile on his face, as if we were doing something naughty. The preacher would hesitate then put his sermon back in his pocket. He would say, 'I think the Lord wants me to preach from the heart.' [**Appendix**: Binding the sermon].

We would be on our way out of a church, and an angel would approach

Appendix, Angels binding the sermon

10ᵗʰ Nov Sunday 1978

<u>Binding the Sermon.</u>

On Sunday evening before church Service we had a time of prayer. There was a new person in our meeting. I knew at once from his bearing he was a Missionary.

When I asked him, he said he was a Minister. This sharp discernment left an impression on me.

That evening he was to preach at our church. As he came to the pulpit to preach I saw an Angel behind him. There were also other Angels.

Angel.

He reached into his pocket to take out his Sermon. He was going to read to us.

I perceived that the reason the Angel was behind was because he had come with an important message.

I turned to Liz and said, "Liz he is going to put his Sermon away."

"Why?" She asked.

"Because the Angel is here. Watch he is going to preach straight from his heart."

To everyone's suprise he put his Sermon away and preached what the lord Wanted.

Q why the presence of Angels? / Heb 1:14. ministering Spirits. *Added 17/6/11*

212

me. I would turn to the person next to me and say, 'Mark, be careful when you approach a roundabout. A lorry will miss you by inches.' It would happen. The angel had come to warn.

After a while, it felt normal, and then I started to take their presence for granted. Their company became part of my everyday life. They stayed on for a while then moved on to other duties or other locations.

From the book *The Heart of Truth* by Charles Finney (1792-1875), a great man of God, the Lord taught me about my patch's governance.

Storm in UK 1987

It was the most catastrophic storm to hit Britain in 300 years, and its effects were disastrous. A substantial amount of damage was done to the country. A few days later, I read an account in the Evening Standard. It showed the damage done in the boroughs of London. [**Appendix** Haringey storm).

It reveals Haringey was protected during this storm. One tree in my patch had fallen, and there was little sign of any damage to the houses. In contrast, in the surrounding boroughs, several hundred trees and homes were damaged.

--- ☆---

Great Storm of 1987 From Wikipedia, the free encyclopedia

The **Great Storm of 1987** was a violent tropical cyclone that occurred on the night of 15–16 October, with hurricane-force winds causing casualties in the United Kingdom, France, and the Channel Islands, as a severe depression in the Bay of Biscay moved northeast.

Among the most damaged areas were Greater London, the East Anglian coast, the Home Counties. Forests, parks, roads, and railways were strewn with fallen trees and schools were closed. The British National Grid suffered heavy damage, leaving thousands without power. That day's weather reports had failed to indicate a storm of such severity.

Appendix, In **1987, we had a storm over the UK.**

It was one of the worst in decades. While many trees were uprooted in the surrounding boroughs of London, in Haringey, there was only tree damage. Did the power of prayer protect this area?

30 Nov 1987, evening standard

Evening Standard Tree Appeal

Camden: 500 trees down with tragic losses in Lincoln's Inn Fields, Russell Square, Coram's Field, Queens Square, Tavistock Square, Red Lion Square and Great Ormond Street.

The City: 50 mature street trees down in the Square Mile and widespread losses in the open spaces owned, managed and maintained by the City Corporation—1000 down on Kent and Surrey Commons, 500 down in Burnham Beeches, including 50 of the ancient beech pollards.

Croydon: The most highly populated borough with many trees. Disastrous damage, 70,000 trees down.

Ealing: Proud of its reputation as a leafy borough, it lost 5500 trees. 1500 of these mature trees lining streets.

Enfield: The most northerly of the boroughs with a lot of green belt. 3000 trees lost, among them fine oaks some more than 200 years' old. Many more forest trees damaged and in need of urgent tree surgery. The superb lime avenue at Forty Hall wrecked with three-

quarters of the trees blown down, a great loss to the park.

Greenwich: Terrific damage, 10,000 trees down. Happily the first and oldest mulberry tree in Britain, planted by King John, survived. So did the Queen Ann Oak in Greenwich Park.

Hounslow: Serious losses. 10,000 trees, a quarter of the borough's stock, destroyed.

Hammersmith: 600 trees down, among them fine mature riverside and street trees.

Harrow: Less green and leafy now. 5000 trees lost.

Haringey: 3500 trees damaged including heavy toll in Finsbury Park. Council launched £30 "adopt a tree" campaign.

Hackney: "Considerable damage" to several thousand trees. Hackney Marshes badly hit. Replanting underway.

Hillingdon: At least 3000 trees brought down including large beech and walnut. Replanting still under discussion.

Havering: Heavily wooded borough severely hit. 5000

woodland still closed because of danger. Replanting campaign launched.

Islington: 1500 trees down including half of trees on Islington Green. Council envisages "severe financial problems."

Kensington and Chelsea: Total 422 lost including rare snowdrop and foxglove trees in Holland Park. Appeal set up.

Kingston: Mayor launched replacement campaign, several hundred lost.

Lambeth: Widespread damage with trees still in dangerous condition. Wyatts Field still closed to public. More than 1000 lost. Operation Acorn launched with schools growing seedlings.

Lewisham: 3500 down in widespread damage estimated at £1 million.

Merton: 3000 trees lost including important species and examples of London plane planted early 1700s. 300 down in Ravensbury Park alone. £120,000 to be spent on replanting this year.

Newham: 12,000 trees down. Continuing survey may mean more will be lost.

Redbridge: More than 3000 down; council leader pledged to replace losses in two-year programme.

Richmond: Severe damage throughout Richmond Park and Hampton Court with

---- ❦ ----

Chapter 51 – Last days in Haringey

I had been in Haringey for 13 years. The intensity of my constant vigil had exhausted me. I needed a break from London, from the church. I had met a lovely girl called Julia in the church. We had been going out for about three years. She wanted to get married, have four children; I was not ready for it. My traumatic life had affected me; put me off marriage for life. It did not feel right to raise a family in a world full of suffering. We broke off and went our separate ways.

I met another lovely girl called Kathy and went out with her. Within a few weeks, she had introduced me to her family and friends and started talking about marriage. Her parents were lovely. Her mother thought I was adorable. Her father was a doctor and a lay preacher in the Church of England. I felt at home with them.

She was gorgeous. Very bright, intelligent, and loved the Lord. I had a troubled childhood; she had had a happy, stable life, a loving family. She made me feel secure, confident. I adored her and considered marriage.

One evening, while we were out walking, happily giggling, in the distance, I saw Julia walking home. She looked lost, miserable. That sight affected me. I had not realized how much she had become part of my life or how deeply I cared for her.

Kathy's latest work took her away from London, and our romance fizzled out. Changes were going on at my work. Our department was closed, and staff relocated to various parts of London. I ended up in Central London. I hated working in Central London and commuting on crowded trains.

Julia and I got together again. This time I proposed to her. She kept me in suspense for a few months then accepted my proposal. I was delighted. Both of us wanted to leave London and move somewhere quieter.

Long hours of prayer, leaflet distribution, caring for others, and sleepless nights were something I could not keep up indefinitely. Before starting my 14th year in Haringey, my 2nd sabbatical year, I brought a verse before the Lord.

'Lord, how are you going to respond to this verse?' It was my turn to ask a question he had asked me many times.

Deuteronomy 15:12, If your brother, a Hebrew man, or a Hebrew woman, is sold to you and serves you six years, then in the seventh year, you shall let him go free from you.

I was mentally and spiritually exhausted. I needed a break. On my second sabbatical year, I handed in my notice at work; put my house on the market. Julia and I were engaged; we planned a life together somewhere different. We could try Canada. I had a brother and sister in Toronto, Canada. Perhaps we could join them. We researched Canada, but the extreme weather, the hot, humid summers, and icy cold winters put us off the idea.

We thought of starting life in South America. We were excited. The proceeds from our house sales would set us up well there. We joined a Spanish evening class. My house sale went through, and I had money in the bank.

Julia thought I should go first and check it out. I had a backpack and travelled for five lovely months-round Peru, Bolivia, Chile, Argentina, Paraguay, and Brazil. My Spanish was reasonable, and it opened doors. Almost every weekend, I was invited to someone's home, wedding, birthday, or other celebration. It was a wonderful break. Five months later, I returned and rented a cottage in Devon.

We got married and made plans about South America. I loved Chile. It was a beautiful country, and I liked its people. Julia got cold feet. She did not like the thought of leaving her family.

I prayed for guidance. I felt the Lord say that whatever we chose, he would go with us. I had the money from my house sale. We put Julia's house on the market and planned to buy a business, something I had always wanted.

Mr Hammond thought I had done the wrong thing giving up secure work and, more importantly, my support for his work. But I was exhausted, burnt out. It was something he could not grasp.

The Lord had taught me a lot about accountability for my patch [remember my parable of mixed fruits. You only need a small piece of apple or pear to get the gist of its taste.]

Need-to-know basis

In my prayers, our Lord Jesus had revealed the gist of his plan for creation. How and why our names happened to be written in his book. About God's desire for creation. He explained why God prepared the good works for us before the foundations of the earth were laid. The reason for Judgment Day and his plans for the New Heaven and Earth. He gave me glimpses of life beyond and my place in the New Kingdom.

I asked him why he was teaching me all these things and confirming it with something I could test. His answer was simple. 'You have the unique ability to grasp God's plans quickly. Because you asked, and it delighted us to share.'

*Mark 4:11, And He said to them, "To you it has been given to know the **mystery** of the kingdom of God; but to those who are outside, all things come in parables,*

Besides, he had other reasons beyond my capacity to understand.

[Kate Adin's Tenet 2]. 'You are unique. There is a greater power that guides your path. Everything that has been made, created is set up for you (for those like you). There are some things, some mysteries that are hidden until the appropriate time.'

---- ☆----

My mind was always buzzing, saturated with knowledge. I needed a break.

At the start of my 15th year in Haringey, we bought a nursing home in Cornwall and moved there.

---- 🐴----

Chapter 52 – Meeting my Wife

The first seven years of my life in the church were what I would call the healing years. I had come through troubled teen years; my social skills and confidence were practically zero. I was a good-looking, athletic, but nervous, and insecure kid, fumbling at the effort to hold onto a job, make friends, or chat with a girl.

By the end of my 1st sabbatical year, some of these wounds were beginning to heal. I started to feel more secure, gained a few promotions at work, and improved my social skills.

Eight years after I joined a church, I was part of a small friendly Christian group. We had lovely weekends, where we would go away for a few days as a group. We would stay at the seaside resorts or go across the sea to Holland or France for an Easter or summer holiday. It was a mixed group of friends, all single, and we had lovely times.

By now, I had improved my social skills, and I was getting better at chatting with girls. There were quite a few girls interested in me, and they would invite me for meals. I enjoyed their company but made sure I kept the relationship platonic. A couple of girls asked me to marry them. I was not ready for a 9-5 job and babies. I loved my freedom.

Deacon's home after church.

After the Sunday evening service, we would meet at a deacon's home and discuss the evening sermon. One mid-September evening in 1984, I turned around and saw a young woman sitting behind me at this group meeting. I watched her. She had beautiful almond-shaped hazel-coloured eyes, ash-blonde hair, and a smooth light olive complexion.

I turned and faced the group leader again, but my mind was somewhere else. When we had finished and people were getting ready to go home, I made a beeline for her. I tried to chat her up. She did not show any interest.

Her name was Julia, and she had recently moved into our area. I offered to give her a lift home, but she said she wanted to walk home alone. The following week I offered to give her a lift but again got a negative response.

The third week I decided I would give it one more try. I needed to change my tactics. After tea and biscuits, I had a small chat with her and mentioned I was giving some people a lift home. Would she like to join us?

My heart was thumping. I thought any minute now, it would probably jump out. She looked around then said yes. We walked up to my car. There were two other girls with us, and they got into the back seats. Julia got in the front passenger seat. I dropped the two girls at their home and then took Julia home.

It was late in the evening. We stopped outside Julia's home, and I turned the engine off. There was an awkward silence for a while. She made no effort to get out. We sat, and my heart was doing a marathon. I didn't want to say the wrong word, and I didn't want to ruin it.

She sat there fiddling with the contents of my glove compartment, looking very English: prim and proper. She had a smart light beige jacket with the collar turned up, a long cotton skirt, horrible flesh-coloured stockings, and two-inch-heel sandals.

I watched her, thinking *it's time for her to stop fiddling with the contents of my glove compartment and leave.* Finally, she turned and asked me a question. I answered her question, and then we started talking.

Soon it was past midnight. I said to her, 'Do you realize it's late? You should go home.'

She was quite blunt. 'I will go home when I am ready.' We talked some more. I was getting worried. She was lodging with a family in the church. I didn't want either of us to get in trouble with them.

I reminded her it was now early in the morning. I got the same answer. I had struggled to give her a lift. Now I was struggling to get her out of my car. ---- 🏵---

Chapter 53 – Invitation

I looked at my watch. It was 1.30 in the morning.

'Julia, I need to go home.' She still did not make a move. 'I need to go home. I have to be in the office by eight,' I said.

She nodded, reached for the door handle, and opened the door, paused, then faced me. I leaned over to hug her. She turned and kissed me on the lips, a peck.

'See you next Sunday,' she smiled. There was a twinkle in her eyes.

'I won't be there,' I replied.

'Why?' The shine in her eyes faded.

'I am going away on holiday on Tuesday. I won't be back for three weeks.'

'Oh.' She sounded disappointed. 'Anywhere interesting?'

'I am meeting a friend in Israel. Don't worry; I will call you when I get back. Write down your phone number.' She did.

Just over two weeks later, I rang Julia. She picked up the phone, and we exchanged greetings.

She asked me, 'How is Israel?'

'Very nice and warm,' I replied.

'Come and see me when you are back.'

'Are you sure?' I asked.

'Yes. I'll cook you a meal.'

'Okay.'

Julia, 'Is that a promise?' I hesitated.

'You don't sound keen.'

'You're inviting me for a meal?' I didn't tell her I was back.

'Yes.'

'Okay, I will be at your house in half an hour.'

---- 🐾---

Chapter 54 – My first date with Julia

On Friday, I took her out. We went to Pizza Hut. The waiter showed us a table near the front window. We sat down and ordered a drink while we looked at the menu.

There were two young girls of about eight years old, with their father on my left side. The girls were smiling and nudging each other as their father surveyed the menu. They caught my eye and smiled. While we were eating, the two girls kept on ogling us.

'Ignore them,' Julia said.

'Why?' I asked as I caught the two girls smiling at me.

'I teach them. They are nice girls.'

A few days later, I had a day off. I went to the primary school where Julia was teaching. It was unplanned. Maybe, if she had time, we could go out for lunch. I got to her school just before lunch break. The receptionist showed me to her class. It was still a few minutes before the class finished, so I stood in the hallway and waited.

Through a small window, I saw her sitting on a child's chair, her legs stretched out, reading a story, surrounded by her class. The children were sitting on the floor. A young girl was delicately stroking Julia's knees as she read a story. The expression on the children's faces was one of adoration for their young schoolteacher. A small boy sitting behind her was stroking the end of her jacket. It formed a beautiful picture of a young blonde teacher surrounded by her adoring fans.

Four months later, this delightful prim and a proper woman asked me to marry her. I said I wasn't ready for marriage. A year later, she introduced me to her family. Four years later, we were married, and we moved to Cornwall. She took a teaching job in a primary school while I managed the nursing home.

For the last 24 years, this adorable and charming woman has been a top-rated primary school Head teacher – a role that suits her well.

She is the best thing that has happened in my life. She brought stability to my life and gave me a sense of belonging. Her parents welcomed me into their family and made me feel at home with them.

I could finally call this green and pleasant country my home.

Chapter 55 – Cornwall; 1989-2006

We sold our properties in London and bought a rundown Nursing Home in Cornwall. We thought that with a matron in charge of the home, it would be easy to manage the business.

Our next five years were taken up with the nursing home.

The nursing home turned out to be a challenge. Within weeks of the purchase, the Bank of England raised interest rates. The country's finances were in a mess, with inflation out of control. The bank kept on increasing the interest rate, and many businesses went bankrupt. The country was in recession.

Thousands of people were laid off. Within six months, our interest payments doubled, our losses mounted. Often I worked 12-14 hours in the home. Julia had found work in teaching, and her wages helped pay for our essentials. In the third year, interest rates stabilized.

At home, I tried to put into practice all the things the Lord had taught me. Every grain of sand counted. Every resident and member of staff counted. I took an intense interest in their welfare and used all our resources to promote their welfare, interest, and happiness.

For the first two years at the nursing home, we struggled to keep it afloat. Each month, we were losing money. We tried everything to reduce costs. Prayed hard to maintain the number of residents. We had more patients passing away than we could replace.

We had kept a substantial reserve when we bought the home. That ran out after 16 months. Our number of residents was way below the breakeven point. I was unable to pay the winter gas bill. I brought the bill before the Lord.

2 Kings 20:3, *"Remember now, O LORD, I pray, how I have walked before You in truth and with a loyal heart, and have done what was good in Your sight."*

Nothing happened. A final notice to pay came in red ink.

In desperation, I wrote to all the hospitals as far as London and

Manchester offering special discounts for people needing nursing care after their treatment at the hospital. We got one call. A small hospital in North Cornwall was closing. They had relocated most of their residents except two. Perhaps, we could take them into our home while a permanent place was found for them. I took our matron to see the manager of the hospital.

She interviewed us. Could we accommodate the two people for two weeks while she looked for a more permanent place? I agreed to take them. That weekend the two patients arrived, and the hospital paid in advance for their care.

I paid the gas bill.

That was the lowest point we reached. After that, slowly, our numbers increased. I asked the staff for their views on improving the home, to reduce the wage bills. They were free to find faults with me, open to criticize me, without fear. I left a notebook in the staff room to air any grievances or for any suggestions, they had.

Since it was in public view, they didn't have to put their names. I read their ideas and inserted action plans to remedy their grievances or act upon their suggestions. When I had fixed something, I initialled and dated it. With their help, we reorganized the home and made it more efficient.

One of my concerns was the low wages we paid. We were losing money, and I didn't have an option to raise wages.

Caring for others

In Haringey, I learned a lot about walking in the spirit, and in Cornwall, I learned about caring for people. It matters a lot to God how we care for others. We are his heirs in Christ. All that is his is ours in Christ.

Saint Paul says, *1 Corinthians 13:1, If I could speak all the languages of earth and of angels, but didn't love others, I would only be a noisy gong or a clanging cymbal.*

Galatians 4:7, *Now, you are no longer a slave but God's child. And since you are his child, God has made you his heir.*

Luke 22:26, *But among you, it will be different. Those who are the greatest among you should take the lowest rank, and the leader should be like a servant.*

I wanted to learn to care for our clients, our staff and implement the words below in practice. (Should church leaders implement this in their pastoral duty, it would improve their relationship with the church members.)

To be kind and respectful, putting the care and safety of our clients first. To help and encourage our clients to participate in decisions about their care. To listen to them, note their concerns, and respect their right to dignity, privacy, and confidentiality.

To share information about their health, care, and treatment with them in a way they can understand. To be open and honest about their care and treatment. To ensure they are safe and reduce as far as we can the risk of mistakes or harm. If mistakes happen, we should promptly apologize to them, explaining what has happened and the likely effects. At all times, to act with honesty and integrity.

To raise concerns immediately if we believe that they are vulnerable, at-risk, or need extra support and protection, paying attention to their wellbeing. To help them to access the care and support that they need.

These are the things the Lord wanted us to learn. Years later, I would realize the importance of this.

Colossians 1:20, *and by Him to reconcile all things to Himself, by Him, whether things on earth or things in heaven, having made peace through the blood of His cross.*

---- ----

Chapter 56 – Firstfruit to the Lord.

Deuteronomy 26:10, So now I bring the first of the fruit of the ground that you, O LORD, have given me." You shall set it down before the LORD your God and bow down before the LORD your God.

By the middle of the third year, we had made a small profit. I discussed this with my wife, Julia, and we went to see our church vicar. We gave him our profit to be used to help the people in the church. By the end of the year, we had a more significant profit, our first share of wages, which again went to help people in the church.

We were in the middle of a recession. In our church, some people were struggling to pay mortgages, electric bills, and other bills. In the church prayer meeting, we would become aware of people's needs.

Our church vicar would walk up to their homes and leave a brown envelope on the doorstep or in the letterbox. A parcel from an unknown person would arrive in the post to meet a distressed family's needs. God does not print money. He moves people's hearts: their generosity. Someone has to donate; take the tab.

It is easy to write a cheque; it is much harder to help the weak and vulnerable and provide human kindness. No amount of money can replace it. Reaching out to the poor and weak takes a certain kind of charity that should flow from within us, a mark of every born again Christian.

1 Corinthians 13:2, If I have prophetic powers and understand all mysteries and all knowledge, and if I have all faith, to remove mountains, but do not have love, I am nothing.

We prayed for ways we could help others. I went and saw the head of a school that cared for special needs children. I asked for his permission to sponsor two classes. We would pay for the children's swimming lessons and outings.

We sought out all institutes' names that cared for children within three miles of us. We made a list of the children's names. At Christmas time, Julia and I wrapped presents for every child, wrote their names on each gift, and took them to the institutes.

God cared for them. Through the example of the wealthy Hindu family, he had shown me a way of life that was pleasing to him.

James 1:27, *Pure and undefiled religion before God and the Father is this: to visit orphans and widows in their trouble and to keep oneself unspotted from the world.*

It still felt like we were just writing cheques. We searched for more ways to help. We found a kindly man called Bob, who ran a soup kitchen in the town centre in the evenings. We volunteered to help him once a week. We helped him in the kitchen, cooking meals for homeless people. That became part of our life.

One of the main lessons I learned in Haringey was, 'God cared for every grain of sand, every leaf, every person irrespective of how they behaved towards him.' The only way to believe this was to live it out. The weak, the poor in our town did not seek us. They asked nothing from us. We reached out to them because we saw God reach out to them.

It does leave some unanswered questions: why do so many people and animals suffer? To say it is a consequence of original sin simply fails to convince me and the vast majority of the world.

In our Hindu Holy books, there is no concept of original sin that I am aware of. The **Bhagavad-Gita**[1] gives a simple answer. It states pain and suffering is due to ignorance, anger, selfishness, and spiritual depravity.

B-Gita chapter 3:10. At the beginning of creation, I blessed creation and set in motion the principle of selfless, sacrificial service to promote the welfare, interest, and happiness of all creation. By this selfless service, all creation would be prosperous, fruitful, and find fulfilment for its desires. 9:33. Even kings and those of noble birth seek this supreme goal. All are born in this temporary world of sacrificial love, pain, and suffering. Therefore, engage in loving service to my creation and me.

[1]*Bhagavad-Gita by Hari Patel amazon com*

Love your Neighbour

Matthew 22:39, 'You shall love your <u>neighbour</u> as yourself.'

1 John 4:8, He who does not <u>love (his neighbour)</u> does not know God, for God is <u>love</u>.

*1 John 3:18, My little children, let us not **love** in word or in tongue, but in deed and in truth.*

1 John 4:20, If someone says, "I love God," and hates his brother (doesn't care for his neighbour)*, he is a liar; for he who does not love his brother* (care for his neighbour) *whom he has seen, how can he love God whom he has not seen?*

A steward of the Lord's parish has the responsibility to demonstrate his thankfulness in deeds to all the inhabitants for the service they provide to his parish and for their contribution (directly or indirectly) to God's kingdom and our salvation.

--- ---

Chapter 57- Conduct pleasing to the Lord

1989-1994 After we were married and moved to Cornwall, Julia and I used to go to the house group together. Surrounded by friends in our previous church, I was relaxed. Here in a new church among strangers, I was cautious, and I kept a low profile.

Then I started to prophesy. The people in the group were uncomfortable with it. It began to affect us, particularly Julia. She could feel my stressed voice as I tried to foretell the day and hour the Lord would answer prayer. She also felt uncomfortable. She could not understand why God wanted me to share things. If God wanted me to share, he should have given me a gift of better delivery, the gift of a born leader.

1 Corinthians 1:27, But God has chosen the foolish things of the world to put to shame the wise, and God has chosen the weak things of the world to put to shame the things which are mighty;

Part of me agreed with her. I was torn between remaining quiet or following what I believed to be from God. In obedience to God, I was prepared to lose friends rather than stay silent. We went to the same church, but Julia and I started going to different house groups. I felt more comfortable without her.

I formed a close friendship with Paul in our church. He was tall, intelligent, and loved the Lord, and we went to the same house group. He was open to the gifts of the spirit and keen to learn from me. We were a good team and enjoyed each other's company. Paul was a bus driver. A few years after I met him, Paul enrolled in a Bible college. He ended up as a vicar in a church in West Cornwall.

Joshua and Benjamin

This story is not real, but it gave me inspiration and encouragement in my early life as a young Christian. I was doubtful I could follow in the steps of Jesus. It's an inspirational story derived from,

Numbers 27:18-20, So the LORD said to Moses, "Take Joshua son of Nun, a man

in whom is the spirit, and lay your hand upon him; have him stand before Eleazar the priest and all the congregation and commission him in their sight. You shall give him some of your authority so that all the assembly of the Israelites may obey.

The Lord God brought the children of Abraham out of Egypt under the leadership of Moses. Joshua was one of the captains who served under Moses. He was a brave man who won favour with Moses, the people of Israel, and God. He was strong, wise, kind, and considerate.

The following is not a real story, but my aspiration based on what leadership should be like from the Bible.

Joshua (Lord) had a friend called Benjamin (me), a special needs little boy of about ten years. He was also an orphan. His legs were weak. He looked a lot smaller than his age, and he strolled. Children did not want to play with him. He had no friends.

As Israel's children moved over Sinai, every day, the cloud of the Lord would lead the people. At dawn, while people camped, the cloud withdrew to the back of the camp and turned into a pillar of fire.

Ben was always the last to settle down for the night. Because he had additional needs, he was often a few miles behind the rest. When everyone else had settled down for the night in their tents and finished their meals, Ben would stagger into the camp. He would walk around the campfire begging for leftovers.

Joshua used to wake up early in the morning, before anyone else. He would have his breakfast with Ben, and then they would start the journey ahead of the others. Later on in the morning, the camp would rise and follow the trail Joshua had left. By lunchtime, they would catch up with Joshua and Ben.

Joshua would leave Ben with the first arrivals and race ahead to scout out the territory. The cloud of the Lord would go ahead of him, seeking out a water supply and a safe place for people to camp. Joshua would instruct the first few arrivals where to camp. He would then race back to find Ben and other weaker people. Because of their condition, they would be far behind the camp, isolated and vulnerable to attacks. Joshua would seek them out and lead them back to safety.

One day, Joshua went out with eleven others to scout out the land of Canaan. Hostile tribes inhabited this land. With much danger to them, they spied on this Promised Land. They returned with some fruit. They gave their report to the elders of Israel.

That night Joshua went looking for his friend. He found him about a mile behind the rest of the camp, near a big rock.

Ben was miserable and felt sorry for himself. No one in the camp seemed to care for him apart from Joshua. He had no family, friends, or companions, and his body ached all the time.

Joshua sat next to him. He understood the little boy's struggles and hardship. He picked up Ben and wiped away the tears. Ben lay in his bosom, tears slowly flowing, and with each tear, his life seems to ebb away from the frail body.

Ben looked at Joshua. 'I will never make it into the promised land. I am a cripple. No good to anyone. Useless.'

Gently, Joshua drew him closer into his bosom. 'Ben, you are like a son to me. I will take you to the Promised Land (Revelation 21, New Heaven, and Earth). Our Heavenly Father has made me a steward of his people, and I will not leave anyone behind.'

Chapter 58 – Tears of Love

Joshua looked beyond the camp of Israel into Canaan. Tears of love and compassion began to flow down his strong face. 'God called me to lead his people (the generation born in the desert) into the Promised Land, and not a soul shall be left behind. Not as long as I live.'

Joshua's relationship with his people was based on his commitment to God. Joshua's trust and strength rested on God's word; in his perfect understanding of his 'TALLACK'; the path God mapped out for **him**[1] before the foundations of Earth were laid.

He understood this life was just a test to see if he was cut out for a more formidable task that lay in the spiritual world, in the sanctuaries. Here, all life forms would come from the four corners of the world, tormented, and tortured; people and creatures whose very fabric of life squeezed out of them, to be healed, consoled, and made **whole**[2].

Like a gold nugget, he was **refined**[3], **tested**[4], and moulded into the future leader in the kingdom of God. That was his inheritance.

He looked at the sky. 'Yes, I can do it,' he cried out aloud as if speaking to the heavens.

--- ☆---

[1] *Ephesians 2:10, For we are His workmanship, created in Christ Jesus for good works, which God prepared beforehand that we should walk in them.*

[2] *Ephesians 2:16, and that He might reconcile them both to God in one body through the cross, thereby putting to death the enmity.*

[3] *Isaiah 48:10, Behold, I have refined you, but not as silver; I have tested you in the furnace of affliction.*

[4] *Zechariah 13:9, I will bring the one-third through the fire, refine them as silver is refined, And test them as gold is tested. They will call on My name, And I will answer them. I will say, 'This is My people'; And each one will say, 'The LORD is my God.' "* ...x..x...

He looked at the half-asleep, exhausted Ben and murmured, 'I have a commitment to you based on love and God's word. For you, I will scout out Canaan and face any danger.

'When I am scouting ahead of others in the enemy's land, I remember your face behind the camp, struggling alone, needing me, wanting me, depending on me. You inspire me; uplift me to face death and danger. I love our Heavenly Father, his people, and **you**[1].'

Ben did not look convinced, so Joshua continued, 'I will show you something. I brought back grapes from Canaan (Valley of Awar-nar), some of them I shared with the elders, but I have kept the best for you.'

Ben took a grape and ate it. 'It's delicious.'

Joshua said, 'I have something better, something I held back from the elders. It is exceptionally good, and it is only for you. Drink this.'

Ben tasted it. 'It's very refreshing. What is it?'

'It's milk with honey. *(Revelation 21 Spiritual gifts and insight into New Heaven and New Jerusalem),* I will take you into the land of milk and honey (New Jerusalem), and we shall sit under a tall guava tree on the bank of a river with sweet waters.'

Ben began to revive in his friend's company. New hope and faith began to take hold of him. The pillar of fire moved closer until slowly, the fire disappeared. In its place stood the Lord. Ben fell onto his face.

The Lord picked Ben up into his arms. 'I am with you always.'

Matthew 28:2, "teaching them to observe all things that I have commanded you; and lo, I am with you always, even to the end of the age." Amen.

--- ☆---

[1] *1 John 4:20, If someone says, "I love God," and hates his brother, he is a liar; for he who does not love his brother whom he has seen, how can he love God whom he has not seen?*

[1] *Galatians 5:14, For all the law is fulfilled in one word, even in this: "You shall love your neighbour as yourself."* ...x..x...

Gently, our Lord put Ben down. Then, pointing at the horizon, he spoke to Joshua, 'you will build the finest church in England[2] and Canada.' *(Some prophecies take a long time, but by **Judgment day**[3] they will be fulfilled.)*

This story has shaped my relationship with the Lord. It gave me hope, a faith that I can fill the ocean with the palm of my hand, account for every atom and grain of sand in my patch.

There are times I have felt like Ben and at other times like Joshua. I had heard the Lord's calling. I saw his might in visions, but the task he wanted me to accomplish, accounting for every leaf, every person in my patch, felt impossible.

There were other times when the Holy Spirit opened up the spiritual world with its immense glory of God and myriads of angels, and nothing seemed impossible to him that believes.

Mr 9:23, Jesus said to him, "If you can believe, all things are possible to him who believes."

---- ☆----

[2] By Judgment Day all prophecies will be fulfilled, e.g., *Genesis 17:8, "Also I give to you (Abraham) and your descendants after you the land in which you are a stranger, all the land of Canaan, as an underline everlasting possession; and I will be their God."*

[3] *Isaiah 55:11, So shall My word be that goes forth from My mouth; It shall not return to Me void, But it shall accomplish what I please, And it shall prosper in the thing for which I sent it.*

---- ----

Chapter 59 – Even a Man of God Can Succumb to Half-truths

This is a story about Jeremiah going to see Zedekiah to warn him of impending doom at the King of Babylon's hands.

*Zedekiah tells Jeremiah **(Jeremiah 38:25-26)**, 'My officials may hear that I spoke to you, and they may say, Tell us what you and the king were talking about. If you don't tell us, we will kill you. If this happens, tell them you begged me not to send you back to Jonathan's dungeon for fear you would die there.'*

v27, Sure enough, it wasn't long before the king's officials came to Jeremiah and asked him why the king had called for him. But Jeremiah followed the king's instructions, and <u>they left without finding out the truth.</u> No one had overheard the conversation between Jeremiah and the king.

When I read this, the Holy Spirit asked me, 'What do you learn from this?'

I thought, 'To save Jeremiah's life, Jeremiah and the king conspired to tell the princes half-truths. They misled the princes. They did not tell any lies, but neither did they tell the whole truth. Even a man of God can succumb to half-truths.'

I pointed out to the Holy Spirit that even though Jeremiah was a great prophet, he was not an heir in Christ in the Kingdom of Heaven. For an heir in the Kingdom of God, a higher standard of conduct was required.

Matthew 11:11 I tell you the truth, of all who have ever lived, none is greater than John the Baptist. Yet even the least person in the Kingdom of Heaven is greater than he is!

I thought maybe those that told half-truths wilfully, to withhold information to further their causes, would be outside the city gates. People whose conduct was displeasing to the Holy Spirit. That is what I learned from this story.

If it were a matter of life or death, I would probably have done the same as Jeremiah.

Later on, the Holy Spirit reminded me, 'You are not judged by a single action but by a consistent pattern in your life.'

---- ---

Chapter 60 – Bank Nurse

Matthew 5:37, But let your 'Yes' be 'Yes,' and your 'No,' be 'No.'

Romans 12:16, Be of the same mind toward one another. Do not set your mind on high things, but associate with the humble. Do not be wise in your own opinion.

Such simple verses, yet when the breath of the Lord passes over them, they reveal layers of wisdom like the rest of the Bible. There is far more value hidden in these simple words. It is about trust, honesty, respect, and acting in a manner that may seem right and favourable for us, yet has hidden deceit built into it.

We employed about 28 part-time staff. One of my temporary Nurse, Megan, (not her real name to protect her identity), worked for us at an hourly rate. It was her choice. She would fill in for staff on sick leave. Often, we had a shortage on Thursday nights, and she was glad to fill this slot. She was a supply staff member, so we paid her a higher rate as she was not entitled to any holiday or sick leave. She was a good worker.

Towards the end of the second year, while we were still making a loss at the nursing home, one of my staff left, and the other staff were glad to increase their hours. However, we had a permanent gap for one night a week. I advertised for this post.

Megan asked me if she could take this slot. This was a permanent post. I said that she would need to sign a new contract, the same as other staff had. She signed the contract.

A month passed, monthly wages were paid. Megan asked to see me. She was nervous and distressed. She showed me her wage slip and said I had made a mistake. I looked at it and pointed out that she was now paid the same rate as the permanent staff.

'I used to be paid at a higher rate,' she said in a timid voice.

'That's true. As a supply nurse, you were paid a higher rate, but you missed out on sickness and holiday entitlement. You now have the same rate as others but also enjoy these entitlements.'

She was disappointed. She had not realized that by signing on, her hourly rate would reduce. She was not interested in other entitlements like holiday pay.

That evening in my accounting for the day, I brought up Megan's pay. The Lord made it clear I was in the right.

Nevertheless, I felt the Holy Spirit was not happy. What is right and acceptable to the heavenly cloud in legal terms is not the same as **spiritually appropriate**.

There is a higher moral law written in the **hearts**[1] of those born of the **WORD of God**[2]. It may not make sense, but the law/principle is,

(**Hari's Tenet 1**] *'The law of the cosmos dictates: No one has a right to gain at the expense of others, not even **God**[3]. Your conscience demands that you have a moral conscience for all life, i.e., you shall not **steal.**[4]'*

The Holy Spirit brought to my knowledge and breathed over these verses.

1 Corinthians 16:14, *Let all that you do be done with love.*

Hebrews 13:5, *Keep your lives free from the love of money and be content with what you have.*

His message was clear. Megan had signed the contract thinking I would pay her usual rate. I hadn't pointed out the new lower rate and its

---- ☆----

[1] *Ezekiel 36:26, "I will give you a new heart and put a new spirit within you; I will take the heart of stone out of your flesh and give you a heart of flesh.*

[2] *1 Peter 1:23, having been born again, not of corruptible seed but incorruptible, through the word of God which lives and abides forever.*

[3] *Lamentations 3:33, For He does not afflict willingly, nor grieve the children of men.*

[4] *Leviticus 19:11, You shall not steal, nor deal falsely, nor lie to one another. ..x..x...*

238

implication to her. I had a duty of care towards her, and I had failed to point out the repercussion of signing the contract.

I wasn't aware of the implication when she signed, but that was no excuse to the Holy Spirit.

The issue was simple in Megan's mind; she had trusted me to pay her usual rate. How was I going to restore her good trust in me?

I was in the right. It would have been acceptable if I did nothing since she had made an error by not reading her contract.

However, worldly right and the **Lord's righteousness**[3] have different values when the Holy Spirit breathes over a verse, and it becomes alive. I have used them as they related to my situation. This is different from its historical application.

The bible states that the words of God (verses) are alive, not dead.

*Hebrews 4:12, For the **word of God** is living and powerful, and sharper than any two-edged sword, piercing even to the division of soul and spirit, and of joints and marrow, and is a discerner of the thoughts and intents of the heart.*

---- ☆----

[3] *Lamentations 19:15, You shall not render an unjust judgment; you shall not be partial to the poor or defer to the great: with justice, you shall judge your neighbour.*

---- 🦖----

Chapter 61 – Doing the right things have unintended repercussions.

Psalms 140:12, I know that the LORD will maintain the cause of the afflicted and justice for the poor.

As I struggled with the issue of Megan', the Spirit brought forth the above psalm. We amended the contract to a higher rate, and I left her entitlement intact.

The following month when I paid the staff, a senior nurse noticed I was paying Megan a higher rate. She told other nurses.

There was a tense atmosphere. I brought the matter before the Lord.

In the evening prayer, the Holy Spirit said, 'Pay them all the same rate.'

'Lord, forgive me, but I am the steward of this business, and I am at liberty to set different rates for my staff. Besides, you know we cannot afford it. We are in financial difficulties. The home is making a loss. It is only a question of time before the receivers take over.' He kept silent. He had spoken.

I shared this with my house group. They said I had two choices. Give the rest of the staff a pay rise or terminate the contract with Megan. Both actions would be right.

Again, I brought the matter before the Lord. He remained silent.

I struggled. With a heavy heart, I gave them all a raise at a time when we were one-step away from receivership.

You may think, 'Ah, the Lord helped you.'

No, he did not. God does not reward people for doing the right thing. It is expected of us.

Things did not work out as you might think. We struggled on losing money for months. We spent restless nights, unable to sleep; we lost all appetite to eat and lost weight. Within a few months, I had aged. ---- ✿---

Chapter 62 – Unhappy days.

There were days I could hardly retain any food in my stomach. We were stressed; there was tension between my wife and me. We each built a protective wall around us. We prayed together, and we prayed separately. Outwardly, we laughed, but inwardly we cried for months.

One day after the registration inspector had done their annual inspection of the home, the matron called me. On previous assessments, on each occasion, they had given me a list of improvements they wanted to be done to pass the next inspection. The two inspectors were waiting in the office with their report.

I greeted them. I was worried; my heart was racing in case they suggested more upgrade work. One of them looked at my tense face and smiled.

'We have carried out a thorough inspection of your home. Our report will mention the improvements you have carried out since you took over this home. All is fine. We both agree your home provides some of the finest quality of care in Cornwall.'

My father would have been proud of me. I did not fulfil his dream of becoming a doctor, but I had achieved looking after people. Sadly, he passed away before he could witness it.

Slowly, the business picked up. By the end of the third year, we had made a small profit. The flowing two years, we had a good harvest. We sold the Nursing Home towards the end of our sixth year there.

--- ☆---

Many years later, on my 6th sabbatical year, as I was going over this matter with the Lord, another similar case arose.

Again, I was in the right. We had signed a contract on a different matter, but the person had misunderstood me and signed the contract in good faith. Again, the Holy Spirit asked me to honour the person's trust/belief. I obeyed at a cost to us.

While I thought about this matter, my mind drifted to an earlier time. I was about six years old. My father and my three uncles had lined all the children up. Something had happened, and one of my uncles was very angry. One by one, my uncle interrogated all the children. It was my turn.

He stooped to face me, looked into my eyes. His face was crimson, full of anger, 'You did it, don't deny it.'

'No, I didn't do it,' I said as I shook my head. He was not convinced. He repeated the question.

My father stepped between us. He said, 'I trust him. He never lies.'

Matthew 5:37, *"But let your 'Yes' be 'Yes,' and your 'No,' 'No.' For whatever is more than these is from the evil one.*

My uncle looked at my father, stared at him; his face flushed, then paused and wisely stepped away.

That trust my father had in me stuck in my memory. It also led me to lots of difficult situations.

----  ---

Chapter 63– Honesty comes at a price

I was in my final year of my A-levels. It was a biology class. We had an excellent teacher, but he was short-tempered and would throw books or even chairs at us if we upset him. (I am glad to say that today his behaviour would not be tolerated in our schools.)

This was his third year at the school. In the previous two years, he had had 100% pass rates for A-level results. He was keen to get the same result for the third year.

We had a mock test. He was going over some of the mistakes we had made. He explained the errors and showed us the correct answers. He then went to a difficult question and showed us the five steps required to answer. It was hard to understand. He asked us to raise our hand if we had not understood the answer.

No one liked to upset him. All the children were petrified of him, and the class remained quiet.

I was the only one to raise my hand. He started again and slowly, methodically, went over five steps, pausing at every step so I could take notes. I failed to understand the last step. He finished and asked me if I had understood.

As I shook my head, he lost his temper, picked up a light chair and threw it in my direction. I was frightened; the whole class was afraid. His face was red, furious. My heart was racing. He turned his back and faced the blackboard. He wiped it clean, dusted off the chalk flakes, composed himself, and walked up to me. He rudely asked the boy next to me to go and sit somewhere else.

He came round me, opened my textbook, and slowly went over the page, explaining the correct way to answer the problem. I could feel his heavy breathing over my shoulder. I was thoroughly scared of him, and his suppressed anger got to me. My mind switched off. I did not understand a single word. He was about to finish when the bell rang.

The other children packed their bags and started to leave the class. He finished.

'It's simple,' he said and walked out.

Six or seven children surrounded me. One of them leaned toward me and asked, 'Can you show us the solution?'

Ephesians 4:15, *But speaking the truth in love, we must grow up in every way into him who is the head, into Christ,*

Honesty has a cost attached. It is easy to keep quiet and be passively dishonest. That day when my father stepped in front of my uncle, his words of trust in me had instilled in me the rule: let your communication be yea or nay.

----  ---

Chapter 64 – Camper van

Psalms 15:1-2, A Psalm of David. LORD, who may abide in Your tabernacle? Who may dwell in Your holy hill? He who walks uprightly, and works righteousness, and speaks the truth in his heart.

We lived in a beautiful part of Cornwall and thought a camper van would be ideal for exploring the countryside with our young children. I went to view a camper van that was for sale. The woman owner was going through a divorce. The van was parked under a tree and neglected. It was covered in six months of bird droppings and dirt. The inside smelled of dampness and mould. She had set the sale price below the market value, but the camper's condition had deterred buyers.

It was a desperate sale. I paid her the asking price, but my conscience was troubled. The Holy Spirit had also noted her dire condition. That evening in my prayers, I thanked the Lord for the camper. The situation had worked well for both the woman and me. We were both pleased with the trade. I was too wrapped up in my excitement to notice that the Holy Spirit was not pleased with my conduct. *[Zak's Tenet; - Guide you with my eye. I can reason with you. I respect your privacy, so I will not press you nor persuade you without your consent.]*

For two years, we enjoyed the use of the camper. We had a lovely time with it. Then we decided to move closer to Julia's parents. I put the camper up for sale and sold it. In evening prayer, I shared with the Lord the two years of joy and happiness this camper had given us, along with a profit of £600 on its sale.

I went to sleep, but my sleep was troubled. I woke up at around 4 am. 'What is it, Lord?'

The Lord said, 'You sold the camper at a profit. How are you going to respond?'

Worldly wisdom would say I had a right to keep the profit to myself. It was my right, and I had earned it.

There is a legal right, moral right, and righteousness based on an awakened conscience sharpened by the Holy Spirit. *[Hari's Tenet 1]* "*The law of the cosmos dictates: No one has a right to gain at the expense of others, not even **God**[1]. Your conscience demands that you have a moral conscience for all life, i.e., you shall not steal.*'

I prayed for wisdom.

Gratitude

Right was on my side. However, to exercise this right was a dishonourable act to the Holy Spirit. The honourable thing was to have no deceit, malice, selfishness in my life. How could he teach such things? It had to come from us without any external influence. That inner divine spring Jesus spoke of, 'Out of you shall flow living waters.' Once that spring had spouted forth, time would release a flood of it.

Hebrews 10:1, For the law, having a shadow of the good things to come, and not the very image *of the things, can never with these same sacrifices, which they offer continually year by year, make those who approach perfect.*

Colossians 1:15, He (and us in Christ) are the image *of the invisible God, the firstborn over all creation.*

To one led by the Holy Spirit. 'Nothing in the Universe should thrive at the expense of another.' One has to have a clear conscience about their conduct. And my conscience, sharpened by the Holy Spirit, led me down a different path.

A few days later, I did the right, the honourable thing. I wrote to the woman, thanking her for the two years of joy the camper had brought into our lives. I shared the profit equally with her. My conscience was finally clear.

[Kate Adin's Tenet 2: You are unique. There is a greater power that guides your path. Everything that has been made, created is set up for you (for those like you).

[Kathy's Tenet 1]. A person, or a relationship, is of eternal value than the things we participate in.]

This and other incidences where I had taken a loss to keep a clear conscience became part of my conduct. The Lord said, 'Out of your heart will flow rivers of living water.'

John 4:10, Jesus answered and said to her, "If you knew the gift of God, and who it is who says to you, 'Give Me a drink,' you would have asked Him, and He would have given you living water."

Rivers of living waters

I struggle to convey what the above verse meant to me. When the above verse takes root in a person's life, it is one of the most treasured moments in God's sight. It is not something that can be taught; otherwise, we would all have it. It is something that springs from within us without any compulsion from God. It is something (way of life, conduct) we have discovered for ourselves and willfully chosen to let it flow from us.

*John 7:38, "He who believes in Me, as the Scripture has said, out of his heart will flow rivers of **living water**."*

*John 4:10, Jesus answered and said to her, "If you knew the gift of God, and who it is who says to you, 'Give Me a drink,' you would have asked Him, and He would have given you **living water.***

Years later, the Lord said to me, 'You will be a director of a company. You will promote your staff and clients' welfare, interest, and happiness, even at a cost to you and the company. The power you wield would be put to Godly use. That is why we need people like you; prepared to account for every leaf in their patch.

'We would move Heaven and Earth for such people. These are some of the most treasured people in God's kingdom, and they're lots of unfilled *vacancies.' (At the age of 66, I was elected a director of a company)* ---- 🕮

Chapter 65 – Move to East Cornwall

1994-2006 Nursing Home

We sold the nursing home towards the end of our sixth year. As part of the deal, our mortgage was paid and we received a cottage in Bedfordshire, Our son Zak was born just after we sold. We moved to Bedfordshire as winter was just setting in. Julia was on maternity leave.

We renovated the rundown cottage and put it on the market. It was a bitterly cold winter. Spring came, and we had not sold the property. Julia's extended maternity leave was up. We locked up the house and moved back to Cornwall. We rented a cottage near her school. She went back to teaching; I stayed home to look after Zak.

Most of our money was invested in the cottage in Bedfordshire. We had some money left over from the sale of the nursing home. I found a large 1860's Victorian house in Liskeard, East Cornwall, for sale. I just loved it at first sight. It was so much like the house I had in London.

It was vacant and had been on the market for more than a year. It needed a major refurbishment. It had structural problems, and banks and building societies would not loan on this property.

I found a builder and asked him to assess the potential of the home. He thought it would be a significant project to fix it, but it could be done in stages. He suggested we could give him two months to fix the first floor and turn it into a temporary three-bed flat. We could then take our time to improve the rest of our home in stages.

We bought the house, and two months later, after the builder had renovated the upper floors, we moved into the upstairs flat. We had run out of money, so the work on the house stopped. I looked after Zak and slowly started to renovate the home.

We did not have a mortgage. Julia's income was sufficient for our needs and left a small surplus each month to renovate the house. We joined the local Anglican Church but kept a low profile.

248

A year later, we managed to sell the cottage in Bedfordshire. I invested the proceeds, which gave us an extra income. I stayed home and looked after our son Zak while Julia went to work and bit by bit renovated the house as the money came in

---- ---

Chapter 66 – My third Sabbath year

A new arrival in the family

1997/8. It was my third Sabbath year, and our daughter was born. Caring for our young children was one of the hardest things I have done. As a stay at home father, I found isolation hard. I would take the children to a toddler group, but most mothers kept to their small, close-knit cliques. It took a long time to win their trust and become a part of their group.

First Fruit

I had time on my hands. I got my diaries out and reviewed all the prayers and house meetings in my notes. By now, I had lost touch with most of the people I had had a fellowship in Haringey. I went over the past prayers and tried to trace the people in my diary.

I got in touch with a few people that remained in Haringey. Rev Hammond had retired some years earlier and had moved somewhere north. There were about 50 names in my prayer diary that I was able to get some feedback on.

Of those people, six had become church ministers or vicars. Among them were Alan and two Pauls I had shared my house in London. Another 24 people had gone into full-time Christian ministry as missionaries or were working for Christian charities. Steve, the vet, had gone to Nepal as a missionary.

About a dozen people from the remaining 20 had become house leaders in their church—the fruit of Rev Jim Hammond's spirit-led ministry and our prayers.

John 17:12, Jesus, "While I was with them in the world, I kept them in Your name. Those whom You gave Me I have kept; and none of them is lost except the son of perdition, that the Scripture might be fulfilled.'

---- ---

Chapter 67– Liskeard Philip.

1996-2005

As mentioned, we joined an Anglican church. I kept a low profile in the church. I was relaxed, calm. We made friends and had a normal relationship with people in the church. I concentrated on family life. We raised two lovely children.

I visited a small Assemblies of God church that met in a small hall. The church's leader was called Pastor Philip, and he had about 20 members. He was open to the gifts of the Holy Spirit, and he encouraged his members to exercise them.

I liked Philip. He was keen to learn about the gift of the Holy Spirit. He wanted me to join his church. I was reluctant.

I wanted a normal life; I was tired of countless nights thinking, planning, and writing down each house group meeting. I didn't want to go back to that lifestyle. Besides, the six years at the nursing home and the constant financial struggle had left me exhausted. I needed a quiet life to recoup, gather my strength.

We formed a strong friendship. Philip had an insight into spiritual things. Straight away, he would grasp the spiritual things we discussed. He needed no convincing. Sharing with him was easy. With him, I could pray in a calm, relaxed voice, share my visions without hesitation, knowing we were on the same level, both men of faith. There was none of the tension I had found in the house groups.

Whenever Philip had something on his mind, he would come to see me. He had a wife and four young children. They lived in a small rented house that was too small for them. With just 20 members, Philip's income from church donations was barely able to keep them afloat. They had young children, and his wife's option to go out and work was not viable.

He had shared his concerns with me a few times. Was he doing the right thing for his family? Perhaps he ought to look for a job.

One day he stopped by my house. He looked worried. I made him a cup of tea and made a sandwich for him. As we talked, I felt his concerns for his family.

'Phil, I am going to pray for your family. The Lord wants you to build his church here. A big church with many facilities for the people of Liskeard. A church with a coffee house, club groups, counselling services, and residential care for people.

'You cannot do the Lord's work while you are struggling to pay your rent. I am going to ask the Lord to provide you with a house.'

He gave me a long look. Phil was a man of God. He believed in miracles, but this was a bit hard to swallow.

Chapter 68 – A great man of God: "Mtu Wa Mungu" (Man of God)

It took him a few seconds to reflect on my words. I loved and respected Phil. He was a great man of God: **Mtu wa Mungu,** and he trusted me.

'Let's pray,' he suggested. We prayed.

A few weeks later, Phil stopped at my house. He had a big smile on his face.

'We have a nice three-bed home. One of my distant aunts left us money in her will.'

Meanwhile, his church membership had increased. They needed bigger premises. He had seen a redundant church that was for sale. He wanted it for his church. However, they did not have the money. He asked if we could pray.

We bowed our heads. While Phil prayed, I waited on the Lord.

When he finished, there was silence. He waited for me to pray, but I remained silent. I could see he was disappointed. Finally, he looked up. He was disappointed I had not supported him in prayer.

I turned on the kettle and made two mugs of tea, and gave Phil one.

I took my time to clear my thoughts. I said to him, 'Phil, the Lord wants you to buy the church. Put an offer on it.'

'But we don't have the money, not even for the deposit,' he replied.

'If the Lord wants you to buy it, he will provide.'

Thessalonians 2:13, when you received the <u>word</u> <u>of</u> <u>God</u> from us, you welcomed it not as the word of men, but as the <u>word</u> <u>of</u> <u>God</u>, which also effectively works in you who believe.

It was easy for me to say it, but it was a massive step of faith for poor Phil. To go and put an offer on a big building when he had no deposit sounded crazy. He did it anyway!

A few days later, he came to see me. This time there was tension in his face. I invited him in. We sat down. Phil was tearful. He had set his heart on this building. He had put trust in my words, and something had gone wrong.

'Phil, what has happened?'

'A property developer had put an offer on the building, and the seller has accepted it.'

Chapter 69– The church is His

I put the kettle on. As I waited for it to boil, I brought the matter before God.

'Tell Phil the church is his.'

2 Corinthians 2:17, For we are not, as so many, peddling the word of God; but as of sincerity, but as from God, we speak in the sight of God in Christ.

When we are so emotionally involved in things happening as planned, we start to believe we hear God. Was this one of those occasions?

Psalms 119:80, May my heart be blameless in your statutes so that I may not be put to shame.

I passed the teacup to Phil. We sat in silence.

Phil asked, 'What do you think?'

I hesitated. 'Phil, this could be just me. I still think the Lord wants you to buy this building and build the type of church we talked about. Our Lord needs such a church. He is going to provide the money. It will take time, so start collecting.'

Phil stared at the cup of tea. 'What about the people who have put the offer in?'

'The Lord is going to find them a better building.'

It would have taken a lot of courage and guts or sheer foolishness on Phil's part to move on a presumption with no real foundation or resources to back it, except belief. *1 Corinthians 4:10 We are fools for Christ's sake.*

A few days later, the people who had put an offer on the church dropped out.

A few months later, Pastor Phil had his building, and some years later, he went on to fulfil the dream we had. He had built a bigger church than what we had prayed. *Matthew 17:20, Jesus told them. "I tell you the truth, if you had faith even as small as a mustard seed, you could say to this mountain, 'Move from here to there,' and it would move. Nothing would be impossible."*

Phil was a genuine man of God. I have come across some very plausible ministers who had grand visions and squandered the church's resources on half-baked ideas. When the money ran out, they moved on to another desperate church seeking a minister, only to squander its wealth as well.

2 Corinthians 11:13, For such are false apostles, deceitful workers, transforming themselves into apostles of Christ.

--- ☆---

Years 2010-11.

In my 5th sabbatical year, as I was going over my diaries, I went over Phil's prayers. Four years earlier, we had moved to Sussex, and I hadn't kept in touch with him.

I rang his church to have a chat with Philip. Sadly, he had moved on. I went on the internet and looked up his church website. He had achieved more than the type of church we had prayed for.

God had enabled him to have a church God had wanted. In Phil, he found a man who had faith to move mountains.

Chapter 70– What shall separate us from those we love?

Romans 8:35, Who will separate us from the love of Christ?

Our children were growing up, and we decided to move to West Sussex. We were concerned about their future. Cornwall is a beautiful county, but it is heavily dependent on farming and the seasonal tourist trade. There are few work opportunities, and many young people have to move out of the county to look for work.

Also, we were too far from my wife's extended family and my brother's family. I had missed family life in my youth, and I did not want my children to miss grandparents, aunts, uncles, and cousins. So we moved to West Sussex, which was much closer to our families.

We bought a house in West Sussex on the coast. We joined an Anglican church and once more kept a low profile.

House group

One evening as I was walking to the house group, these two scriptures came to my mind.

Romans 8:35, *Who will separate us from the love of Christ? Will hardship, distress, persecution, famine, nakedness, peril, or sword? V39 nor height, depth, nor anything else in all creation, will be able to separate us from the love of God in Christ Jesus our Lord.*

I shared the above verses at the house group and what they meant to me. A few days later, Ken, whose house we used to meet, asked me if I could do him a favour.

Over 30 years ago, they had a student from Kenya called Joseph Cxxx *(Name deleted under the UK Data Protection Act. UK)* who had lodged with them. He used to call them Papa Ken and Mama Ann. He had returned home to Kenya and worked as a telephone engineer. Meanwhile, Ken and his wife had moved home and lost touch with him.

Ken knew I had grown up in Kenya. He asked me if I knew anyone in Kenya who might be able to find his friend.

The only lead I had was his name, which happened to be very common in Kenya, and the fact that he had been a telephone engineer at one time.

As I gave an account in the evening prayer to our Heavenly Father, I brought before God Ken's request. I lifted the scripture to the Lord and asked him how he was going to respond to it.

I went to sleep.

--- ☆---

Around five in the morning, I got up and went in search of Joseph on the internet.

Chapter 71 – Tracking Liz

Two weeks later, I had an e-mail from Kenya. I gave the e-mail to Ken. They were reunited.

My mind went back to a time I was in Haringey. One day in late August (29 August 1984), we were celebrating a friend's birthday. I was sitting at the table, enjoying the birthday cake. A piece of the packaging of the cake was in front of me. People were talking. My gaze fell on this piece of paper.

Romans 8:35, *Who will separate us from the love of Christ?* This scripture ran through my mind.

'What does it say to you?'

I thought about it.

When I joined Rev Hammond's church, I made some friends a bit older than me. However, they were married, and as a single person, I needed friends in my age group. After a few months, two young girls called Liz and Megan joined the church. They had moved into the area. I got to know them and began to spend some time with them.

They came from happy families, and often on weekends, they would return home to see their families or visit their friends. On rare occasions, when they were not busy during the weekend, they would feel sorry for me and invite me for dinner. In return, I would mend anything in their flat that was coming apart.

For me, it was a big occasion. I had the company of people my age. I enjoyed their company. It was an oasis in the desert of my otherwise non-existent social life, a rare occasion when I could relax. As time went on, I got closer to Liz. She was lovely, easy to talk to, and I could share my thoughts with her. She encouraged me to explore my spiritual side in depth. I started to share my visions with her.

Liz had many friends, a loving family, and a busy social life. I was alone. We were fond of each other and enjoyed each other's company. We started going out. We got on very well. She helped me to learn to drive, relax, and joined me in jogging. My social life began to improve. I became dependent on her.

I started to force too much of my time on her. I got jealous of her family, friends, and I wanted her to spend more time with me. The relationship was uneven. I was demanding, often erratic in my behaviour. The closer we got, the more demanding and erratic I became. She found my demands hard to cope with. Finally, she broke all ties with me and moved to another town.

I was devastated. I was lost without her. In those early days, she was the only close friend I had in Haringey. I missed her. My demanding and possessive behaviour had driven away the one person who had shown me love and care. I cried for days.

I brought the matter before the Lord. He taught me to come to terms with our breakup. *(Liz's Tenet 1) 'If you love someone, you have to let them go. If they love you, one day they will return.'*

I learnt from the Lord; we were temporarily parted and would be reconciled one day. He had taught me that just as my prayers had a ring of permanency, the same applied to our relationship.

Four years later, I still missed her. At this birthday party, the scripture came to life**,**

Romans 8:35, *'who shall separate us from the love of Christ.'*

To me, it read as, 'Who shall separate us from the love of Christ (and those in Christ?), shall tribulation, or distress, or persecution, or famine, or nakedness, or peril, or sword?'

As I looked at the empty cake box, I felt her pain. She was alone, lonely. Was she thinking of me? I felt her spirit call out to me.

Chapter 72 – Picture

I started drawing on the base of the cake box. A friend of mine had told me that Liz had moved to a small town in Oxfordshire called Witney, a place that was unknown to me.

I drew a picture of Liz, me, and the Lord on a bridge, on that piece of birthday box. I drew two bridges on the river and tall trees on the right bank of the river. The flow of water was south to north. On the right side of the bridge would be a unique stone. This stone would somehow lead me to Liz. I marked the spot on my map—[**Appendix** Finding Liz].

Then the vision changes; it is late afternoon, around 6 pm. As I observe the bridges, a young girl walks onto one of them, followed by a young man. They stop and have a cuddle.

Five weeks later, on 6 Oct 1984, my friends Kate, Maggie, and I went to Witney to find Liz.

I wanted to find Liz. We found a country park with two bridges on the river and tall trees on the river's right bank, just as I had marked on my map. I took the bearing of the water flow. It was south to north, as I had noted. There were tall trees on the right bank of the river. Late evening at 6 pm, we saw a girl walk onto the bridge, followed by a young man. They stopped and have a cuddle, just as I had seen in my vision.

Kate and Maggie looked in amazement as I crawled on the grass, looking for this unique stone on the right side of the bridge. I searched the area but didn't find it. In my mind, this stone would somehow lead me to Liz. It was getting dark, and I had to give up the search. I was disappointed.

We find the unique stone by accident, or perhaps a greater power had a hand.

We left the park, headed back to the car park, passed through a residential area and lost our way. We walked through a narrow alleyway. Then we walked past some homes. Suddenly, I froze. My heart

Appendix   Finding Liz

9ᵗʰ Oct 1984
20.20 hrs.

On Saturday the 6ᵗʰ Oct 1984, three of us, Margarete Julian, Kate Adiv and myself went to Oxford for a day trip. At about 4.00pm we left Oxford and headed towards Witney where Liz lives

We arrived there at about 4.30. In the village we asked about if there were any bridges. We were told there were three bridges near the church

The first bridge we found was wrong one. We went to next one. There were two near by. Both were quite similar. With the compass I took the bearings. Water was flowing from S→N. It was bushier on the right and it had wooden rails. The second bridge was similiar but it was bushier on the right. We tried to look for the stone but couldn't find.

So we went further away and had a picnic. Kate asked how do we know which bridge 'Well,' I said,' Let's wait for the last confirmation. We will see a girl in jeans come and stop of at the bridge.' A few minutes later a girl came and she stood on the bridge at the exact place I had drawn her. She was with her boy friend. They were cuddling on the bridge.

After our picnic I took some photo's and then we went to search of the stone.

We couldn't find any peculiar stone. As it was getting late we came home.

We also found her house as we walked back to the car.

started to beat fast. Something caught my view in the window of one of the houses. I could see through the window into the room. On top of the Television was a small wooden sailing boat.

It was the present I had bought for Liz from Canada many years ago! We found the unique stone! I noted the address.

We went home. I wrote a letter to Liz. A few days later, I received an invitation to meet her, and we were reconciled. It was amazing to spend some time with her. I was at peace.

....

At 6 pm, just as I had seen in the vision, we saw a girl walk onto the bridge, followed by a young man. They stop and cuddle.

---- ❀ ----

Chapter 73 – Finding Maggie

When Julia and I moved to Cornwall, I lost touch with many of my friends. Twenty years later, I made an effort to track Maggie down. She had been a very good friend of ours. She had helped me find Liz, and now I was in search of her.

The last time I had seen her was at my wedding. I had her address in London. I made inquiries, but she had moved on. The church in Haringey had changed. People I had known had moved out of the area.

There was someone in Haringey church who had known Maggie. She said Maggie had left the church about ten years earlier and may have gone to Sri Lanka. Her parents had been missionaries to Sri Lanka, where Maggie was born. On retirement, they had returned to Cornwall. They had both passed away.

I wanted to trace her; I had prayed for her in Haringey and continued to uplift her in prayer every seven years. I wanted to see how she had fared. I was getting no leads, so I prayed for her whereabouts.

I went on the internet; put her full name in Google search for Sri Lanka. Nothing. The thought came to me that she was probably married and would have changed her surname.

The only lead I had was her name, in a country with a population of 20 million. I prayed again and went to sleep.

I woke up at 4 am and went on the internet. I am not sure how I was led from one thing to another to a photograph of theological college staff in Sri Lanka.

There were about 40 people in the photograph. Among them, I recognized her face. I wrote to the college and a few days later received a reply from Maggie. She was married to a church pastor and had a different surname.

A few months later, she came to the UK to visit her family. We took her out for a meal. ---- 🐝---

Chapter 74 – Heart Surgery; Pain and Suffering are Part of Life

2 Kings 10:15, Is your heart right.

A few months after we had moved to West Sussex, in August 2007, I had heart surgery to replace my right aortic valve.

About three months before the surgery, the Lord placed a verse in my mind. **2 Kings 10:15,** *"Is your heart right, as my heart is toward your heart?"*

I thought on the matter and felt the Lord was warning me about the surgery going very badly.

The Holy Spirit said, 'I want you to get fit, start exercising.' I spent every day doing strenuous exercises. The day before surgery, I wrote the above verse on my heart with permanent ink. I wanted to warn the doctors, as I knew there were going to be complications.

I had surgery on Monday. They replaced my Aortic valve with a metal valve, and it seemed to have gone well. By Thursday, they were arranging for me to go home on Saturday.

On Saturday, I got up early and took a shower. I was excited. I wanted to get home, sleep in my bed. I got out of the shower and got dressed. I took a few steps towards the bathroom door and felt dizzy.

I returned to my bed and called a nurse. I was having difficulty breathing. Then I passed out. They did a scan of my chest. I had massive internal bleeding (haemorrhaging). My **INR**[1] reading was over 10; it should have been below 3. My face had turned grey. I was struggling to breathe.

---- ☆----

[1] **INR** *or international normalised ratio- measures the time for the blood to clot. In healthy people, an INR of 1.1 or below is considered normal.*

An INR range of 2.0 to 3.0 is generally an effective therapeutic range for people taking Warfarin to stop blood clotting on the metal valve.

If the INR is too high, there is an increased risk of bleeding. ...x..x...

The anticoagulant, Warfarin (also used in rat poison), had over-thinned my blood, and it was seeping out into my chest, constricting my lungs and heart. I was feeling like a poisoned rat, in and out of a coma. Around 11 am, I went into a deep coma.

At 1 pm, they took me into the theatre and drained just under a litre of blood from my chest.

I spent another week in hospital. On the fourth day, the surgeon who had operated on me came to see me. He said, had they operated half an hour later, it would have been too late. My fitness and the nurse who had carried out a blood transfusion on me had saved my life.

He asked me about the bible verse on my chest. I explained why I had written it on my heart. He stood there looking at me. He was a Greek Orthodox Christian, and I do not know what went through his mind. It took me about six months to recover.

Hip joint

Eighteen months later, in March 2009, I had intense pain in my hip. I was rushed to the hospital.

Five years earlier, I had a right hip resurfaced with a metal joint. They diagnosed metal ions in my blood, and these ions had damaged my right leg and knee muscles, causing tumours and nerve damage. I was in acute pain and given the maximum dose of morphine every four hours, and it seems to make little difference.

I have a very high pain threshold. At the dentist, I usually do not take any injection for fillings. But on this occasion, they had to put me in an isolation unit because of my screams. There was constant pressure on my femoral nerve. It felt like my hip was caught in a vice.

There were times when the pain got so bad that I would hold a pillow over my face to muffle my screams. After seven days, my pain eased. Three days later, still in pain, they sent me home with a box of strong painkillers to await further tests.

I had a series of **CT**[1], MRI, and cardio echo scans over the next few months.

[1] *Both MRIs and CT scans can view internal body structures. A CT scan is faster and can provide pictures of tissues, organs, and skeletal system. An MRI is highly adept at capturing images that help doctors determine if there are abnormal tissues within the body. MRIs are more detailed in their pictures.*

In August, they did a biopsy of two tumours, each about 8 cm long, in my hip at a specialist hospital in Oxford that dealt with ion poisoning. I had muscle and nerve damage, and I could not raise my right leg due to nerve damage.

The specialist consultant on metal ions read my report. He was going away on holiday, and the earliest he could operate would be November.

He planned to remove the tumours and have a plastic surgeon seal the scars from the tumours and repair the nerve. Then replace the metal hip joint with a ceramic joint. He said it was going to be a long, complicated surgery.

Chapter 75 – Power of prayers

My wife asked our small church to pray for my surgery.

I was confined to the house while I waited for the operation. I could not place any weight on my leg, walking around the house on two crutches. I would wake up with burning pain in the hip and leg. Sitting, walking, and sleeping were difficult. Climbing stairs to go to the bedroom was extremely difficult, and I hated being dependant on my wife.

Julia and the children were excellent and did their best to make my life easier. She would help me get changed at night and dress in the mornings before she left for work.

In November, I had my surgery. It went well. A few months later, I checked-up with the original consultant at our local hospital who had diagnosed metal ions, nerve damage, and tumours. He sent me for x-rays, and then two weeks later, I had another appointment with him.

He studied the x-rays and praised the surgeon who had operated on my hip. He said, 'The hip orthopaedic surgeon and his team have done a fine job on your hip joint and nerve damage. And I see they successfully removed the tumours, and you have no scars there?'

I replied, 'The hip orthopaedic surgeon told me it was a straightforward operation. There were no tumours and no nerve damage when they operated.'

His mouth opened wide. 'But I have X-rays and CT scans and biopsy results here.' (I have my Medical Record to show this, **Appendix 15**)

I repeated, 'Yes, I had tumours and nerve damage at the time of biopsy of the tumours, but there were no tumours or nerve damage when they operated. It's in my medical records.'

During my hip operation, my right knee had swollen, and it had seized. The consultant assured me it was temporary. I had physiotherapy, but months went by, and there was a slight improvement. I still needed

Appendix 15 My Medical record, Hip joint-Tumour

On Admission

Problem and Diagnosis: Pseudotumour right hip compressing on the femoral nerve.

Procedure/ Done: Revision cemented total hip replacement.

Clinical Course: Uneventful intraoperatively.

Result status:	Auth (Verified)
Performed by:	Chan , Esther on24 November 2009 15:36 GMT
Verified by:	Chan , Esther on24 November 2009 15:45 GMT
Visit info:	NOC, Inpatient, 18/11/2009 -

* Final Report *

Nuffield Orthopaedic Centre NHS Trust

Discharge Information Form

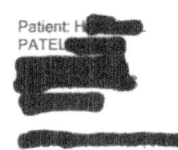

GP: Dr ▇▇▇▇
FLANSHAM PARK HEALTH CTR
▇▇▇▇
WEST SUSSEX
▇▇▇▇

Date: 24-NOV-2009

NHS No: ▇▇▇▇
MRN: 10061408

Patient: H▇▇▇
PATEL▇▇▇

Consultant at Discharge: D▇▇▇▇ Trauma & Orthopaedics   (Tel: 014 1444 4444)

Ward: NOC-Ward E   Admission Date: 18-NOV-2009   Discharge Date: Type Here
26|11|09.

Problems & Diagnosis - Present Admission   **Problems & Diagnosis - Lifelong**
 Pseudotumour right hip compressing on femoral   Mechanical heart valve
nerve

Procedures / Investigations Done:
Revision Right Resurfacing to Total Hip Replacement
Procedures / Investigations Pending:
Revision cemented total hip replacement (Ordered: 03-SEP-2009 11:03)
Allergies: None Recorded.

Chronic Disease Register Tests: Cholesterol: None   HDL.: None   HbA1c: None   T4: None   TSH: None

Patient Capability: Self Caring: Yes   Continence: Fully Continent   Mobility: Fully Mobile

Outcome: Home

Clinical Presentation: Corin Hip Resurfacing 3 years ago. Presented with a large haematoma secondary to carp malalignment and him being on warfarin for mechanical heart valve.
Significant Investigations: Type here
Clinical Course: Admitted two days pre-op to ensure INR <1.5 prior to surgery. During that time he was given LMWH. Uneventful intraoperatively. Warfarin was restarted 24 hours post-op. Post-op Hb 10.5. Check Xray was satisfactory. Continued to receive LMWH until INR >2.5.

Information Given To Patient: Mobilise full weight bearing

Follow up Arrangements: Out-patient follow-up with Mr Whitwell at 6 weeks
Social Support Arrangements made by Hospital:
Meals on Wheels: Y / N   Home Help: Y / N   Home Care: Y / N   District Nurse: Y / N

269

*Problem & Diagnosis. Pseudo tumour right hip compressing on femoral nerve. Uneventful intraoperatively

Details

Ward: NOC-Ward E   Admission Da

Problems & Diagnosis - Present Admission   F
✳ Pseudotumour right hip compressing on femoral
     nerve

Procedures / Investigations Done:
✳ Revision Right Resurfacing to Total Hip Replacement
Procedures / Investigations Pending:
Revision cemented total hip replacement (Ordered: 03-SEP-2C
Allergies: None Recorded.

Chronic Disease Register Tests: Cholesterol: None

Patient Capability: Self Caring: Yes   Continence: Fully

Outcome: Home

Clinical Presentation: Corin Hip Resurfacing 3 years ag
malalignment and him being on warfarin for mechanical heart
Significant Investigations: Type here
Clinical Course: Admitted two days pre-op to ensure INR
✳ Uneventful intraoperatively. Warfarin was restarted 24 hours
  receive LMWH until INR >2.5.

crutches to walk. Ten months later, I had an endoscopy surgery that made it worse. I changed my normal routine. I had to be careful. I functioned reasonably well with a crutch as long as I did not lift heavy objects and limited myself to short walks.

Car journeys were painful. Every time we went over a bump, a sharp jab of pain would shoot past the knee. These were painful years, sleepless nights.

Six months later, I could walk without crutches. There were times I hit deep pockets of depression. I didn't think I would live to see my 60th birthday.

My children were in their teens, and seeing them happy and cheerful gave me strength. I wanted to see them grow up into adults.

It took three years for my right knee to regain a 110-degree bend. Then in 2014, I had kneecap surgery to ease the pain. It worked very well. My walking and sleep pattern improved, and a year later, I was almost back to normal. My quality of life greatly improved. Thank you, Lord.

I have had my share of pain and suffering. To me, it is part of life. It is also a tool to learn to cope with pain and empathise with others.

Ray, a close friend of mine, asked me, 'You have prayed for healing for others. You are close to the Lord, so why didn't he intervene?'

My reply was, 'It's an excellent question. I don't know the answer.'

Years later, when I was going over my diaries, I asked the Lord about my friend's question.

His answer was, 'I intervened in the heart operation and kept you alive. I intervened in nerve damage and tumours which I healed. Doctors did what they could, and I intervened where they had no expertise.'

Chapter 76 – The Church Hostility

We had been in West Sussex for some years. We went to a small Anglican church, and Sunday school was suitable for the children. However, I found the church service dull, as there was no scope to participate, apart from sitting in the pews and going through the church rituals.

A few years later, I joined a charismatic evangelical church. I thought it was time to participate in this church. After a few weeks of keeping a low profile, I felt it was the right time to exercise my spiritual gift in a house group.

I joined a house group. I noticed some presence of the Holy Spirit in their prayers. Initially, I kept a low profile and said little in the house group. One day I couldn't hold back. Before we began the prayer, I turned to a young person and asked him the time. He looked surprised but looked at his watch and said, 'it's 7.45.'

I quoted the verse in **Matthew 18:20**, *For where two or three are gathered in my name, I am there among them.*

I said, 'If the Lord is in our midst, we should be able to hear him answer our prayers, just as this young man has answered my question.' They looked surprised but said nothing.

John 10:27, *"My sheep hear My voice, and I know them, and they follow Me.*

They prayed for a young girl looking for work and a few other things. There was nothing definite or explicit in their prayers. Then I prayed, 'Lord, thank you for answering our prayers. She will receive a letter on Wednesday from her second job interview offering her work.'

There were three reasons to pray in this manner. I explained the first reason to the group. To fulfil the scriptures, i.e., to manifest the presence of the Lord in our midst.

The second, more important reason I kept to myself. Go home, pray and make it happen (principle: fix the radiator and grow in faith), bring the scriptures to life.

Thirdly, he wanted me to witness something in the spiritual world and note it in my diaries. The answered prayer would confirm it.

This went on for two more weeks. They would pray, but I would be particular in my prayers. Then in the fourth week, when I entered the house group, the house leader took me to the back of the house. He said the group was not happy to have me among them. I was misleading them, making them feel very uncomfortable.

They had asked him to remove me from the group!

In his group were men and woman well-versed in the Bible. For a while, I listened as he criticized my faith and my belief. My views were a danger to the church; the weak could be misled into false doctrine. I had the scriptures wrong. I was an instrument of Satan and doing these things with his guidance to mislead them.

I was seething with hot raw anger. I held my breath, silently counting to ten repeatedly.

Galatians 5:22, but the fruit of the Spirit is love, joy, peace, longsuffering, gentleness, goodness, faith.

It was a personal attack on our Lord and me. What made me furious was them stating that the Devil could do miracles to deceive people. They were implying the Devil led me. The things I was able to do could be the works of Satan.

Our Lord also suffered such accusations. *Mark 3:22, And the scribes who came down from Jerusalem said, "He has Beelzebub," and, "By the ruler of the demons He casts out demons."*

I said to him, 'Everything I have prayed for has been in the name of Jesus as the Lord taught us. Do you seriously think the Devil would respond in the name of Jesus?' I spoke in a quiet, quivering voice, desperately trying to remain calm, controlling my tone. 'I may be wrong about my faith, my understanding of scriptures, but I know the voice of my Lord. Do you?'

Now the group leader took that as a personal attack on his faith.

I asked, 'Has your house group a special prayer request? You will all pray, but I will give you the day and hour the Lord will bring it to **pass**[1]. Shall we test it?' I was referring to Elijah's challenge to the prophets of Baal.

1 Kings 18:26, *So they took the bull which was given them, and they prepared it, and called on the name of Baal from morning even till noon, saying, "O Baal, hear us!" But there was no voice; no one answered.*

He was confused, frightened. He knew enough about me to know my **words held power.**[2]

He asked me to follow him to the hallway. The rest of the group watched me through the open door of the living room. I looked at them. They avoided any eye contact.

--- ☆---

[1] *John 10:27, "My sheep hear My voice, and I know them, and they follow Me.*

[2] *1 Thessalonians 1:5, For our gospel did not come to you in word only, but also in power, and in the Holy Spirit and in much assurance, as you know what kind of men we were among you for your sake.*

Chapter 77 – I appointed them

He was a person I greatly respected. He was a kind and humble person, but not then. In a quivering voice, he said, 'We don't want you in our group; please don't come here again.'

I was hurt. I felt rejected and angry that they regarded me as a vessel of the Devil. It also meant I had lost the friends I had made. My purpose in that church felt wrong. That evening I brought the matter before the Lord. He said nothing.

It took me a few months to calm down. I avoided churches. The Bible and its teaching were causing me grief, first with my family, now in a church. I was too emotionally upset. I spent weeks in limbo, not sure what to do.

Then one evening, when I was in a better, receptive mood, I felt the Lord open this issue.

'I understand you are upset, but you need to understand. They spotted a **flaw**[1] in your scripture use. I have a covenant with you. Even if you are wrong, I will honour your trust. If you make a mistake, I will correct your error and answer your prayer when the moment is right. I will correctly guide you—*[Zak's Tenet; Guide you with my eye. I will reason with you. I respect your privacy, so I will not press you nor persuade you without your consent.]*

'They are not so forgiving. Your anger towards them is unjust. They are my people. I appointed them.'

Romans 13:1 *Let every soul be subject to the governing authorities. For there is no authority except God, and God appoints the authorities that exist.*

I read the story about David and Saul. **1 Samuel 26:9,** *And David said to Abishai, "Do not destroy him; for who can stretch out his hand against the LORD'S anointed, and be guiltless?"*

Months later, I was still sulking at them. I was also lost. I had not been to

---- ☆----

Flaw[1] *Refer to end of Chapter*

275

a church for months. Reading the Bible had almost cost me, my family, now even the church was closing its door to me. I didn't feel confident about joining another church. After the turmoil with my family in Kenya, I was extra-sensitive to rejection. Doubts began to cloud my views. I just didn't know what to do. I couldn't get the balance right.

I didn't seem to fit anywhere. I kept away from the church and made some friends outside the church. They accepted me as I was. I felt at peace. I was relaxed, devoted my time to my family, and did voluntary work for a charity looking after asylum seekers. Life was more manageable and happier outside the church.

Years went by. My wife and children still went to the small Anglican Church, and sometimes I went with them, sitting at the back of the church and kept a low profile.

Sixth sabbatical year

On my sixth sabbatical year, as I was going through my diaries, I came across this incident. I brought it before the Lord again. Over the weeks, a picture began to emerge. I was now more at ease with myself. These people, who had shaped my past few years, were the Lord's people. I was no longer angry with them. I had got over the rejection.

I sat before the Lord. I felt the Holy Spirit guide me. These church members were hard-working, decent people trying their best to put bread on their families' table. They worked hard, faced daily struggles to fit in the demands and stresses of work, raising a family, trying to build his church. They were not used to the movements of the Spirit. They were not ready for the likes of me in their church. I had been a round peg in a square hole.

Jesus had gone without food for four weeks. He left his father, mother, and family for the sake of the kingdom.

Matthews 12:48-49, But He answered and said to the one who told Him, "Who is My mother and who are My brothers?" And He stretched out His hand toward His disciples and said, "Here are My mother and My brothers!

He faced rejection; his works were questioned and ascribed to the devil. He had laid out his life for others, and God empowered him and glorified him.

2 Peter 1:17, *For He received from God the Father honour and glory when such a voice came to Him from the Excellent Glory: "This is My beloved Son, in whom I am well pleased."*

The people of the church were uncomfortable with my approach. I had made a fatal mistake. *Zak's Tenet: you can reason with them. You will respect their privacy; you will not press them nor try to persuade them without their consent. I understood my mistake.*

'I am sorry, Lord. It was my fault.

1 Corinthians 15:46, However, the <u>spiritual is not first</u>, but the natural, and afterwards the spiritual.

'<u>I ran ahead before they were ready</u>. I needed to earn their trust, respect, confidence first.'

He had taught me, 'There are some hills that are too high to climb. You have to lay the matter before me and go round the hill. Some day when you are strong, you will be able to climb the hill.'

I asked the Lord, 'Why didn't you point out my error earlier?'

'I will reason with you, but I will not press you without your consent. I did not have your consent until now. You were not ready to climb the hill until now.' *[Liz's Tenet 1: It is not wise to reveal all (climb) before it's time.]*

The Lord said, 'I think it is time you joined a church. And we will make it the finest in England.'

The cloud that had hung around me for years lifted.

---- ☆----

They spotted the <u>flaw</u> in your scripture use.

I am aware that I may have made some unintentional mistakes in this book. This book is my sole effort, devoid of any professional editing and the help of any publishing house. Hence, it is not for sale.

I am certain there are hundreds of Christians better equipped to write this book. They have the resources, the backup of academics, the publishing houses—all the resources they need.

Nonetheless, I felt the Lord wanted me to write this book. I had my doubts. I prayed about it, and I needed strong evidence that it was from the Lord. One night around 3 am, I woke up and started to write numbers in a cube.

In the next 8 months, the number sequence grew from 9 to 27, all adding up to the same number in 8 dimensions. Each number had its own 27 sub cubes number, and I wrote down the sequences for each number; for each sub-cube, I should say with the aid of a £1 pocket calculator—**appendix 10 end of the book.**

The Lord said to me, 'Hari, if you can do this complex mathematical cube, you can write my book.

I remembered what the Lord said when I was making the gospel leaflets in Haringey, and the deacons tried to stop me due to my poor spelling; 'Hari, they asked for <u>someone to warn them</u>. If they are earnest to seek me, it will make no difference to them if your leaflets (book) had spelling, grammatical, or scriptural mistakes. **'It is the overall content of the message that matters.'**

--- ☆---

I will be happy to receive any corrections from you. Your contribution would be appreciated.

harxpatel@gmail.com

---- 🦠---

Chapter 78 – Good works

Review of my diaries during my sixth sabbatical year.

I wondered if I should have gone into intercession for Terry Waite (Chapter 30) in 1987 to secure his release, as I had done for Marko. I put this thought before the Lord so I could learn from it. The gist of his first question was: 'If there had been a ransom demand for £5m, would you have picked up the tab?'

My answer to the Lord was, 'If I had that kind of resources, I might have contributed towards it.'

The Lord said, 'You made a big donation (took the tab). You did that when the appeal went out on TV, the date you quoted in public, and you quoted the arms **deal** playing a part in his crisis.'

The second question put to me by the Lord was, 'why pick up a massive spiritual tab?'

One of the good works prepared for me before the foundation of Earth was laid was spiritual warfare. I learned about that in the spiritual battle for Marko's release and Silvia's healing. There was no need to replicate it again. I had to move on to the next level.

Another lesson about spiritual warfare I learned was from the prayers for Ethiopia. This time it was to teach me about control over the clouds/rain and working with angels. They played a massive part in bringing about the rain and releasing seeds, agricultural tools, and funds.

Angels

Matthew 2:13, *Now when they had departed, behold, an angel of the Lord appeared to Joseph in a dream,*

The Bible has many stories about angels in both the Old and the New Testaments. <u>Even Jesus needed the help and comfort of angels.</u>

Luke 22:42, Jesus said, "Father, if it is Your will, take this cup away from Me; nevertheless not My will, but Yours, be done." v43 Then <u>an angel</u> appeared to Him from heaven, strengthening Him.

They have often volunteered to come into my life to help. They enjoyed the task and the privilege of working with us. I never commanded them. It was always a polite request in the name of Jesus for help. They were his ministering angels. There was also an eternal bond of friendship formed with our spiritual colleagues.

*Revelation 19:10 And **I fell at** his feet to worship him. But he said to me, "See that you do not do that! I am <u>your fellow servant and of your brethren</u> who have the testimony of Jesus. Worship God! For the testimony of Jesus is the spirit of prophecy."*

One day we shall judge them. A better word would be to assess them, their potential.

Working with them, I learned to assess their potential, dedication, and immense joy at working with us, the future heirs in Christ.

I cannot understand why some churches suppress the discussions about angels, almost denying their existence. They are part of our family. The hardship and joy we share with them bind us closer to them. In tough times, your real friends stand by you, and when your friends are unable to come to your assistance, and you are fortunate to see angels, they will be there.

Chapter 79 – Angelic and Spiritual realm

Ephesians 6:12 For we do not wrestle against flesh and blood, but against principalities, against powers, against the rulers of the darkness of this age, against spiritual hosts of wickedness in the heavenly places.

Some of us, led by the Spirit, are going through the most challenging times any being in the universe has encountered. The first person to complete this race was Jesus.

And those God has called to be heirs in Christ are meant to go through very tough times if they are to be part of his elite troops, spiritual warriors. He did not spare Jesus, and he will not spare you if you have given him your full consent (Zak's Tenet). The Universe is a tough place, and only the strongest in Spirit will qualify to receive their entire inheritance. God does not hand over his pearls to those who are lazy, lethargic, unwilling to run the race with all their heart, mind and strength.

Hundreds and thousands of Christians want their entire inheritance. To claim it, they should be prepared to make the sacrifices needed to overcome the world?

*Romans 8:18, For I consider that the sufferings of this present time are not **worthy** of being compared with the glory which shall be revealed in us.*

*2 Thessalonians 1:11, Therefore, we also always pray for you that our God would count you **worthy** of this calling, and <u>fulfil</u> all the good pleasure of His goodness and the work of faith with power.*

For God to fulfil the works of faith in you, he needs your full consent and willingness to be at his command day and night, ready at a moment notice, even if it is four in the morning and you just had two hours sleep. Moreover, he doesn't want to drag you out of your bed screening.

He wants a response where he whispers in your ear, and you are up. That is what you get on a battlefield. Spiritual warfare is a battleground where God trains his warriors. Cowards choose to remain in the background away from the battle with lazy, pious, pompous people, avoiding getting their hand dirty but clamour for the glory and attention of their flock.

If only Christians could comprehend the glory that awaits those that overcome the world.

Angels

Angels understand the sacrifices needed to overcome the world, and they want to support us, just as they helped Jesus. They desire to be part of our family. They don't have children. They want to understand the passion we feel for our loved ones, the pain and sacrifices we make for families and friends.

They seek answers to questions like why do so many of us put up with work we hate. Where do we get this strength, the motivation to go to a dull, dreadful work day after day? Is it so there is bread on the table for our loved ones? That is an outstanding commitment and sacrifice of self for others.

They are perplexed when they see parents who show no such love, leaving behind parentless children and wives/husbands in misery to further their interests. The angels shake their heads and wonder, 'What makes humans so selfish, so self-centred?'

They admire our tenacity to face hardships for our loved ones, our church, our Lord, our country. It is an act of love, and love is the driving force of the universe.

1 Corinthians 13:1, Though I speak with the tongues of men and angels but have not love, I have become sounding brass or a clanging cymbal.

They want to understand the pain they see on a parent's face when their child is sick or dying. The lifelong pain scarred into a young child's memory when the mother fails to return home from the hospital. How will this child fare in a hostile world?

Latent sacrificial love

The angels and I want to learn more about the latent sacrificial love we all have, including animals. This life on Earth is an excellent opportunity for that. Where else in the universe will you find this sacrificial love?

The Holy Book of Hindus, the Bhagavad-Gita, which I learned from four, states, *Gita 3:16. The Vedas (Hindu scriptures) say that the Universe rotates on the axle of sacrifice. Brahman (Word of God, as in John 1:1) the creator set this law in motion to train, discipline, and enlighten all in the principle of sacrifice. Those who choose to live only for this world live in vain.*

The mighty archangels call out to the Heavenly crowd, 'Come down to Earth if you want to learn about love. There are plenty of vacancies on Earth. Sign here and adopt an Earthly family.'

Hebrews 12:1, *Therefore, we also, since we are surrounded by so great <u>a cloud of</u> (Heavenly) <u>witnesses.</u>*

They want to understand selfishness and the evil surrounding it. How is it that so many of us can ignore the suffering of our neighbours? How is it we can calmly take pleasure in fancy holidays, displays of wealth, while our neighbours starve?

Why do some of us leave our Elderly relatives or very young children emotionally starved for affection? Leaving them feeling alone, helpless, thinking no one cares, that no one makes an effort to understand or support them.

Where do humanity's cold greed and selfishness come from? Why doesn't God intervene often enough?

Please, allow them to understand the two sides of our nature, the sacrificial and the callously indulgent.

--- ☆---

Hebrews 1:14, Are they not all ministering spirits sent forth by God to minister for those who will inherit salvation?

1 Corinthians 6:3, Do you not know that we shall judge angels? How much more, things that pertain to this life? ---- 🎕---

Chapter 80 – The Aim of Good Works

God read the good works written in his book for me before he gave me life. Each was carefully chosen to teach me/us a specific thing about God and our role in his kingdom, on Earth and in Heaven. Authority over government (Uganda), authority over sea, rain, aid (Ethiopia and Korea), spiritual powers (Marko), healings (Paul's friend, Colin and Silvia, Miss Staking), angels (timing of delivery of letters, healing), money/material, and spiritual tabs (Raymond, my home, wealth, time).

Each good work has a spiritual aim, has eternal nourishment for our spiritual growth, and will bring forth fruit on Judgment Day.

Gold and silver[1] that will pass the Judgment Day.

We are meant to be the Vessels of gold fit for the holiest of **holies[2]** in the **New Jerusalem[3]**. This is part of our inheritance.

Moving in the spirit was exciting. There were days I found it hard to sleep. I would feel that God would do something in the church or for a person, but I wanted to get more accurate information. To work out the date, then the hour and the precise minute, which is very hard because people's watches can vary by a minute or two?

I was getting fixated on precise minutes. It developed into an obsession. The angels would say something like, 'we could arrange the delivery of the letter around the fifth or sixth.' That wasn't good enough for me. They would say we don't control the hospital administration or the post office sorting office. The letter could arrive two days early. My suggestion

--- ☆---

[1] *2 Timothy 2:20, But in a great house, there are vessels of gold and silver and wood and clay, some for honour and some for dishonour.*

[2] *Hebrews 10:19, Therefore, brethren, having boldness to enter the Holiest by the blood of Jesus,*

[3] *Revelation 21:2, Then I, John, saw the holy city, New Jerusalem, coming down out of heaven from God, prepared as a bride adorned for her husband. ...x..x...*

would be, hide the letter; let it slips to the floor until the day. Delay things; use your initiative. Then they would say, 'The postman can be early or late on his round. We don't control him.'

'Well, delay him; make sure his car doesn't start.' I would spend hours going over minute details. It was developing into an addiction. There were times over two to three week periods where I was so fixated for a specific hour that I would lose interest in food or sleep and lose 5-6 lbs in weight.

This unhealthy obsession was damaging my health, my wellbeing, my relationship with others. I didn't care. I was caught up in something too exciting to let go of.

Parable of Seven Sons[1]

If I had seven children, one of whom was exceptionally gifted in all things, blessed in every gift in Heaven, and one child with additional needs, I would teach my family to treat the weak one with utmost kindness and care. I would teach my family to regard the child as a gift to the family for our perfection of compassion and charity.

The strong one should use his ability to serve his siblings to promote their welfare, interest, and happiness. That is the lesson God taught me and to acquire the wisdom to reconcile all things in Christ.

As a child of 10 years, I cried out, 'If there is a God, I will make him account for all the suffering in the world.'

I believe he heard me. He gave me an idea of his plans. He showed me the principle, *[Hari Tenet 2]* '*The law of the cosmos dictates: No one has a right to gain at the expense of others, not even **God.** Your conscience demands that you have a moral conscience for all life, i.e., you shall not steal.*'

--- ☆---

[1] ***This is my standard.*** *I would not recommend it to anyone unless they had the necessary resources to implement it. Sometimes it is wise to go round a hill until you have resources essential to climb it*

...x..x...

Moreover, before this creation ceases to exist (Revelation 21:1), God will **judge**[2] all and make everything and every one whole. As part of our inheritance, I/we have an active role in this reconciliation and restoration process.

Acts 3:21, whom (Christ & us as God's heir through Christ, Galatians 4:7) heaven must receive until the times of restoration of all things, which God has spoken by the mouth of all His holy prophets since the world began.

Creating life, moral responsibility

If someone creates life, they are accountable to the least and the greatest of their living subjects. They have a moral duty of care to compensate for all the pain and suffering inflicted on their creation. Something I learnt from God when he was teaching me to look after Haringey on his behalf.

He taught me to be part of this process, to reconcile every bite of energy, atom, sand, leaf, living thing in my 'patch'. Life on Earth is too short to grasp this fully, but I got the gist of it (my patch: Haringey, part of East Cornwall, and part of West Sussex).

--- ☆---

[2] God does not want anyone to perish, but his justice demands this for some.

Chapter 81 – Cost of our salvation

Php 2:12, Therefore, my beloved, as you have always obeyed, not as in my presence only, but now much more in my absence, <u>work out</u> your salvation with fear and trembling;

This is my view, and I do not wish to impose it on anyone.

Lesson 1: This lesson has to do with the perfection of my/our salvation. Christ redeemed us on the cross and by the blood of innocent animals. The sin offering is just a symbol of it. ***Exodus 29:36*** *Also, every day, you shall offer a bull as a sin offering for atonement.*

I struggle to find the right words. In essence, we in Christ were **chosen**[1] from the beginning because God **foreknew**[2] who would respond. Some of us took the challenge to seek out and work out our salvation. Others like Esau sold their birthright. ***Genesis 25:33,*** *Then Jacob said, "Swear to me as of this day." So he swore to him and sold his birthright* <u>(as the eldest son)</u> *to Jacob.*

For those who would follow his call, certain things were needed to work out our salvation. He needed a place like Earth, but it meant a considerable amount of pain and suffering for the rest of creation.

He wanted me to grasp the <u>tremendous cost of my salvation, borne by</u> him, and creation. I am considerably more than just a citizen of God's Kingdom, a joint heir through Christ, handpicked by him, called to be perfected to the full **stature**[3] of Christ the firstborn.

--- ☆---

[1] *Ephesians 1:4, just as He <u>chose</u> <u>us</u> in Him before the foundation of the world, that we should be holy and without blame before Him in love,*

[2] *Romans 8:29, For whom He <u>foreknew</u>, He also predestined to be conformed to the image of His Son, that He might be the firstborn among many brethren.*

[3] *Ephesians 4:13, till we all come to the unity of the faith and of the knowledge of the Son of God, to a <u>perfect man,</u> to the measure of the <u>stature</u> of the fullness of Christ.* ..x..x...

The bar the Lord set for his heirs is incredibly high; many are called, but only a handful will give him the time and commitment required to finish the race set before them.

Hebrews 12:1, *Therefore, since so great a cloud of witnesses surrounds us, let us also lay aside every weight and the sin that clings so closely, and <u>let us run with perseverance the race that is set before us.</u>*

I say it in love. If Church leaders want God's blessing, they should be running in the race set before them.

I believe many are just walking, not running. It is not for me to judge them but to reason with them in love. *2 **Corinthians 13:5,** Examine yourselves as to whether you are in the faith. Test yourselves. Do you not know yourselves, that Jesus Christ is in you? — unless indeed, you are disqualified.*

Many church leaders will face Judgment Day and cry. Their crime will be great because they sold their birthright and misled their church, which is a spiritual crime against God and their followers. However, they have time to change.

There is God's rebuke for them in **Ezekiel 34**. I applied this to myself at one time and spent years learning to meet his requirements, and I am still learning.

V1 And the word of the LORD came to me, saying,
2 "Son of man, prophesy against the shepherds of Israel (England & Canada), prophesy and say to them, 'Thus says the Lord GOD to the shepherds: "Woe to the shepherds of Israel who feed themselves! Should not the shepherds <u>feed the flocks?</u>
3 "You eat the fat and clothe yourselves with the wool; you slaughter the fatlings, but you do not feed the flock.
4 "<u>The weak you have not strengthened</u>, nor have you <u>healed</u> those who were sick, nor <u>bound up</u> the broken, nor <u>brought back</u> what was driven away, nor sought what was lost, but with force and cruelty, you have ruled them.
5 "So they were scattered because there was <u>no shepherd</u>, and they became food for all the beasts of the field when they were scattered.

Also, in **Matthew 25:1-12,** our Lord warns them, quoting the five foolish virgins' parable.

"Then the kingdom of heaven shall be likened to ten virgins who took their lamps and went out to meet the bridegroom.

V2, "Now five of them were wise, and five were foolish.

3 "Those who were foolish took their lamps and took no oil with them,

4 "but the wise took oil in their vessels with their lamps.

5 "But while the bridegroom was delayed, they all slumbered and slept.

6 "And at midnight, a cry was heard: 'Behold, the bridegroom is coming; go out to meet him!'

7 "Then all those virgins arose and trimmed their lamps.

8 "And the foolish said to the wise, 'Give us some of your oil, for our lamps are going out.'

9 "But the wise answered, saying, 'No, lest there should not be enough for us and you; but go rather to those who sell, and buy for yourselves.'

10 "And while they went to buy, the bridegroom came, and those who were <u>ready</u> went in with him <u>to the wedding</u>; and the door <u>was shut.</u>

11 "Afterward, the other virgins came also, saying, 'Lord, Lord, open to us!'

12 "But he answered and said, 'Assuredly, I say to you, I do not know you.'

It is also the responsibility of church elders and deacons to appoint the right candidate for their church.

The Holy Spirit in my early days as a young Christian said to me, 'Hari, I do not want the day of the Lord to be a day of tears for you, a day of lost opportunity. I do not want you to enter the Kingdom of God, pass through the gates of Heaven, with no idea of what awaits you, like those who walk in ignorance, virgins whose oil will run out.

'I gave you several visions of the Day of Judgment so that you might aspire to be a refined vessel of gold in our house, not a vessel of wood or clay.'

2 Timothy 2:20, *But in a great house, there are vessels of gold and silver and <u>wood and clay</u>, some for honour and some for dishonour.*   ---- 🜨---

Chapter 82 –An obligation to God and creation for the perfecting of my salvation

Romans 13:9, For the commandments, "You shall not commit adultery," "You shall not murder," "You shall not steal," "You shall not bear false witness," "You shall not covet," and if there is any other commandment, are all summed up in this saying, namely, "You shall love your neighbour as yourself."

Lesson 2. What I derived from the above verse. He needed to instil in me/us the principle: 'Nothing in the universe should gain at the expense of another.' I grasped this.

In my conscience, I felt a moral obligation to him, **creation**[1] and my neighbours for the perfecting of my salvation. My spiritual birthright was worked out at his expense and the expense of **others**[2]. As an act of gratitude to all, I sought his help to participate in **reconciling**[3] all things in Heaven and on Earth (all the creatures in **my Patch**[4]). When I had

---- ☆----

[1] *Romans 8:28, And we know that all things work together for good to those who love God, to those who are called according to His purpose.*

[2] *Romans 8:22, For we know that the whole creation groans and labours with birth pangs together until now.*

[2] *Genesis 3:17, cursed is the ground because of you; in toil, you shall eat of it all the days of your life.*

[3] *Ephesians 2:16, and that He might reconcile them both to God in one body through the cross, thereby putting to death the enmity.*

[3] *Colossians 1:20, and by Him to reconcile all things to Himself, by Him, whether things on earth or things in heaven, having made peace through the blood of His cross.*

[4] *My Patch. My sense of gratitude extends to all; all the creatures and people, even my enemies. For they have all intentionally, or not, contributed to my salvation. Hence, my reaching out to all the homes on my Patch with leaflets, offering services and my home to anyone in need.*

...x..x...

grasped this, my conscience was clear. With the Lord's help, I would make restitution to all in this life or the hereafter for the pain and suffering my life brought to others on Earth/my Patch.

Lesson 3. For me. Compensation and restitution may make up for some of the harm my/our salvation may inflict on family and neighbours, such as reading the bible and the problems it created for my parents/uncles. Wounds can heal, but the Scars/emotional wounds become part of those affected by our actions. They remain—an eternal reminder of the high cost to them for my/our salvation.

An obligation I feel I will have to make up for. Most believers have no grasp of this debt; we owe those affected by our actions and God. It is part of our work in heaven, with God's help, to reconcile all things and make restitution to others (make them whole) for the cost they incurred for our salvation.

A King may bestow an estate upon a warrior. However, a good, honourable warrior has a duty of care to the King, and his subjects to manage them well. A fair-minded steward makes compensation and restitution to his subjects for his errors as he learns to govern.

This is my view; you do not have to agree. I came from a culture where we were vegetarian and brought up not to harm but to live in harmony with all.

Gita 6:30-31. I am present to those who have realized me in every creature. Seeing all life as my manifestation, they are never separated from me. They worship me by showing compassion to all living things. Hence, all their actions proceed from me. Wherever they may live, they abide in me.

I would not impose this standard on others. I consider it gross **selfishness**[1] to seek my happiness/salvation at the expense of God,

---- ☆----
Selfishness. *Ezekiel 36:2, "I will give you a new heart and put a new spirit within you; I will take the heart of stone out of your flesh and give you a heart of flesh. ...x...x.*

neighbours, creation, and its creatures, if I am not prepared to make them whole with God's help, for whatever loss they suffered, either on this earth or in the hereafter.

I am now clothed with a new heart and a **new Spirit**[1] that has heightened my conscience. My old self with a heart of stone is now crucified with Christ, and a man with New Heart and New Spirit has emerged with a new heightened **conscience**[2].

---- ☆----

[1] Ezekiel 36:26, "I will give you a _new heart_ and put a _new spirit_ within you; I will take the _heart of stone_ out of your flesh and give you a heart of flesh.

[2] Acts 23:1, Then Paul, looking earnestly at the council, said, "Men and brethren, I have lived in all good **conscience** before God until this day."

Chapter 83 Jacob's ladder.

Revelation 3:18, I counsel you to buy from Me refined gold in the fire that you may be rich; and white garments, that you may be clothed, that the shame of your nakedness may not be revealed; and anoint your eyes with eye salve, that you may see.

First step. This is the gist of what the Lord taught me. A gold nugget must be refined and purified by the fire.

Genesis 3:10, So he (Adam) said, "I heard Your voice in the garden, and I was afraid because I was naked; and I hid myself."

He brought before me the story of Adam and Eve **(Genesis 2:22-24.)** Their existence may be actual, or it could be just a story. It is not essential to me; critical is the message I got from this story and how I would respond to it.

When they disobeyed God, he does not condemn them straight away. It was part of the learning process to trust, admit, and learn. Due to their inbuilt self-preservation instinct triggered by fear or ignorance, they would try to protect themselves: run, hide, or fight back. God expected that natural reaction from them, an innate self-preservation instinct of all creatures and mine.

Lesson one. Disobedience, fight/running away is part of my nature.

Jacob's ladder. The second step for Adam and Eve.

To find shelter and calm down, to reflect on their actions, their deeds and fear. To analyse what they had done and how they felt. It was time for them to learn not to hide anything from God. Learning to trust him without fear was a big issue here.

1 John 4:18, There is no fear in love, but perfect love casts out fear, for fear has to do with punishment, and whoever fears has not reached perfection in love.

God gave them until evening to do this. *[Kathy's Tenet 1. A person, or a relationship, is of eternal value than the things we participate in.]* They failed to trust him; instead, they tried to make excuses.

Hebrews 11:6, And without faith (or trust) it is impossible to please God,

Lesson 2. I have the evening prayer time to reflect on the day's events under the gaze of the Holy Spirit.

Jacob's ladder. Third step.

When our Lord came to see them in the evening, he would have liked them to share the day's events. Share their joy or suffering. Admit any disobedience without fear and learn from God. If God forbids anything, there is a reason.

When trust is breached, there are consequences for the person and others. It is essential to admit errors to those they had hurt, and with the Lord's help, make restitution.

Lesson 3. Admit any disobedience without fear and learn from God.

Jacob's ladder. Fourth Step.

Gratitude and obligation. Finally, there would have been a growing sense of gratitude and debt owed to God for our salvation. It is a chance to learn from mistakes and harm done to others, learning from God to put right, making restitution (make whole), and reconciling everything.

No amount of restitution can make up for the emotional harm done to a soul *[Su Anne's Tenet 1; - scars are for eternity]*. Therefore, it is essential we learn quickly, take great care in our conduct with others, and avoid getting into the same situation again.

I am learning to be thoughtful, considerate, and careful.

Making mistakes doesn't mean we sinned. God waited. Adam and Eve had a chance to follow the above steps. They denied any wrongdoing and blamed others. They were not prepared to learn, trust God, and put things right; that was their sin.

A wall opens between them and God. It was due to their failure to change, to learn from their mistakes; he taught me never to follow their example.

'Lord, what if I keep on making mistakes?' I asked. **Matthew 18:21** *Then Peter came to Him and said, "Lord, how often shall my brother sin against me, and I forgive him? Up to seven times?"*

V 22, Jesus said to him, "I do not say to you, up to seven times, but up to seventy times seven.

Lesson 4. Exercise Gratitude, obligation and make restitution (make whole) and reconcile all things.

Our Lord would take the tab for our mistakes and make restitution to others until we are mature enough to take care of our responsibilities. That requires us to be willing to be guided in the correct way to make amends for our mistakes.

Consider how the Lord reacts to the thief who follows the above rules. **Luke 23:39-43,** Then one of the criminals who was hanged blasphemed Him, saying, "If You are the Christ, save Yourself and us." But the other, answering, rebuked him, saying, "Do you not even fear God, seeing you are under the same condemnation? We indeed justly, for we receive the due reward of our deeds, but this Man has done nothing wrong. Then he said to Jesus, "Lord, remember me when You come into Your kingdom." And Jesus said to him, "Assuredly, I say to you, today you will be with Me in Paradise."

Jacob's ladder. Fifth step.

We bring before God our day. He doesn't want to correct all our inappropriate conduct in a single day. He wants a chance for the Holy Spirit to take at least one behaviour in 7 months to change (a lot more if you are a fast learner).

That is 12 conducts corrected by sabbatical year (in 7 years) and 98 in an average lifetime. That is more than enough to transform us, radically change us.

Ezekiel 36:26, *A new heart also will I give you, and a new spirit will I put within you: and I will take away the stony heart out of your flesh, and I will give you a heart of flesh.*

*[Janet Warrington's Tenet 1] Everything that happened to you, every experience, good and bad, thought, feeling, tears, laughter, joy, will turn one by one into a positive force for good, for your spiritual growth, and maturity, to fulfil your place among us. You are not alone. **We**[1] (Hebrews 12:1 heavenly witnesses) are <u>with you,</u> and **we**[2-3] will be with you until the end of time.'*

---- ☆----

[1] *Isaiah 41:10, Fear not, for <u>I am with you;</u> Be not dismayed, for I am your God. I will strengthen you, Yes, I will help you, I will uphold you with My righteous right hand.'*

[2] *Matthew 28:20, "teaching them to observe all things that I have commanded you; and lo, <u>I am with you</u> always, even to the end of the age." Amen.*

[3] *Hebrews 12:1, Therefore we also, since we are <u>surrounded</u> by so great a <u>cloud of witnesses,</u> let us lay aside every weight, and the sin which so easily ensnares us, and let us run with endurance the race that is set before us,*

---- ----

Chapter 84– Jesus Prays

*Luke 6:12 Now it happened in those days that he went out to the mountain to pray and continued **all night** in prayer to God.*

Why is it difficult to grasp that life on Earth was difficult for Jesus, and the same may apply to us? He had to fast for 40 days before he could start his ministry.

He waited upon his father each night, sometimes for the whole of the night and sought the good works God had ordained for him the following day, learning to suppress things he wanted to do.

Hebrews 5; 7, who, in the days of His flesh, when He had offered up prayers and supplications, with vehement cries and tears to Him who was able to save Him from death and was heard because of His godly fear. Though He was a Son, yet He learned obedience by the things which He suffered. And having been perfected, He became the author of eternal salvation to all who obey Him.

The knowledge and plans his father had ordained for the next day did not fall into his lap. It was hard work to seek them out and suppress his desires and wishes. There was a choice between waiting upon his father or seeking the allure of a warm, comfortable bed.

God chose these steps for Jesus to walk in to build his obedience, iron will, firm discipline, and commitment to a higher calling.

*Ephesians 4:13, till we all come to the unity of the faith and of the knowledge of the Son of God, to a perfect man, to the measure of the **stature** of the fullness of Christ;*

If I wanted to reach the full stature of Christ, I would need to make the same effort as him. A choice we make every day if we are to follow in the steps of Jesus.

Our Lord's abilities were reduced to our level so that he could understand the trials and problems we would encounter. He would have gone through the same kind of doubts, anxiety, confusion, uncertainty we now face.

Jesus has experienced the issues we would meet, and, having overcome them, he can teach us systematically to do the things he could.

Jesus Prays All Night. Luke 22 v 24

This is a complex subject for me to explain. I do not have the linguistic ability, but I will try. *1 Corinthians 2:16 We have the mind of Christ.*

Hundreds of people have claimed to have seen Jesus, but when was the last time they asked him what a typical day in his life on Earth was like?

Or in the evening as he prayed, what went through his mind as he went about seeking his father's plan for him for the following day?

I asked the Lord, 'Can you show me, one who was often called a retard at school (glad, a term no longer in use today) in a simple manner I can understand, step by step, how you prayed and sought from God the father, revelations about your heavenly stature? How did God reveal the good works he had chosen for you? How did this revelation come to you?

I know Jesus wanted me to experience what he had to do to make a miracle happen the following day and the difficulties he faced on Earth. These thoughts went through my mind.

It was evening, Jesus was tired, cold, and his body ached for rest. He needed sleep, but he had a sense of responsibility to his Father to account for the day.

As the moon shone, he bowed his head while nearby, the angels and his disciples waited and watched. He entered into communion with his father, giving an account of every word he had spoken that day, its implication on his disciples. Together, they assessed the day's work and what needed to be done the following day.

Romans 14:12, So then each one of us shall give account of himself to God. *Ephesians 2:10,* For we are his workmanship, created in Christ Jesus for good works, which God afore prepared that we should walk in them.

His every thought was examined under the light of the divine gaze or scriptures. *2 Corinthians 10:5,* casting down arguments and every high thing that exalts itself against the knowledge of God, bringing every thought into captivity to the obedience of Christ.

Even though he was God's son, he had to learn through such works (being tired and worn out) to be made perfect.

Hebrews 5:7-9, *In the days of his flesh, Jesus offered up prayers and supplications, <u>with loud cries and tears,</u> to the one who was able to save him from death, and he was heard because of his reverent submission. Although he was a Son, he <u>learned obedience</u> through what he suffered; and having been <u>made perfect</u>, he became the source of eternal salvation for all who obey him,*

The weakness of the human body and mind tried to make Jesus give up his prayers. Thoughts entered his mind; you are tired, go to sleep. You have a hard day ahead of you; multitudes will be waiting for your words. You need rest/sleep. Each temptation was resisted and overcome.

Jesus was under complete submission to his father's gaze. He did nothing to displease his father.

The greatest evil I fear is not the Devil, but my inner desire to take the easy path, give up without a good fight, lack willpower, or lack creative life.

Eternal life

The words I have spoken in spirit are alive, have the power to transform lives. Hence, I have a duty to the Holy Spirit, our Lord, and God to regularly account and nourish them until Judgment day.

Then on that day, I will see its whole fruit—a long-term commitment. I have grabbed that eternal life with both hands.

Jeremiah 30:2, "Thus speaks the LORD God of Israel, saying: 'Write in a book for yourself all the words that I have spoken to you.

*Philippians 2:16, holding fast the word of **life**, so that I may rejoice in the day of Christ that I have not run in vain or laboured in vain.*

---- ❦ ----

Chapter 85 – We have the mind of Christ

1 Corinthians 2:16 For "who has known the mind of the LORD that he may instruct Him?" But we have the mind of Christ.

The angels saw that through that weak human body of Christ radiated iron self-discipline and control. A mind that could control and evaluate thoughts and insight in the proper priority, considering that which was eternal above temporal. The words he would say the next day were carefully thought out in terms of eternity and spoken to bring fruit on Judgment day or before.

With much thought, care, and love, he shared his views about the disciples, the multitude, and the hostile crowd with his father.

Through visions about his past glory, his place in the WORD (John 1:1), by taking him back into the beginning and through such revelations, his father showed him things and good works (Ephesians 2:10) he had prepared for Christ, i.e., the ten lepers would come to him for healing, and only one would come back to thank him. Jesus then prayed and discussed with his father how and what he ought to say to them and do. To heal all or just one?

His father would give him visions about the heavenly realms, insight into judgment day and beyond. The physical healing would confirm the knowledge he had gained of the spiritual world, his past, and future and strengthen the father-son bond.

Hebrews 1:5, For unto which of the angels said he at any time, Thou art my Son, This day have I begotten thee? And again, I will be to him a Father, And he shall be to me a Son?

The angels and Satan recognised his superiority over them, even though the mortal body limited his abilities. One by one, the holy angels came to acknowledge, having seen his ways and his thoughts that he was far above the rest of men and angels. That even the great Satan could not defeat him. He, Jesus, was without fault.

Revelation 4:11, "You are worthy, O Lord, To receive glory and honour and power; For You created all things, And by Your will, they exist and were created."

Angels bowing down before him, acknowledging his authority. He had proved worthy of their and our adoration, worship and respect. He was worthy of leading us against Satan and his kingdom.

Revelation 17:14, these (Satan and his follower) will make war with the Lamb, and the Lamb will overcome them, for He is Lord of lords and King of kings; and those who are with Him are <u>called, chosen, and faithful</u>.

After his death, God raised him from this Earth to the highest place in **Heaven**[1], next to him. This mortal earthly body no longer limited him. There was not a single angel found to challenge him.

The Holy Spirit said to me, 'Hari, the WORD (John 1:1) of God and I are sent to bring into your life what was real in Jesus. We want to exercise your spirit, educate you, and develop you into the full stature of Christ. The training and hardship Christ underwent, you will go through. Your life is not going to be easy. We need your consent.'

He had my consent.

Ephesians 4:13, *until all of us come to the unity of the faith and of the knowledge of the Son of God, to maturity, to the measure of the <u>full stature of Christ</u>.*

I wrote down in my diary what the Lord had taught me about his life on Earth. If he went through a tough time trying to live a life pleasing to his father, the same was required from me/us, that is for those of us who want to run the race <u>as one who runs to win</u> the whole inheritance in Christ.

That weekend Mr Hammond gave a sermon based on the book of Hebrews. This is a summary of it.

The human tendency is to settle down; there is no settling down with

---- ☆----

[1] *Hebrew 10:12, But this Man (Christ), after He had offered one sacrifice for sins forever, sat down at the <u>right hand </u>of God. ....x...x...*

301

God. Keep moving. Hebrews 11. People of faith confessed that they were strangers and pilgrims on Earth. Christians are pilgrims, ever moving.

Hebrews 11:16, He has prepared a City.

We are settlers, but not on the Earth. The City of God is our conscious goal. We move towards it only as we follow the spirit. Once we settle down, we have lost our keenness for God and the City.

This world has nothing worth spending life for (in pursuit of earthly gains). I have seen a goal far too great to miss. If I am a true pilgrim, I must be led by the spirit, even in details. We seek a better country. Tradition says Jews' houses must have some part unfinished to bear testimony to the world that its occupant is only like Abraham, a pilgrim and a stranger upon the Earth.

[This is a fantastic sermon by Rev Jim Hammond. One of his greatest.]

---- ✤ ----

Chapter 86 –Father and Son and a Grocery Store

Genesis 28:12 Then he dreamed, and behold, a ladder was set up on the earth, and its top reached to heaven, and there the angels of God were ascending and descending on it.

The way I was taught to enter into spiritual warfare. It worked for me. It may or may not work for you.

On the 1st step of Jacob's ladder, reaching Heaven. Month 1

The son takes an order for 5 apples, 9 oranges, and 15 bananas. He starts to pack the items. However, he cannot count. He asks his father for help, and the father teaches him to count up to 5. The son places five apples in the box, and his father does the rest. The son delivers the parcel.

All is well, i.e. we pray a particular prayer with date and time, and God makes it happen. A simple prayer.

On the 2nd step. Month 2.

The following order is for 9 apples, 15 oranges, and 18 bananas. The son waits upon his father and learns to count up to 15. He packs 9 apples and 15 oranges, and his father does the rest. He delivers the parcel.

All is well, i.e. we pray, and God says, 'Now enter into spiritual warfare and overcome your opponents.' We learn the art of spiritual warfare, where God is our shield. A specific prayer is answered.

On the 3rd step. Month 3.

The following order is for 10 apples, 12 oranges, and 20 bananas. The son waits upon his father and learns to count up to 20. He packs 10 apples, 12 oranges, and 19 bananas. He has made an error.

His father smiles and corrects the error. 'For now, it will do. Tomorrow I will teach him to correct his error.' *Luke 2:52, And Jesus increased in wisdom and stature and in favour with God and man.* When we have made our best

effort, and there is an honest error; God will correct it and honour our work.

The son delivers the parcel. He is nearing the full stature of Christ. *Ephesians 4:13, and of the knowledge of the Son of God, to a perfect man, to the measure of the stature of the fullness of Christ.*

Again all is well, i.e. we pray. We walk in heavenly realms, enter spiritual warfare; God intervenes and helps us. A specific prayer is answered.

The 4th order is repeated as above.—Month 4.

The son repeats the same error. This time the father does not correct the error. The son makes up the order and delivers it. On his return, there is a message from the client. There has been a mistake, i.e. God only answered the first half of the prayer.

The son had worked hard to learn and got confident, excited; things were going well. He was beginning to enjoy his work, but now he is doubtful. The mistake and the rebuke from the customer have dented his confidence.

It has been a hard, long struggle to learn to run his father's business. He is devastated. Perhaps he is in the wrong trade. Doubt clouds his mind.

To get specific prayers answered, he had entered spiritual warfare but made some mistakes. This time God does not intervene. He wins some battles but loses the main conflict. Only part of his prayer is answered, i.e. the date but not the time.

We should all have gone through these periods. So did Jesus. *Luke 22:43, and there appeared an angel to him from Heaven, strengthening him. V 44 and being in agony, he prayed more earnestly: and his sweat was as it were great drops of blood falling to the ground.*

People find it difficult to grasp that Jesus wants us to learn to do miracles. Not to convince the world, but as a means to encourage us that the walk in the spirit is real, has power and is transforming us into his image and sometimes those around us.

In our walk with him, we will make honest errors, and he will reach out and correct them, or he will teach us to fix them. Mistakes are part of learning. Supernatural things will happen even when we have made errors. He leaves it to the Holy Spirit to choose an appropriate time to teach us to correct our mistakes.

He can teach us to count, but he wants us to have the pleasure of figuring out that 2+2+3=7. The joy, the excitement of self-exploration and discovery brightens our lives. He wants us to have lots of it.

Furthermore, God wants us to enjoy life, view the beauty of the Rocky Mountains, the joy of gazing into the eyes of our beloved partner or children and let the miracle happen just as we prophesied.

This is because we will come across steep hills in our walk with him, which will reduce us to tears, despair, and we may even fill suicidal.

If we want to hear that voice from heaven saying, *Mr 9:7, And a cloud came and overshadowed them; and a voice came out of the cloud, saying, "This is **My beloved** Son. Hear Him!"*

To be God's shepherd comes at a price; blood, sweat and tears.

---- ----

Chapter 87 – Inspiration

*John 7:38, "He who believes in Me, as the Scripture has said, out of his heart will flow **rivers of** living water."*

People or beautiful locations can inspire us, but no one can teach us about the delights of self-discovery. They are springs of living water that flow from within us, encouraging us, giving us the strength to climb to impossible heights. They come from within us just as the desire to walk upright before the Lord.

There was no desire in Adam and Eve to walk upright before the Lord. The Lord God chose us because he saw the keenness in us to learn. Seventy times seven, we shall fail him, and he shall pick us up.

God saw the potential in us and handpicked us. We can fulfil our calling. God wants us to keep trying, and one day he will carry us over the hill if we lack the strength as long as we are willing.

I like to ask for a date, time, and particular things in public, before a crowd, so there is no mistaking the hand of God in all our lives. The primary reason for the display of God's power was to convince me that the things I saw in visions were genuine.

Secondly, to encourage me to seek more and continue pursuing the path of good works he had prepared. Each good deed had a lesson for me, to spiritually build and mature me, to make me fit for my inheritance.

Thirdly to bless others and demonstrate the Lord's presence among us.

***Matthew 8:3,** Then Jesus put out His hand and touched him, saying, "I am willing; be cleansed." Immediately his leprosy was cleansed. V4, And Jesus said to him, "See that you tell no one; but go your way, show yourself to the priest, and offer the gift that Moses commanded, as a testimony to them."*

Why tell no man?

I believe the previous night, the Heavenly Father had revealed to Jesus something meaningful that would happen the next day, like a confrontation with the **Pharisees** or meeting the woman at the well.

God, the father, would prepare him for the following day's meeting. What he should say and why. It meant a long night in prayer, reassuring Jesus that it was not his imagination but one of the good deeds prepared for him and confirming it the following day.

The same method he is using now on me.

None of us is perfect yet. There have been some very rare occasions when what I had prophesied did not transpire, like the grocer's son making a mistake, and God allowed it to happen for a reason. I have been embarrassed. I had to admit my error in public, and I had to go back to God to learn from it.

Failures like these have shaken my beliefs, my motives. I had to go into long prayers and with many tears, learn from failure.

Chapter 88 – City Gates

Revelation 21:10, And he carried me away in the Spirit to a great and high mountain, and showed me the great city, the holy Jerusalem, descending out of heaven from God.

The Lord said, 'Hari, remember the woman with the radiator. You taught her to fix the problem. You are going to learn to do miracles yourself. When you do that, your faith will be strong.'

I don't have the linguistic ability for this, but I will try. My words are not perfect and maybe challenging to follow. I can only apologise for my poor skill at expressing what follows. I pray the Holy Spirit will guide you on this journey with me.

First, let me share a vision I had from the Lord. It was a role model for me to follow.

We were in a house group at St James Church Muswell Hill, London. Someone had asked for a prayer for a woman who had been admitted to the hospital. People prayed for her. It was natural to ask the Lord to heal her, to make her better.

As I waited on the Lord, I felt the Lord speak to me. 'Watch, observe and learn.'

Vision

Before me opened up the vision of the future New Jerusalem, ***Revelation 21:1,*** *Then I saw a new heaven and a new earth, for the old heaven and the old earth had disappeared. And the sea was also gone.*

The Lord said, 'I want you to walk in the city. See if you can find her.'

I walked and searched for her but did not find her.

The Lord said, 'Go outside the city gates and search for her.'

Revelation 21:12, *The city wall was broad and high, with twelve gates guarded by twelve angels. And the names of the twelve tribes of Israel were written on the gates.*

I searched for her and found her outside the city. The Lord continued, 'Pray as I guide you.'

I prayed. My voice was tense; I was nervous, fearful of people's reaction. I was going to pray, and it was not going to comfort them. My words would sound mean and cruel.

I prayed, 'Lord, I lift her in prayer. She will be released from the hospital, but she will pass away very soon from an illness that has <u>nothing to do with her medical condition.</u>'

My voice was stressed as I obeyed the Lord. I don't blame people for feeling tense. I was tense. It's not the kind of thing people ask to be prayed for.

I hated doing things like this, but I knew the Lord had a purpose in showing me this vision to teach me about the city's entry requirements.

Revelation 22:14, Blessed are those who do His commandments, that they may have the right to the tree of life, and may <u>enter</u> through the gates into the city.

To confirm my vision, he would make sure my prayer would happen.

---- ☆----

Test. A few weeks later, it was announced in the church that the woman had passed away from a new illness.

Now I could place more trust in the vision I had. What was the lord trying to teach me?

Chapter 89 – Who are these people.

*Revelation 21:27, But there shall by no means enter it (holy Jerusalem in the new heaven) anything that defiles or causes an <u>abomination</u> or **a lie.***

Something the Lord taught me, 'creating wealth is acceptable but indulging in my own salvation, happiness, a bigger home and expensive holidays, while neglecting my neighbours' spiritual needs is an <u>abomination</u> to the Lord. (Moreover, I should say especially for a church ministers).

*Revelation 22:15, <u>Outside the city,</u> are the dogs — and all who love to live **a lie.***

We can lie subtly, keeping quit when we have the truth and use the cowards' way of remaining silent to hide the truth from others. We often use the other person's ignorance to our advantage. We say, 'I didn't lie. I kept quiet, his fault if he is ignorant of the facts.' That is deceitful, living <u>a lie.</u>

I gave an example when I was at school, and our teacher asked if we had understood his method. Many in the class remained silent because they were afraid to admit they hadn't understood. They were living a lie.

After the vision of the woman outside the city gates, I spent a couple of months trying to find the reason for it. This vision was about her after Judgment Day, and the old Earth has gone. We are now talking about the new Earth and Heaven.

Q 1. Revelation 22:15. Why does the Bible call people outside the city gates dogs and <u>liars</u>? Why was this Christian woman outside the city? Was she a habitual liar and deceitful? Is that what awaits such people?

Q 2. Who are the blessed ones who can walk through the city gates? What are their qualities?

Q 3. Will I be one of the saints that will return with Christ? What preparations have I undergone to prepare for this task?

Q 4. Where will I be? In or outside the city of God?

I put these questions to church leaders to inspire them to seek the truth so that they may be a blessing to their church.

Q 1. What role has God called you for in his eternal city? How is the Holy Spirit preparing you for this role so that you can account for every atom, leaf, a person in your Patch? (To get the gist of it, because I/we just do not have enough time on Earth to fully grasp this).

Q 2. He prepared good works for you to walk in before the foundations of the world were laid. Make a list of good works that you have walked in?

Q 3. On the Day of Judgment, will your works achieve gold or silver standard or burn to ashes as wood and straw?

Q 4. Has God carried out regular mock tests of your works? Have the mock tests strengthened you? *Psalms 139:23, Search me, O God, and know my heart; Try me, and know my anxieties;*

New Jerusalem

Over the next few years, I saw more visions of the city and inquired about people's qualities in the city and those outside. I searched the Word of God, asked the Lord to breathe over relevant verses in the bible to put life into them, and reveal the mystery that St Paul talks about, now revealed to the saints.

Mark 4:11, And he said to them, "To you has been given the secret of the kingdom of God, but for those outside, (the city gates) *everything comes in parables;"*

Ephesians 1:9, he has made known to us the mystery of his will, according to his good pleasure that he outlined in Christ,

Colossians 1:26, the mystery hidden throughout the ages and generations has now been revealed to his saints.

I walked among the people outside the city gates, many claiming to have been born again Christians. They asked me many times, 'Why did you not warn us? We sold our birthright because you did not warn us.'

My answer has always been, 'You should have read the story Jesus quoted about the rich man and Lazarus.'

Luke 16:30. *The rich man replied, 'No, Father Abraham! But if someone is sent to them from the dead, then they will repent of their sins and turn to God.' 31 But Abraham said, 'If they won't listen to Moses and the prophets, they won't listen even if someone rises from the dead.'*

---- ----

Chapter 90 – Wait Upon the Lord for Specific Direction

Level 1 of Jacob's 2nd Ladder.

Matthew 6; 8, "Therefore do not be like them. For your Father knows the things you have need of before you ask Him."

In my early days in our house group, in a prayer meeting, people would pray, and that was the end of the matter. I would wait upon the Lord.

What is the scripture encouraging us to do? To wait upon God. I would <u>wait</u> upon him during the week, and far away, someone would be praying. In response to their prayers, he would give me an insight into the matter or date and hour for healing or answered prayer.

Because I gave our Lord the time to prepare me during the week, when I am in a house group, I let people know that rather than pray, I will thank the Lord and let them know how and when he will answer a prayer request.

Ephesians 1; 4, just as He <u>chose us</u> in Him before the foundation of the world.

It translated to me as, 'I chose you. When you pray, you will ask me for a specific day and hour for the prayer to be answered, so that they shall know I am in the midst of them.' *Matthew 18; 20, 'For where two or three are gathered in my name, I am there among them.'*

But the primary reason would be to trust the vision he had given me earlier. *John 14; 29, And now I have told you this <u>before it occurs</u>, so that when it does happen, you may believe.*

Note, <u>you</u> will believe, not the world.

I have followed these rules. I pray or state a specific thing that others can test, like a day and hour. The primary reason is the confirmation of the vision received earlier and the lesson that goes with it.

Romans 8; 14, For all who are led by the Spirit of God are children of God.

1 Corinthians 2: 4, My speech and my proclamation were not with plausible words of wisdom but with a demonstration of the <u>Spirit and of power</u>.

In my early days, it was easy. He would give me the date, time, and hour of healing, i.e. 'Tuesday 14th February 10 AM, the hospital will ring to say the cancer results are all clear. There is no sign of cancer.' And it would happen. [**Appendix 5: Silvia and Colin**]

Level 2 of Jacob's Ladder.

Then it got more complicated. His message was clear. A word of knowledge was for God's prophets. *Luke 7:28, I tell you, among those born of women no one is greater than John; yet the least in the kingdom of God is greater than he."*

Lord, 'Your calling is much more demanding than that of the prophets. Remember the story about the grocer's son.'

Ephesians 1; 3, Blessed be the God and Father of our Lord Jesus Christ, who has blessed us in Christ with <u>every spiritual blessing</u> in the heavenly places.

'Exercise that blessing.'

As time passed, spiritual warfare became harder. As I contemplated the healing of a fellow Christian, his message was clear to me.

Ephesians 6; 11, put on in the whole Armour of Christ.

Ephesians 6: 17, And take the helmet of salvation....., and the sword of the Spirit, which is the word of God.

Revelation 22: 2, -the tree of healing. (Use it; you are lifted in heavenly places with Christ).

I knelt. 'Holy Spirit, please lift me on the cross with Christ.'

Romans 6:6, We know that our old self was crucified with him.

I continued in prayer, 'I put my thoughts, deeds, and unrighteousness on the cross. I wait for the Holy Spirit to convict me of any sin. If he does, I acknowledge and confess it.

I am dead to the world, self, and foe, and alive unto the Lord. I plead for the blood of Christ to cleanse me of all unrighteousness. Holy Spirit, please lift me, in the heavenly places in Christ.'

Galatians 2:20, *"I have been crucified with Christ; it is no longer I who live, but Christ lives in me, and the life I now live in the flesh I live by faith in the Son of God, who loved me and gave Himself for me.*

Ephesians 2:6, *and raised us up together and made us sit together in the heavenly places in Christ Jesus.*

Ephesians 3:10, to the intent that now the manifold wisdom of God might be made known by the church to the principalities and powers in the heavenly places.

I am in the heavenly realms. If this is just in my head as an illusion, nothing will happen. If I come back with a firm date and time for specific prayer, and it happens, then I have credibility in the heavenly realms and on earth.

As I kneel before the throne of God, an incredible warm blanket encompasses me. That glow of warmth, assurance permeates through my being. I feel creation was built just for my perfection, so overwhelming is the love from the heavenly cloud that surrounds me.

It is something we all are meant to experience.

Ephesians 3:19, to know the <u>love of Christ</u> which passes knowledge; that you may be <u>filled with all the fullness</u> of God.

---- ☆----

What does it mean to be filled with all the fullness of God?

To me, it means the ability to account for every leaf, every person in our parish and a lot more. That comes from personal experience. That is just the starting point.

Hebrews 11:6, But <u>without faith,</u> it is impossible to please Him, for he who comes to God must believe that He exists and that He is a rewarder of those who diligently seek Him.

Chapter 91 – And the heavenly cloud of witnesses are watching.

Hebrews 12:1, Wherefore seeing we are also compassed about with so great a cloud of witnesses, let us lay aside every weight and the sin that does so easily beset us. Let us run with patience the race that is set before us.

I am in the spirit, in the heavenly place. And the heavenly cloud of witnesses is watching.

I wait for the Holy Spirit to lead me. I need to walk up to the tree of healing. But before I do that, I have certain obstacles to overcome. First, is this one of the good works that God had prepared for me? I need to find out. If it is, then he has some lessons for me to learn. What are they?

He wants me to grasp that I was there, hidden in Christ before the foundation of the Earth was laid. He prepared good works for me. It was time to learn about this period, my position in his plans.

Proverbs 8:22, *"The LORD possessed me at the <u>beginning of His way,</u> Before His works of old.*

V23, I have been established from everlasting, <u>from the beginning</u>, before there was ever an earth.

V24, When there were no depths, I was brought forth, when no fountains were abounding with water.

V25, Before the mountains were settled, before the hills, I was brought forth;

V26, While yet He had not made the earth or the fields, or the primaeval dust of the world.

V27, When He prepared <u>the heavens, I was there</u>, When He drew a circle on the face of the deep,

V28, When He established the clouds above, When He strengthened the fountains of the deep,

V29, When He assigned to the sea its limit, So that the waters would not transgress His command, When He marked out the foundations of the earth,

V30, Then I was beside Him as a master craftsman; And I was daily His delight, Rejoicing always before Him,

The Holy Spirit breathes over them, and they come to life. Daily I stand before the throne of God. I wait upon him and learn how to claim the power and glory given to us. A process that takes many months of learning. (Unless the Holy Spirit breaths on it, nothing will happen.)

Healing. Make it happen! The First Time.

I put on the whole armour of Christ.

Ephesians 6:11, *Put on the whole armour of God so that you may be able to stand against the wiles of the devil.*

In the past, I had been opposed by spiritual foes. I had stood my ground quoting: ***1 John 4,*** *for the one who is in you is greater than the one who is in the world.*

The Lord said, 'Walk up to the tree of healing, take the leaves and its fruits, and take them to the person in need.' I had grasped the concept, which many will struggle to understand; in God, the past, present and future are **one**[1]**.**

Hebrews 4:4, *For in one place it speaks about the seventh day as follows, "And God rested on the seventh day from all his works." **Hebrews 4:3** For we who have believed enter that rest, just as God has said, "As in my anger I swore, 'They shall not enter my rest,'" though his works were finished at the foundation of the world.*

The only way to grasp this is to let the Lord make you walk there and unleash its power.

Galatians 5:25, *learn to walk in the spirit.*

--- ☆---

[1] *God created time. He is outside as well as inside time. And so can we in the spirit.*

Chapter 92 – Someone has to pay the bill.

As I walked up to the tree of healing, the Lord called out, 'Hari, in Haringey, I taught you to account for every atom, every tree and person. There is a bill to pay for this fruit from the tree of healing. Someone has to pay the bill.'

I looked at him. I sat down. 'Lord, I am tired; my spirit is tired. This course is getting harder and harder. I don't think I can go on any further.'

A great sense of depression and defeat engulfed me. I buried my head in my lap. 'I am tired. I am exhausted. I don't think anyone has ever walked as far as I have.'

He came and sat beside me. For a long time, neither of us said a word.

Finally, he spoke. 'Your journey has just started. Take the leaves and their fruit. He/she will be healed on the date and time you chose, I will pick up the tab/bill, but you will have to pick up the tab in the future. You are my younger brother. You have to learn your trade, i.e., do the things I did.'

(I don't know if this makes sense to you. The gist of all this is that we give a tenth of what we earn to the Lord for his kingdom on Earth. In the spiritual home, in his father's house, as priestly people, we keep a tenth of what we earn and give the rest towards building the Kingdom, his people.)

For Silvia's healing to take place, it took me two weeks of intercession and learning the art of spiritual warfare before I could reach the tree of healing. Once I was there, I was confident of victory. During this time, I had lost a stone in weight. The time, the commitment, and the struggle to make the healing happen while employed in full-time secular employment are challenging and doesn't leave much time for other activities or much sleep.

I managed it with God's help to see her blessed, my contribution to the tab and in the process; I lost a couple of night's sleep and a stone in weight.

The lesson was clear; we are spiritual warriors learning spiritual warfare by following in Christ's steps.

Ephesians 2;10, *For we are His workmanship, created in Christ Jesus for good works, which God prepared beforehand that we should walk in them.*

He wanted us to learn to account, take responsibility, to make miracles happen, just as Jesus had made them happen on Earth. To make this happen, someone has to put in time and effort until victory. Such victories reflect our genuine love for Christ.

John 14; 12, *Very truly, I tell you, the one who believes in me will also do the works that I do and, in fact, will do greater works than these because I am going to the Father.*

Jesus expects us to exceed him. It is his will. It needs commitment, an iron will, and determination and the whole heavenly crowd is watching. Who will rise to take this challenge and glorify Christ and the father? Whoever loves him enough to take this challenge, let him step forward.

Matthew 22:14, *'For many are called, but few are chosen.'*

Level 3 of Jacob's Ladder

I am sure many people sought Jesus for healing, and he would have felt compassion for them. There were times he would have walked away because they were not part of his father's good works for that day.

His indwelling spirit clearly showed me that it would cost me time and suffering to be made perfect. If it was hard for Jesus to make miracles happen, it would become harder for me. There were hard lessons ahead of me, and there was a reason for this.

Philippians **2:12,** *'wherefore, my beloved, - work out your salvation with fear and trembling.'*

I spent long hours waiting upon the Lord to understand what 'work out your salvation with fear and trembling' meant and what level of commitment was required. ---- 🌼---

Chapter 93 – Bringing every thought into captivity to the obedience of Christ

Level 4 of Jacob's Ladder

2 Corinthians 10:5, bringing every thought into captivity to the obedience of Christ.

It's challenging to learn to bring every thought in subjection to the Lord, but it is possible.

My mind has a habit of wandering during the day. As I walked to work or did my job, every glance, every thought was monitored by the Holy Spirit. Was that an appropriate way to think, look at a woman, or talk to my colleagues? Was my attitude to work up to the high standard God required? Was I right to lose my temper at the rude man on the train?

He taught me to begin each morning with a prayer. If I felt guilty about any stray thought, I should lay it on the cross. In his own time, the Holy Spirit would give me the strength to overcome it. It was pointless to try to overcome it in my power. I was not to be embarrassed about any thoughts or deeds. The Holy Spirit knew me, understood me better than I did.

Each prayer session was a fresh start. To bring my thoughts before him and account for them, and to plan for the day ahead. To make sure there was spare time (emergency time) between plans. Things didn't need to be rushed. If I hurried, I made mistakes and learnt little. Mistakes can cost more time and resources to put right.

Then, in the evening, I would go over my thoughts and deeds for the day with the Lord. Why did I lose my temper on the train? What was a better way to have dealt with the rude man? What kind of conduct would please the Lord?

What does the scripture say about our conduct?

Galatians 5:22, but the fruit of the Spirit is love, joy, peace, longsuffering, gentleness, goodness, faith.

How should I have responded to the rude man in light of the scriptures? 'Teach me, O Lord, your way.'

The Holy Spirit would pick specific incidents during the day and from scriptures, show me my errors. He would show me the right way to respond. *Psalms 5:8, Lead me, O LORD, in Your righteousness because of my enemies; Make Your way straight before my face.*

He would point out the harm caused to others by my errors and how to compensate them.

Luke 19:8, if I have taken anything from any man by false accusation, I restore him fourfold.

This is what the Lord was after, transforming me, changing my thinking.

Ezekiel 36:26, a new heart also will I give you and a new spirit will I put within you.

Romans 12:2, And do not be conformed to this world, but be transformed by the renewing of your mind, that you may prove what is that good and acceptable and perfect will of God.

Jesus spent long hours in prayer, <u>learning obedience and being perfected,</u> and he wanted me to follow his example.

Hebrews 5:8-9, though He was a Son, yet He learned obedience by the things which He suffered. And having been <u>perfected</u>, He became the author of eternal salvation to all who obey Him,

(Luke 6:12) It was a compulsory requirement for the Kingdom of God. If I wasn't prepared to do it, my birthright as **firstborn**[1] in Christ would go to someone else. I would have a secure place in heaven, but as the second born in a family, one not entitled to receive his entire inheritance.

My mind had to be focused, disciplined, governed by the written Word,

---- ☆----

[1] *Hebrews 12:23, to the general assembly and church of the **firstborn** who are registered in heaven, to God the Judge of all, to the spirits of just men made perfect. ...x...x...*

made alive by the indwelling Holy Spirit. A mind of Christ. Once I had that, the Lord could start to do great things.

The hard part was the daily discipline to bring every thought in subjection to Christ. With lots of practice, it became easier.

Chapter 94 – Barriers of time

Then he began to teach me how to cross the barriers of time, an item he had created. For in God, there is no past, present or future; they are all one. I have grasped this concept. You can only learn this if you have walked in it, like my parable earlier of the woman fixing her radiator.

I ask the Holy Spirit to take me to the period before the foundations were laid. *Ephesians 1:4, just as He chose us in Him before the foundation of the world, that we should be holy and without blame before Him in love.*

I need to open the eternal scrolls. I need to read about my role that is written here. *1 Corinthians 1:30, But of Him you are in Christ Jesus, who became for us wisdom from God — and righteousness and sanctification and redemption.*

Ephesians 2:10, for we are his workmanship, created in Christ Jesus to good works, which God hath before ordained that we should walk in them.

Ephesians 3:11, According to the eternal purpose, which he purposed in Christ Jesus our Lord:

Psalms 40:7, Then said I (Word + Christ + us, hidden in Christ), "Behold, I come; In the scroll of the book, it is written of me. V 8 I delight to do Your will, O my God, And Your law is within my heart."

John 1:10, He (Christ + us) was in the world, and the world was made through Him + us. (I/We are participating with Christ in making this world and the restoration and reconciliation process through Christ).

Christ knew about his past before the foundations of the earth were laid, so can we. We have the mind of Christ. This gift is available to those who meet its requirements.

Again, I have grasped the above. I opened the scrolls and read about the good works ordained for me. Why were these good works chosen for me? I will soon find out.

I have part of my answer. I head into the present, then into the future, where the tree of healing is.

Revelation 22:2, In the middle of its street, and on either side of the river, was the tree of life, which bore twelve fruits, each tree yielding its fruit every month. The leaves of the tree were for the healing of the nations.

I wait under the tree for three days. The tree has not yielded her fruit. I hear a noise and turn to see the Lord. I kneel.

The Lord says, 'To bring about healing is not easy.'

'I am so close, Lord, maybe one or two more days, and the tree will yield her fruit.'

'Then what?'

'I will take the leaves to the person in need.'

'Before you do that, you need to seek the guidance of the Holy Spirit.'

Isaiah 55:11, so shall my word be that goes out from my mouth; it shall not return to me empty, but it shall accomplish that which I purpose, and succeed in the thing for which I sent it.

I grasp the concept. However, I struggle to explain it. I don't have the right words. I will try it. If God sends his Word, it has a purpose, and on the Day of Judgment, it must have borne his desired fruit. Not any fruit but what it was meant to achieve. Therefore, we need to have a good understanding of the requirements of Judgment Day.

Our Lord has given us the authority within the above guideline to send a Word out in his name with power. In the name of Jesus, we ask. We need to show what fruit we want, a method to implement it, and take responsibility for it until Judgment Day. And prove to him that we have the determination and the will to meet his requirements.

Hence, the reason every 7th month, 7th year, I bring before God every prayer, house group, scripture verse quoted by me, and to uphold it before God until the Judgment day. It is a huge task and a big commitment.

The Holy Spirit said, 'I know you will nurture this healing and its impact on the person until the day of the Lord. But would the recovery have brought about the required fruit on the Day of Judgment? Would this act of charity have benefited the person when seen from the Day of Judgment?

Only the sons of God, the **first-born** in Christ, filled with the Holy Spirit, can answer this.'

1 Corinthians 15:23, But every man in his own order: Christ the firstfruits; afterwards they that are Christ's at his coming.

2 Thessalonians 2:13, God from the beginning chose you for salvation through sanctification by the Spirit and belief in the truth.

The Lord said, 'Let us try. Close your eyes. Let the Holy Spirit lead you. The person is healed. Their life flashes before you up to Judgment Day. What do you see?'

I replied, 'I see the healing made the person feel she was exceptionally blessed, favoured. It made her arrogant and careless.'

'What do you learn?'

'Before I administer the healing leaves, I should make it clear that the healing will be an act of grace from you. An act of charity, nothing to do with her merits.'

'You tell her that, now witness her life flash before you until the end. What do you see?'

'That didn't work. Let's try again,' I plead.

---- ☆----

Babies in Christ suck milk and leave it to the Lord to carry the tab. Mature warriors make it happen.

1 Corinthians 3:2, I fed you with milk and not with solid food; for until now you could not receive it, and even now you are still not able.

Hebrews 5:13, For everyone who partakes only of **milk,** is unskilled in the word of righteousness, for he is a babe. ---- 🐾---

Chapter 95 – Full stature of Christ

Ephesians 4:13, until all of us come to the unity of the faith and of the knowledge of the Son of God, to maturity, to the measure of the <u>full</u> <u>stature</u> of Christ.

I spent three days repeatedly going over different scenarios. I was exhausted. I said before; it gets more challenging as we progress. Another reason I am now reluctant to take the spiritual tab for another.

Finally, the Lord said, 'Go, she will be healed on the day and hour you state. When that happens, you will know what has transpired was not your imagination. It will take you many months to fully grasp what you have seen.'

Why is it more demanding as we progress?

[Lesson. We have the mind of Christ, but it's another thing to acquire the skills to use it according to God's purpose.]

John 14:12, *Very truly, I tell you, the one who believes in me will also do the works that I do and, in fact, <u>will do greater works </u>than these because I am going to the Father.*

Why does he want me to learn this? Why does he want to make it a reality in my life?

2 Corinthians 4:18, *while we do not look at the things which are seen, but at the things which are not seen. For the things which are seen are temporary, but the <u>things which are not seen</u> are eternal.*

Someone with a terrific imagination can have such thoughts. How does one prove the existence of <u>things, which are not seen</u>?

To test its reality, stand before a church meeting and state how the prayer will be answered. If it happens, not once but often, they have some measure of spiritual truth in their remarkable life.

Level 5

In prayer, account for every grain of sand, leaf, tree, animal and person in your 'patch'. Why?

1 Thessalonians 3:13, *so that He may establish your hearts blameless in holiness before our God and Father at the coming of our Lord Jesus Christ <u>with all His saints</u>.*

Matthew 24:30, *Then the sign of the Son of Man will appear in heaven, and then all the tribes of the earth will mourn, and they will see the Son of Man coming on the clouds of heaven with power and great glory.*

Matthew 25:31, *When the Son of Man comes in His glory, and all the holy angels with Him, then He will sit on the throne of His glory.*

Revelation 20:4, *and they lived <u>and reigned with Christ</u> a thousand years.*

When he reigns, he will <u>need perfected saints</u> filled with the power of the Holy Spirit, able to do the above.

It is possible; it requires a trained, forceful, disciplined mind. A mature spiritual mind like that of Christ: and we have that mind of Christ.

1 Corinthians 2:16, *For "who has known the mind of the LORD that he may instruct Him?" But we have the <u>mind of Christ.</u>*

---- ---

Chapter 96– Use God's creative power

Level 6

Again, I have a linguistic problem here. I have grasped this concept, but I cannot convey it. What follows is written in a simple, almost childlike way. It's the best I can do.

We should be in the **holiest of holy**[1] in the **temple**[2], with Christ. From here, we can use God's creative power as a responsible and accountable being, one who can pay the tab for the abilities he uses, according to God's **eternal plan**[3].

That's what Jesus wants us to experience, this spiritual reality for our faith to grow.

John 17:24, Father, I want these whom you have given me to be with me where I am (in the heavenly temple). Then they can see all the glory you gave me because you loved me even before the world began!

This is not something for the future. It should be our current position. I walked there and read the names of those who had come before me and will come after me.

Ephesians 3:11, This was in accordance with the eternal purpose that he has carried out in Christ Jesus our Lord.

--- ☆---

[1-2] *Hebrews 10:19, Therefore, brethren, having boldness to enter the Holiest by the blood of Jesus,*

[2] *2 Timothy 1:9, who has saved us and called us with a holy calling, not according to our works, but according to His purpose and grace which was given to us in Christ Jesus before time began,*

[3] *Ephesians 3:11, according to the eternal purpose which He accomplished in Christ Jesus our Lord,*

 ---- 🦁----

Chapter 97 – The result should fulfil God's eternal purpose.

We need to understand his plans and have a good idea of the good works he had ordained for us. Otherwise, we are just wasting time pursuing the wrong goals, just as Adam and Eve chose to follow their own dreams. We are building the kingdom of God with our own hands, ideas, and plans, i.e. our strength.

As far as God is concerned, his work was completed from the beginning. He has chosen us to tidy up the loose bits for our spiritual growth, for the perfection of our salvation. To make us feel we were part of building his kingdom, participating in its formation and having a sense of belonging in our eternal home.

Luke 10:9, "And heal the sick there, and say to them, 'The kingdom of God has come near to you.'

Genesis 2:2, and on the seventh day, God finished his work which he had made, and he rested on the seventh day from all his work which he had made.

Hebrews 4:3 For we who have believed do enter that rest, as He has said: "So I swore in My wrath, 'They shall not enter My rest,'" although the works were finished from the foundation of the world.

John 17:9, I pray for them. I do not pray for the world but for those you have given Me, for they are Yours.

John 17:2, as You have given Him authority over all flesh, that He should give eternal life to as many as You have given Him.

Acts 13:48, and as many as had been destined for eternal life became believers.

John 17:16, They are not of the world, just as I am not of the world.

John 17:18, As You sent Me into the world, I also have sent them into the world.

Lastly, everyone has a moral duty to promote the whole universe's welfare, interest, and happiness. We see this principle written in two Holy books. God says all testimony has to be confirmed *(Matthew 18:16) 'by the mouth of two or three witnesses every word may be established.'*

First testimony Bible *John 3:16,* "For <u>God so loved</u> the world that He gave His only begotten Son, that whoever believes in Him should not perish but have everlasting life. (his son who gave his life to promote the universe's welfare, interest, and happiness).

Second testimony, ***Bhagavad-Gita 3:10****,* The Supreme Lord of creation continued: At the beginning of creation, I blessed creation and set in motion the principle of selfless service to promote the welfare, interest, and happiness of all creation. By this selfless service, all creation would be prosperous, fruitful and find fulfilment for its desires.

This moral law should reach out to the universe. It cannot be enforced. It has to come from within a person, and that is his spirituality. This is the new heart, a new spirit he has given us. Either we have it, or we don't.

We have the ability to convert thoughts into energy, into matter /antimatter, Sub-atomic particles, atoms, and life. We have the mind of Christ. We have the power of resurrection. With this mindset comes the moral obligation to be answerable to the least and the greatest. Such power is given to those who can fulfil the above requirement.

Right now, some of Christ's people are **being trained**[1] to use this power/ability. That is the gift of God open to us in Christ. It is for us to prove we **merit it**[2]. No other religion offers this gift.

When one has reached this level on Jacob's ladder, there awaits the right hand of fellowship from the 24 Elders and our Lord. *Revelation 19:4 and the <u>four and twenty elders</u> and the four beasts fell down and worshipped God that sat on the throne, saying, Amen; Alleluia.*

---- ☆----

[1] *Ephesians 4:13, till we all come to the unity of the faith and of the knowledge of the Son of God, to a perfect man, to the <u>measure of the stature</u> of the fullness of Christ.*

[2] *Matthew 7:6, "Do not give what is holy to dogs, and do not throw your pearls before swine, or they will <u>trample</u> them underfoot and turn and maul you.*

..x..x..

Matthew 25:34, Then will the King say to them on his right hand, Come, ye blessed of my Father, <u>inherit the kingdom</u> prepared for you from the foundation of the world:

Level 6 b.

To have access to the inner mind of God. *Job 38:4, Where were you when I laid the foundations of the earth? Declare, if <u>you have understanding</u>.*

(The Bible states some of us were there in God's plan; that is, if we have spiritual understanding.)

We get some glimpses from verses like: *John 17:24, for You loved Me (WORD + Jesus + us in Jesus)) before the foundation of the world.*

*1 John 5:7, For there are three that bear record in Heaven, the Father, the Word, (Word + Jesus + **us in Jesus**[1]) and the Holy Spirit: and these three are one. (Is he referring to Jesus only or us as well?)*

1 Corinthians 6:17, But he who is <u>joined to the Lord</u> is one spirit with Him.

1 Corinthians 2:16, For "who has known the mind of the LORD that he may instruct Him?" But we have the <u>mind of Christ</u>.

Ephesians 1:4, even as he chose <u>us</u> (Word + Jesus + us) in him before the foundation of the world.

To whom does <u>us</u> refer?

I do not expect people to agree to any of my concepts. That is their freedom.

With all my imperfections, God has chosen to overlook them in the process to transform me. He does not judge me nor honour me by my/our level of

---- ☆----

Revelation 4:4, Around the throne are twenty-four thrones, and seated on the thrones are **twenty-four elders**, dressed in white robes, with golden crowns on their heads.

Revelation 19:4, and the <u>four and twenty elders</u> and the four beasts fell down and worshipped God that sat on the throne, saying, Amen; Alleluia.

..x..x..

331

knowledge, but what kind of person I am. I/we matter more to him than what I/we will ever achieve.

It is the quality of a relationship that matters to him and me.

---- ☆----

Revelation 4:4, Around the throne are twenty-four thrones, and seated on the thrones are **twenty-four elders,** dressed in white robes, with golden crowns on their heads.

Interestingly in Bhagavad-Gita, this was compiled before the New Testament in 3rd BC

*Chapter 10:6. The Supreme Lord passed unto Brahman **(WORD of God)** the breath of life. From Brahman came the seven great sages. Four other great sages, Sanka, Sananda, Santana and Sanat-kumara, and fourteen Manus, were manifested before them. Together they form **twenty-five Elders** of the Universe.*

I wonder if they are including Christ as one of the Elders!

---- ----

Chapter 98 – He chose us

1 Corinthians 6:17, But he who is joined to the Lord is one spirit with Him.

Ephesians 1:4, even as he chose <u>us</u> in him (Jesus + us) before the foundation of the world.

Ephesians 1:11, In Him also we have obtained an inheritance, being <u>predestined</u> according to the purpose of Him who works all things according to the counsel of His will,

You and me. Isn't it amazing that God chose us from the beginning? And if he chose us, he will finish the work he set out to do provided we do our part.

Hebrews 1:10, You, LORD, in the beginning, laid the foundation of the earth, and the heavens are the work of Your hands.

Hebrews 4:3, although the works were finished from the foundation of the world.

Ask yourself, what works is he talking about? Why does God say they were finished?

Jesus finished the work set before him on Earth, and so did St Paul.

<u>Jesus in</u> *John 17:4,* 'I have glorified You on the earth. I have <u>finished the work</u> which You have given Me to do.'

<u>St Paul in</u> *2 Timothy 4:7,* 'I have fought a good fight, I have <u>finished my course</u>, I have kept the faith.'

When my time is up, in a few years, I will be able to say, 'I have finished my course, I have kept the faith.'

--- ☆---

There are some people whose names were not written in the book of life. Why?

Revelation 13:8, And all that dwell upon the earth shall worship him, whose names <u>are not written</u> in the book of life of the Lamb slain from the foundation of the world.

Revelation 17:8, they whose name <u>hath not been written</u> in the book of life <u>from the foundation of the world</u>,

Why are some excluded from the beginning? Is it to do with God's **foreknowledge[1]?**

*Romans 8:29, For whom He <u>**foreknew**</u>, He also **predestined** to be conformed to the image of His Son, that He might be the firstborn among many brethren.*

Questions that I struggle with. Who and why were some chosen before anything came into existence? Why were some people excluded before they were born or walked on this Earth?

And some are given preferential treatment. Is it fair?

For me, it was a struggle. The gist of it was that God the father called all of us. He foreknew the vast majority of humanity would follow the path Adam and Eve chose. Therefore, he decided not to purify them, to put their names in his book.

Perhaps, he foreknew that most would drop out of the race set before them on encountering difficulties. They would take the more comfortable option, to be just citizens of his kingdom, i.e., like Esau, when the race/life got difficult, sell their birthright to the likes of Jacob.

In Heb 11:20, By faith, Isaac blessed Jacob and Esau concerning things to come. (Jewish exegesis thinks Jacob has precedence because God foresees Esau's negligence.)

Hebrews 12:17, For you know that afterwards when Esau wanted to <u>inherit</u> the blessing, he was rejected, for he found no place for repentance, though he sought it diligently with tears.

---- ☆----

[1] *Romans 11:2, God has not cast away His people (Likes of Esau) whom He foreknew.*

[1] *Romans 8:30, Moreover whom He predestined, these He also called; whom He called, these He also justified; and whom He justified, these He also glorified.*

..x..x..

God does not cast the likes of Esau away. We read about them in the New Heaven living outside the Holy City. It is not a pleasant description.

Revelation 22:15, But outside are dogs and -- whoever loves and practices a lie.

Many things do not make sense to me. I have many questions for God awaiting answers. However, I know what God called me for, both in this life and the hereafter. And most of the good works he had devised for me were meant to prepare me for the afterlife, that more permanent home, prepared for my family and me.

For example, delivering my testimony and the gospel message to every home in my Patch may not have produced much fruit. Still, it certainly prepared me for the hereafter to qualify on the Judgment day to stand beside the Lord.

To be an eternal priest in his tabernacle.

Psalms 2:8, Ask of Me, and I will give You The nations for Your inheritance, And the ends of the earth for Your possession.

What a beautiful gift of God.

Chapter 99 – There Are Two Kinds of People in God's Kingdom

Those who have been purified and perfected live within the city gates (Revelation 21), and the unpurified ones live outside the city gates. We make our own choices to accept the invitation to dwell in New Jerusalem or outside the city.

Matthew 22:1-13, Parable of marriage feast for the king's son.

22:2, The kingdom of Heaven is likened unto a certain king, who made a marriage feast for His son.

Matthew 22:12, "So he said to him, 'Friend, how did you come in here without a wedding garment?' And he was speechless. v13 "Then the king said to the servants, 'Bind him hand and foot, take him away, and cast him into outer darkness; there will be weeping and gnashing of teeth.'

Alternatively, the Parable of ten virgins.

Matthew 25:1, Then shall the kingdom of Heaven be likened unto ten virgins, who took their lamps and went forth to meet the bridegroom.

Matthew 25:10, And while they went away to buy, the bridegroom came; and they that were ready went in with him (Into the City) to the marriage feast: and the door was shut. V11, Afterward came also the other virgins, saying, Lord, Lord, open to us. V12 But he answered and said, Verily I say unto you, I know you not.

I despair. Why is it that many church leaders, deeply steeped in bible knowledge, cannot ask the father in Jesus' name, things that non-Christians can verify?

John 15:16, "You did not choose Me, but I chose you and appointed you that you should go and bear fruit and that your fruit should remain, that whatever you ask the Father in My name He may give you.

What is the fruit that will on Judgment day pass the test of fire and endure eternity?

I plead with you to step out in faith. The Lord needs courageous, dedicated people to build his kingdom. If necessary, spend all night in prayer until the

WORD of God that dwells in you returns, fulfilling what these words were sent out for. That is eternal life.

1 Timothy 6:12, *Fight the good fight of faith, lay hold on <u>eternal life,</u> to which you were also called and have confessed the good confession in the presence of many witnesses.*

Chapter 100– House Group Leader

Many years ago, one evening, after I had led a house group, I sat down and read Ezekiel 34. The Holy Spirit convinced me of my poor spiritual state. I realized I didn't meet the scriptures' requirements and wasn't fit to be a group leader.

That Sunday, the sermon was on Ezekiel 34; I knew the Lord was speaking to me. I gave up leadership and asked the Holy Spirit to teach me to fulfil the scriptures' requirement. I put all my heart, mind, and strength into learning his ways and gave him whatever time and attention he required.

Ezekiel 34:1-4, And the word of the LORD came to me, saying,

V2, Son of man, prophesy against the shepherds of Israel (<u>my interpretation</u> England and Canada), prophesy and say to them, 'Thus says the Lord GOD to the shepherds: "Woe to the shepherds of Israel (England and Canada), who feed themselves! Should not the shepherds feed the flocks?

V3, You eat the fat and clothe yourselves with the wool; you slaughter the fatlings, but you do not feed the flock.

V4, The <u>weak</u> you have <u>not strengthened</u>, nor have you <u>healed</u> those who were sick, nor <u>bound up</u> the broken, nor <u>brought back</u> what was driven away, <u>nor sought</u> what was lost.

(He called you once, and now he is calling you to learn to walk in a spirit-led way. This rebuke is given in love to England and Canada's shepherds because God has a plan to raise these two nations to Great heights. These two nations are incredibly blessed.)

Two of England's greatest gifts to the world were the King James Bible and the English language.

Canada is the future of God's people. Together, these two countries will continue to punch way above their weight if a remnant of his people continues to walk upright before God.

That spiritual task falls in your lap. God bless you.

Chapter 101- God' Soldier

Parachute Regiment, Territorial Army.

Being in the Army helped me get a good grasp of **Romans 8:28,** *And we know that all things work together for good to those who love God, to those who are called according to His purpose.*

I was a volunteer in the Territorial Army in parachute regiment from 1974-76. To gain the regimental beret, we had to pass specific tests. One of the hardest was the assault course. Every obstacle was well chosen, deliberately crafted with risk and some unknown challenges. These unpredictable risks helped to make our training realistic and kept us on our guard. Ignore these risks, and we could get badly hurt. I am glad I passed the training to gain my beret.

Later, we trained to use weapons, anti-tank missiles, machine guns, hand-to-hand combat, and house-to-house combat. Evasive measures from Ariel attacks. Use of protective gear to protect us from biological and chemical attack. All good works pre-ordained and pre-destined for another life at the front. Most of it would be of no help in my current civilian life.

Similarly, God chose the good **works**[1], our assault course on Earth, for each of us. To train us, to make us fit for his eternal **purposes**[2] in the afterlife.

---- ☆----

[1] *Ephesians 2:10, For we are His workmanship, created in Christ Jesus for good works, which God prepared beforehand that we should walk in them.*

[1] *Ephesians 1:4, just as He chose us in Him before the foundation of the world, that we should be holy and without blame before Him in love,*

[2] *Romans 9:11, (For the children being not yet born, neither having done any good or evil, that the purpose of God according to election might stand, not of works, but of him that called;)*

...x..x...

Chapter 102- God' Calling

Ephesians 1:11, In Christ, we have also obtained an inheritance, having been destined according to the purpose of him who accomplishes all things according to his counsel and will.

From the earliest days of my Christian journey, God made clear what my calling was. Not to be a great evangelist or preacher but to follow him into the holiest place in the Universe. *Hebrews 9:3, and behind the second veil, the tabernacle is called the <u>Holiest</u> of All.* Just as at the age of four, on my first day for school, my father walked with me to school, at the gate, leaned down, and said, 'I want you to be a doctor one day.'

Buddha taught, "The mind is everything. What you think, you become," People's perspectives may differ from mine. I respect that.

Army. Some obstacles during my training were just awful. If one fell 30 feet from a narrow plank, a test designed to help one overcome the fear of heights, one could suffer serious injury. Many soldiers called such obstacles evil. Our trainers installed these evil things. Now, if I fell and died, the army would have to make compensation to my family.

Similarly, my view is that God designed the Earth as an obstacle course to perfect his adopted sons and daughters. Moreover, he allowed some very nasty, evil **angel**[1] in the garden of Eden and later on permitted evil **people**[2] to flourish. Satan, the deceiver, was in the garden before Adam and Eve disobeyed God.

---- ☆----

[1] *Genesis 3:1, Now the <u>serpent</u> was more cunning than any beast of the field which the LORD God had made. And he said to the woman, "Has God indeed said, 'You shall not eat of every tree of the garden'?"*

[2] *1 Peter 3:12, For the eyes of the LORD are on the righteous, And His ears are open to their prayers; But the face of the LORD is against those who do <u>evil</u>."*

[2] *Hosea 7:2, But they do not consider that I remember all their <u>wickedness</u>. Now their deeds surround them; they are before my face. ....x..x...*

Most people in my patch are honest, hard-working people contributing (intentionally or not) to his kingdom and our salvation. If anyone in my patch were to suffer the consequences of the evil God permits, God has to make them whole. It makes perfect sense to me that God has a moral duty to them, if not in this life, then in the afterlife.

Nonetheless, Evil people will stand before him on Judgment day and account for their action. God will judge and punish them justly in front of the whole creation.

Fellow Workers[3]

If the army were to take me into their confidence and involve me in designing the assault course, my attitude would differ. I would see these nasty parts of training as necessary obstacles that we helped create. I would now be part of my fellow workers in perfecting our activity in this elite unit. I would see all things as working for my **good.**[4]

In the same way, God gave us the chance to involve ourselves in his Earth's history, to change its course. He gave us the **gift**[5] of the Holy Spirit to heal the **blind**[6], make it rain or topple evil heads of government. A chance to change the course of every leaf, every tree, every person's destiny in our patch.

---- ☆----

[3] *1 Corinthians 3:9, For we are God's fellow workers; you are God's field, you are God's building.*

[4] *Romans 8:28, And we know that all things work together for good to those who love God, to those called according to His purpose.*

[5] *Acts 11:16, "Then I remembered the word of the Lord, how He said, 'John indeed baptized with water, but you shall be baptized with the Holy Spirit.'*

[6] *Luke 4:18 & (Isaiah 61:1), "The Spirit of the LORD is upon Me, Because He has anointed Me To preach the gospel to the poor; He has sent Me to heal the brokenhearted, To proclaim liberty to the captives And recovery of sight to the blind, To set at liberty those who are oppressed;*

....x..x...

What a tremendous gift. An eternal inheritance so many are neglecting, for the comfort of a soft bed and pleasures of this world.

Matthew 13:44, "Again, the kingdom of heaven is like treasure hidden in a field, which a man found and hid; and for joy, over it, he goes and sells all that he has and buys that field.

In my early days, God was trying to teach me, going out to convert the world without first being armed with the right tools is a waste of time.

This is my testimony as a joint heir in Christ. There is still time for you to rise and claim your inheritance.

Philippians 3:14, I press toward the goal for the prize of the upward call of God in Christ Jesus.

Chapter 103– From the beginning (Ephesians 1:4. & 2 *Thessalonians* 2:13).

Ephesians 1:4, just as He chose us in Him before the foundation of the world, that we should be holy and without blame before Him in love.

We were in spirit (past, present and future are one in God) with God from the **beginning[1]**. We can, in spirit, with the Holy Spirit's help, go back to that time and amend our record in the Lamb's **book of life[2]**, now with informed knowledge. That is a privilege we have as **fellow brothers and sisters[3]** with Christ, making an informed choice, to plan our **good works[4]** in consultation with God, to finish the **race[5]** set before us.

Furthermore, we can help design the race to make it harder or easier for us to complete. That privilege is granted to us but wasn't presented to the

---- ☆----

[1] *2 Timothy 1:9, who has saved us and called us with a holy calling, not according to our works, but according to His purpose and grace which was given to us in Christ Jesus before time began,*

[1] *2 Thessalonians 2:13, But we are bound to give thanks to God always for you, brethren beloved by the Lord, because God from the beginning chose you for salvation through sanctification by the Spirit and belief in the truth,*

[2] *Revelation 21:27, But there shall by no means enter it anything that defiles or causes an abomination or a lie, but only those who are written in the Lamb's Book of Life.*

[3] *Hebrews 2:11, For both He who sanctifies and those who are being sanctified are all of one, for which reason He is not ashamed to call them brethren,*

[4] *Ephesians 2:10, For we are His workmanship, created in Christ Jesus for good works, which God prepared beforehand that we should walk in them.*

[5] *Hebrews 12:1, Therefore we also, since we are surrounded by so great a cloud of witnesses, let us lay aside every weight, and the sin which so easily ensnares us, and let us run with endurance the race that is set before us,*

[5] *Ac 20:24, I do not count my life of any value to myself unless I finish my course and the ministry that I received from the Lord Jesus to testify to the good news of God's grace.*

...x..x...

prophets. It is for us to claim it or let it pass by.

In spirit, with the help of the Holy Spirit, I went back into the past. A privilege granted to us in Christ and made an informed choice to amend my destiny for the race that was set before me. I helped devise the assault course. Now the race/course was developed with my consent. A privilege given to us when he chose us **before the foundations**[6] of the world were laid. This is part of our inheritance, which some of us who are brave and courageous are willing to claim and use to grow spiritually.

God helps those who are determined to get over the assault course and **clothes**[7] them with glory for his good pleasure. They will be tested, and He will crown them one day because they have overcome the assault course.

Lord, 'Everything that has lived on this planet, **we will make whole**. What you have experienced is the tip of the iceberg, a fraction of my commitment.' And I believed him because I had informed knowledge and chose to work with him.

The only way to feel this is to ask God to make it happen in our life, to experience it, like when I taught the young woman to fix her radiator. That's what he taught me, how to be an overcomer, by making me walk in it.

All this can come from a good imagination. I needed a reality check. I asked God to give me something that would prove to me that I had been able to do it. The following few chapters will deal with it.

When we have experienced this, we can start to exercise faith in our rich inheritance. Until then, it is just intellectual knowledge but no real power.

----- ☆----

[6] *Ephesians 1:4, just as He chose us in Him before the foundation of the world, that we should be holy and without blame before Him in love,*

[7] *Revelation 3:18, I counsel you to buy from Me gold refined in the fire, that you may be rich; and white garments, that you may be clothed that the shame of your nakedness may not be revealed; and anoint your eyes with eye salve, that you may see. ...x..x...*

Chapter 104 – Attitude

Romans 8:28 And we know that <u>all things work</u> together for good to those who love God, to those who are the <u>called according to *His* purpose.</u>

In this world, everything works for our **good.**[1] That makes me feel a sense of gratitude and thankfulness to this world and my Patch.

Furthermore, I am a **steward**[2] of God on my patch, and I have undertaken to **account**[3] for everything in it to God daily, a task I have volunteered for. I should say I could only do this with the help of the indwelling Holy Spirit.

I want to (this is my view, and others may disagree) acknowledge my gratitude to my patch by starting to bring about the process of **reconciliation**[4] with everything/everyone in my patch. If not in this world, then in the hereafter.

The things I am learning and used in my perfection have repercussions for everything in my patch. Their pain and suffering is, in a small way, a result of my purification and sanctification. My salvation comes at a cost to my neighbours, Mother Earth and all its creatures. *(**Romans 8:22,** For we know that the whole creation <u>groans</u> and labours with birth pangs together until now.)*

I have a thirst and a desire to make everything whole in my patch,

----- ☆---

[1] *Romans 8:28, And we know that <u>all things work</u> together for good to those who love God, to those who are <u>called according to His purpose.</u>*

[2] *Luke 12:42, And the Lord said, "Who then is that faithful and wise <u>steward,</u> whom his master will make ruler over his household, to give them their portion of food in due season?*

[3] *Hebrews 4:13, And there is no creature hidden from His sight, but all things are naked and open to the eyes of Him to whom we must give <u>account</u>.*

[4] *2 Corinthians 5:19, that is, that God was in Christ <u>reconciling</u> the world to Himself, not imputing their trespasses to them, and has committed to us the word of <u>reconciliation</u>. ...x..x...*

Currently beyond my power.

Also, I believe God is responsible for creation and its joy, pain and suffering. Their happiness, pain, and suffering, are temporary; my understanding is God has undertaken to **reconcile**[5] and make all things whole. As his steward, I desire to intercede on their behalf daily and help make them whole. It's not from a feeling of guilt but a proper recognition that my salvation has come at the cost of suffering to them.

And even if I don't have an obligation to them, I still would like to do it. God gave me the gift of the Holy Spirit, and I would like to learn to use its power to do good. God put me on this **earth**[6] to learn, and I am using this opportunity to do just that.

*Acts 23:1 Then Paul, looking earnestly at the council, said, "Men and brethren, I have lived in all good **conscience** before God until this day."*

1 Timothy 3:9, Holding the mystery of the faith in a pure conscience.

Training

One of the first goals of our training in the army was getting fit. Each morning before breakfast, we had to run five miles. On the first day of training, we ran for about half a mile, and many of us were physically sick. Some of us vomited by the roadside. The instructors shouted and scowled at us to make us run. I did not complete the run. By the end of the week, we had managed to achieve a two-mile run. Three weeks later, most of us were able to run the five miles. Those who could not were removed from the regiment and sent home. The last half mile, a few of us would sprint

---- ☆----

[5] *Colossians 1:20, and by Him to reconcile all things to Himself, by Him, whether things on earth or things in heaven, having made peace through the blood of His cross.*

[6] *Genesis 2:15, Then the LORD God took the man and put him in the garden of Eden to till it and keep it.*

...x..x...

back to the barracks. I was one of them. It taught me that I could do ten times what I would consider possible if I had the right motivation and trainers.

God has set a race before us. **Hebrews 12:1,** *Therefore we also, since we are surrounded by so great a cloud of witnesses, let us lay aside every weight, and the sin which so easily ensnares us, and let us run with endurance the race that is set before us,*

2 Timothy 2:3, *You, therefore, must endure hardship as a good soldier of Jesus Christ.*

This is my simple understanding, a speck of dust trying to comprehend the unfathomable mind of God.

Every thought and emotion of defeat and despair, every tendency towards suicide we have ever felt, God has felt. Yes, he has had thoughts beyond our imagination. The difference is he found a way to overcome it all.

He turned that negative energy into a positive, creative life. He created the Universe, something he wants us to learn about, appreciate, and become creative like him.

Some of us have experienced a portion of such despair. We need to learn how to release the creative power that God has given us and how to account for it. That power is in us, the WORD of God that gives us life. Many have no idea how to activate their true potential.

Yes, you do.

How?

Allow the Holy Spirit to teach you to walk in the spirit. For that, you need to give him time and a commitment to obey.

Revelation 21:5, Then He who sat on the throne said, "Behold, I make all things new." And He said to me, "Write, for these words are true and faithful." --- 🐝---

Chapter 105 - Build my Spiritual Sanctuary

Exodus 15:17, You will bring them in and plant them in the mountain of Your inheritance, In the place, O LORD, which <u>You have made For Your dwelling, The sanctuary</u>, O Lord, which Your hands have established.

One could apply this to a place on earth. However, I believe the Holy Spirit is looking at it from a long-term view, i.e. in a spiritual home where he has established God's sanctuary.

The Lord said, 'Hari, You will build my/our spiritual sanctuary.'

This concept is beyond my intellectual ability to explain. All I have is a gist of it. Our Lord has established his sanctuary outside time. How long did it take? Seven days; - periods, stages, each could have been a few billion years.

Our heavenly Father and our Lord built it; my role was more like a five-year-old child helping his father decorate a home. In the beginning, there was nothing. It began with a thought/vision, which turned into energy, plasma, the first subatomic particle (K-matter). He asked me to name it. I called it 83.450. (**Appendix end of book**) Every particle, every atom was fashioned individually, documented, and added to the inventory.

The first night (start of the early stage), I went to sleep. I was excited. I knew something strange would happen. I woke up at 3 p.m. and, on the internet, read about magic squares where the total number in all directions is the same. Then over the next few nights, I would wake up and start writing numbers. Then I drew a cube and starting giving the 27 cubes numbers.

Finally, I had a cube with eight dimensions with the exact 777 at each corner; its outward force—(**Appendix Fig A**) and a further two dimension with a force of 699.3 its inward force. Total of ten dimensions. One night I woke up, turned my computer on, and looked up Universe's shape on Google search (**Fig B** end of the book).

There on the screen was a picture of the Universe inside a cube and some more pictures of galaxies.

Over the following nights, I would get up and add more information to it. I drew a diagram showing the total forces on the surface of the cube (Universe). Then I inserted them into a map, drawn to scale. It showed the shape of the Universe as an egg.

Similarly, I received numbers for another cube. When I sketched it to scale, it produced an image that looked like what scientists had drawn for an atom. **Fig C**

Then he asked me to overlap two cubes of No 92 and use their combined numbers to form a single balanced cube again. I did it and created a cube of 183 with one surplus unit. The second cube of 178 with six surplus units. The words Helium and fusion came to my mind. I went and looked up fusion on the internet. **Fig D**

I had things going through my mind that were way beyond my comprehension. To me, the gist of it was that the indwelling Holy Spirit could teach me how the Universe was created. Various forces (gravity, dark matter) kept it in its current form and how changes in one sector would change the number (gravitational force, dark energy) in another sector (galaxy) to retain the outer constant. I could draw such balanced cubes mathematically, but it was getting beyond my mental ability to grasp its significance.

The number sequences to add up to a single number (777) from 8 dimensions is a complex sequence with two negative numbers. I had managed to put it all together. I asked a family member, a physic professor if he could work out what was the possibility of arriving at this sequence with a pad and a £1 calculator. He had a good look at it for a couple of days. His highly sophisticated university computer could not do such sums because he didn't know the formula.

To come up with these numbers in sleep is just incredible. He gave these numbers to confirm I had the mind of Christ to grasp his design for the sanctuary. *1 Corinthians 2:16, For "who has known the mind of the LORD that he may instruct Him?" However, we have the mind of Christ.*

By the WORD of God, the sanctuary was built. I assisted in a childlike manner, sub-particle by sub-particle. This was a small sanctuary, one of many they made, and its length, height, and breadth were 4.3 light-years. Each cube has eight outward pull dimension and two inwards.

John 14:2, "In My Father's house are many mansions; if it were not so, I would have told you. I go to prepare a place for you.

[Each cube has a 27-sub cube, having 270 dimensions, and each sub-cube has another 27 cubes, the total for all is 2,980 Dimensions. The force on the circumference for all these dimensions is **777**[1]. I have the mathematical calculations for all individual units. I have not reached the intellectual level to comprehend its significance or mystery.]

O, how I wish I were a young man again. With the indwelling Holy Spirit's help, I would unlock the secrets of the universe, the atom, anti-gravity, and much more. As I drifted into these thoughts, the cloud of heavenly saints from every faith on earth that had surrounded me all my life appeared together with a host of angels.

I heard a voice say, 'My son, all these glories awaits you when you come home.'

*1 Corinthians 2:9, But as it is written: "**Eye has not** seen, nor ear heard, Nor have entered into the heart of man The things which God has prepared for those who love Him."*

----- ☆----

World Population

[1] **A** few days after I had finished cube 777, I felt the Lord standing beside me. He had a message for me.

I laughed, 'No way, Lord. How do I test this?'

He said, 'Check the world population.' I checked on the internet.

www.worldometers. Info/world-population

World population (live) 02-10-2018 13:17:06. Current population. Clock: 7.7 Billion People.

---- ❀ --

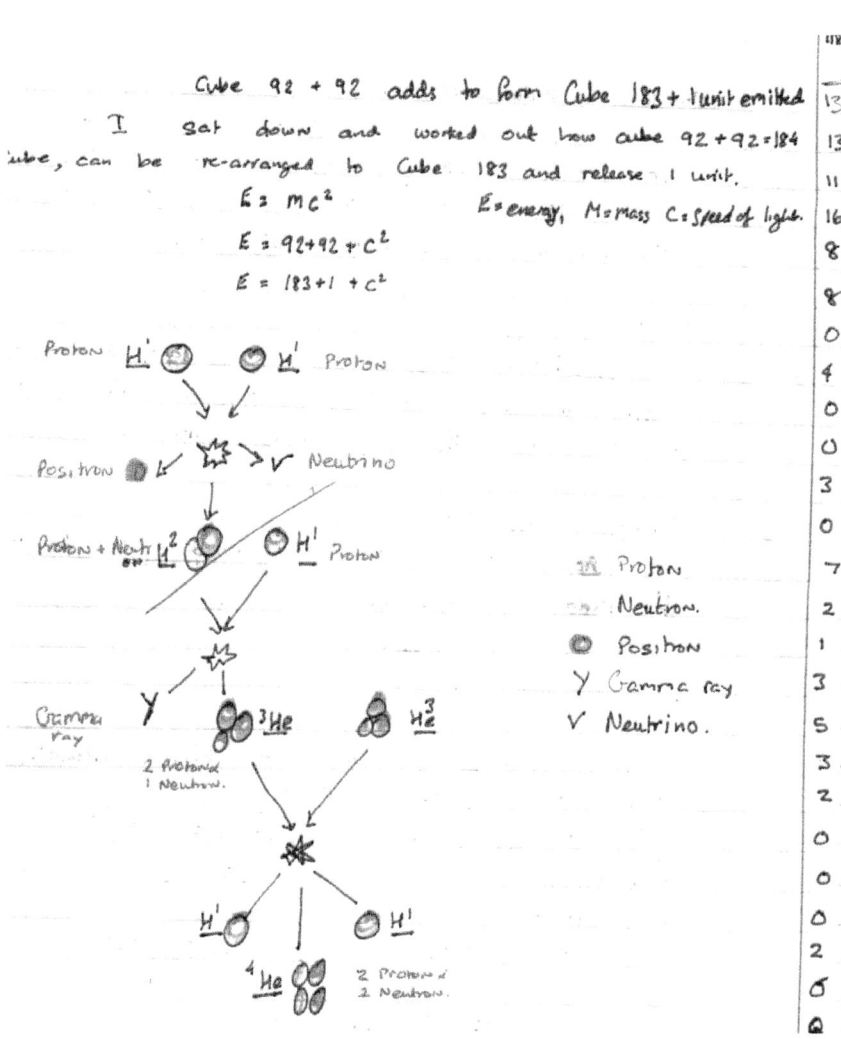

Cube 92 + 92 adds to form Cube 183 + 1 unit emitted

I sat down and worked out how cube 92 + 92 = 184 ube, can be re-arranged to Cube 183 and release 1 unit.

$$E = mc^2$$

E = energy, M = mass C = speed of light.

$$E = 92 + 92 + c^2$$

$$E = 183 + 1 + c^2$$

Proton, Proton

Positron, Neutrino

Proton + Neutron, Proton

Gamma ray

³He, ³He (2 Protons 1 Neutron)

H¹, H¹

⁴He (2 Protons 2 Neutrons)

Proton
Neutron.
Positron
Y Gamma ray
V Neutrino.

Chapter 106 Programmer

We had an old-fashioned thermostat in the hallway to regulate the heating systems installed in our home. It was a temperature sensor with a switch. I removed it and replaced it with a Programmable Thermostat. I read the instruction book, followed its instructions, and wired the programmer to the heating system.

Then set the time for the heating and the water system to come on during the week and weekend. I tested it. The programmer worked fine, but the heating failed to come on.

I called the helpline listed on the instructions booklet, and he found I had made a mistake in the wiring. I corrected it and tested the system. The heating came on time and switched off as programmed.

However, the hot water system did not work. Once more, I called the helpline, and he helped me correct another mistake. Finally, everything worked fine. I had made mistakes, but with the help line's assistance, I had learned to read/follow the instruction correctly.

Moral of the story.

The Bible is like the instruction book. If you follow it correctly, you can set the day and hour for things to happen, heal the sick, and many other things. If you do not follow the Bible correctly, still drinking the **milk**[1], your prayers may fail. You may believe it has been answered differently, but in all honesty, nothing has changed.

You call the church leaders the experts in reading the instructions in God's book. If they are skilled in the word of God, then the prayers will work,

----- ☆----

[1] *Hebrews 5:13, For everyone who partakes only of **milk,** is unskilled in the word of righteousness, for he is a babe. ...x...x..*

352

whatever it may **be**[2].

If you want to follow the Lord's instruction with **power**[3], ask the indwelling **Holy Spirit**[4] to teach you to read the Bible correctly and help you to correct your mistakes.

I will guide you with My eye

Ps 32:8, Lord, 'I will instruct you and teach you in the way you should go; I will guide you with My eye. Lord said to me,

1. 'I want you to build me three different Cubes, each ten-dimensional cube, whose sum total at each corner comes to the same number 777.
2. It has to be up to five decimal points.
3. Within the cube are 27 other cubes. They all have a number. Each number has to meet the above requirement.
4. You have to use a simple pocket calculator (costing less than £2).

The indwelling Holy Spirit will guide you.'

----- ☆----

[2] *Luke 4:18, "The Spirit of the LORD is upon me because He has anointed Me to* preach the gospel *to the poor; He has sent Me to* heal *the broken-hearted, to proclaim liberty to the captives. And* recovery of sight *to the blind,* to set at liberty *those who are oppressed.*

[3] *Mark 16:17-18, And these signs shall follow them that believe; In my name shall they cast out devils; they shall speak with new tongues; They shall take up serpents; and if they drink any deadly thing, it shall not hurt them; they shall lay* hands on the sick, *and they shall* recover.

[4] *Thessalonians 1:5, For our gospel did not come to you in word only, but also in* power, *and in the Holy Spirit and in much assurance, as you know what kind of men we were among you for your sake.* ...x...x..

I sat down and drew a cube. Over the next few weeks, I followed his instructions. I made many mistakes, learned to correct them, and finally had the three cubes, all with different numbers. However, ending with the same number.

Lord, 'You have done this; it holds the mystery of the universe, atom, and gravity. Now you are ready to build me a spiritual **sanctuary**[5].' And we did it.

----- ----

[5] *Ex 15:17, You will <u>bring them in</u> and plant them in the mountain of Your inheritance, in the place, O LORD, which You have made for Your dwelling, the <u>sanctuary</u>, O Lord, which Your hands have established.*

[5] *Ps 78:69, And He built His <u>sanctuary</u> like the heights, like the earth, he has established forever.*

[5] *Heb 8:2, A minister of the <u>sanctuary</u>, and of the true tabernacle, which the Lord pitched, and not man.*

---- ---

Chapter 107 - Sanctuary

Isaiah 51:16, And I have put My words in your mouth; I have covered you with the shadow of My hand, That I may <u>plant the heavens</u>, Lay the foundations of the earth, And say to Zion (my Church), 'You are My people.'

The sanctuary's purpose is to make whole all who lived in my patch, the exception being the evil people. To thank them, show gratitude, and acknowledge their contribution to God's kingdom and my salvation by making them whole.

To make restitution for their pain and suffering. In the end, nothing should cry out that my/our salvation or God's kingdom (Revelation 21) was achieved at their expense.

The Universe's moral law is that nothing should thrive at the expense of another, i.e. you shall not steal. This <u>reconciliation</u> process is part of my/our inheritance in God/Christ.

Colossians 1:20, *and by Him to <u>reconcile all things</u> to Himself, by Him, whether <u>things on Earth</u> or things in Heaven, having made peace through the blood of His cross.*

The Lord said, 'Hari, when we have built it, and the whole creation has been made complete, your <u>conscience</u>[1] will be clear.

----- ☆----

[1] **1 Timothy 3:9,** *holding the mystery of the faith with a <u>pure conscience</u>.*

Chapter 108 – Make whole

Romans 8:29, For whom He foreknew, He also predestined to be conformed to the image of His Son, that He might be the firstborn among many brethren.

There is a considerable cost attached to the process to make all things whole. My understanding is that God will fund this tab for two reasons: his honour and because of his investment in me/us.

My/our value to him is beyond my comprehension. He has waited billions, maybe trillions of years, for the glorious day when he can reveal his firstborn in Christ to the heavenly cloud.

I pray the Holy Spirit would open your eyes to the mysteries hidden from ages, now revealed by his saints to the principalities and powers in the heavenly places.

Ephesians 3:10, to the intent that now the manifold wisdom of God might be made known by the church to the principalities and powers in the heavenly places.

Mr 4:11, And He said to them, "To you it has been given to know the mystery of the kingdom of God; but to those who are outside, all things come in parables,

Colossians 1:26, the mystery hidden from ages and generations, but now has been revealed to His saints.

I pray that this rich inheritance of ours is not squandered away in ignorance or pursuit of earthly gains, but that in all things, you yield to the indwelling Holy Spirit.

1 Corinthians 2:9, But as it is written: "Eye has not seen, nor ear heard, nor have entered into the heart of man the things which God has prepared for those who love Him."

We cannot comprehend the physic laws at the sub-atomic level because they are outside the scope of our current understanding. Our world and our thinking rotate on axes of the known laws of physics. This world provides us with answers we can test. God, like subatomic particles, functions at a level outside of our understanding.

So close your eyes and look deep inside you. Your body and mind are made of atoms formed a fraction of a second after the **Big Bang**[1]. Before that, your mind (atoms) was in that flux of the Big Bang, and what came prior to that; you were pure energy. And that pure energy was with God from the beginning.

We were with God from the beginning, perhaps in a different form as pure energy.

*Ephesians 1:4, just as He chose us in Him **before the foundation** of the world, that we should be holy and without blame before Him in love,*

*2 Thessalonians 2:13, But we are bound to give thanks to God always for you, brethren beloved by the Lord, because God **from the beginning** chose you for salvation through sanctification by the Spirit and belief in the truth,*

....

[1] *The Big Bang hypothesis states that all of the current and past matter in the Universe came into existence at the same time, roughly 13.8 billion years ago.*

Suddenly, the Singularity began expanding, and the universe as we know it began.

---- 🥠 ---

Chapter 109 – Knowledge is progressive

Our ancestors used to believe the Earth was flat. Later, they thought that Earth was the centre of the Universe. Now we know we are a speck in a galaxy.

Tomorrow the mystery of quantum physics and black holes and singularities will unravel. It will transform our lives; perhaps project us into a world of fusion and limitless cheap energy. Space travel and colonization of planets could follow.

Great leaps in knowledge require corresponding growth of wisdom, virtue, moral value, and spirituality.

Matthew 18:3, *and Jesus said, "Assuredly, I say to you, unless you are converted and become as <u>little children</u>, you will by no means enter the kingdom of heaven.*

In the past, our ancestors regarded Earth as flat. They were content with a simple explanation of 7-day creation, the story of Adam and Eve, to a generation unable to grapple with the speed of light, the infinite Universe, quantum physics.

There are certain things Jesus wants us to grapple with using a childlike attitude. At the same time, he advises us to grow up and have a mature outlook.

Hebrews 5:12-13, *For though you ought to be teachers by this time, you need someone to teach you again the first principles of the oracles of God; and you have come to <u>need milk</u> and not solid food. For everyone who partakes only of milk is unskilled in the word of righteousness, for he is a babe.*

The doors to quantum physics and nanotechnology are opening, so too is the door to what we should call our quantum spirituality. Doors only the bravest of the brave will walkthrough.

The price of might and greatness is accountability. As we enter the atomic age, we will need faith and moral guidance more than ever.

That responsibility rests in your hands.

Numbers and Love can be generated spontaneously out of nothing.

Maths is numbers. God is love.

Blot out numbers, and you do away with Maths

Blot out God, and you do away with love.

Without love, we are nothing.

---- ☆----

Not just any love, but a universal love for all things, all creation, all people, with a sense of respect, responsibility, accountability and a higher moral obligation to all things, to make all things whole (restitution, reconciliation).

When we can look in a mirror and say, 'I live in a universe at no expense (cost, hardship) to anyone.

I am pure energy.

I was, am, will be pure.

I have finally returned to my Father's bosom,

In whom, past, present, future is one.

1 Corinthians 13:2, *And though I have the gift of prophecy, and understand all mysteries and all knowledge, and though I have all faith, so that I could move mountains, but have <u>not love, I am nothing.</u>*

Chapter 110 – Books

Kathy's Tenet 1. You matter more than the things we do and have done together. It is the relationship that matters.'

Years later, as I reviewed my life in the 6th sabbatical year, the pieces of the puzzles the Lord had shown me over the years started to fit together. An overall picture emerged, and I felt the Lord say, 'I want you to write a book.'

He wanted me to convey the message, 'You matter more than the things we do and have done together. It is the relationship that matters.'

Isaiah 51:16, *And I have put My <u>words in your mouth</u>; I have covered you with the <u>shadow of My hand</u>, That I may plant the heavens, Lay the foundations of the earth, And say to Zion (my Church), 'You are My people.'*

I felt him say, 'I have led you so far, beyond the imagination of most men. I have taken you to places where no human or angel has been.

[King David's Tenet: - Father's love for his child].

The Lord said, *"I understand the pain and sorrow in your heart. Trust me; when our Heavenly father leads his child through the valley of death, he has a reason and a good purpose. For every tear you shed, he has shed more because his loving hand has allowed the pain on your being. His motives, his intentions are for your betterment and growth. Your tears inflict deep wounds into him, yet he has chosen this path through the valley of death for both of you. Love comes at a high cost. Moral character and compassion are refined in the fire of grief, suffering, and joy, just as gold is refined in the fire."*

'God has witnessed every pain you have gone through. It is no easy task to see a beloved child suffer. It was the only way we could teach you the crucial things -values in life that matter in the hereafter.

'We have felt your pain, and we have tried to bridge the gap. We have given you a unique insight into our mind because you asked.

'Because you matter more to us than we matter to you. There are billions of people in God's Kingdom, but very few who are striving to reach the full stature of Christ.'

Ephesians 4:13, until all of us come to the unity of the faith and of the knowledge of the Son of God, to maturity, <u>to the measure of the full stature of Christ</u>.

My struggles

This is my personal feeling. The hurt I felt as a child, my family's rejection, the pain of innocent animals killed still flows through me. I laid my life before God to understand my pain and the pain of the Universe if it is ever possible to do.

Distant future

Finally, I am at peace with God, my neighbours, Mother Earth, and all its creatures.

I stood at his feet, at that spiritual point in the far future. The whole of creation and the new heavens flashed past me. He has shown me things that very few have seen.

The Lord said, 'Come, cross the bridge with me. On the other side is a new beginning.'

I stood apart. 'Forgive me, Holy Father, my spirit is tired, exhausted. I have no energy to cross the bridge with you, not today. I have gone as far as I can. I hope I paved the way for my brothers and sisters in Christ to follow you and cross the bridge.

'One day, I may be strong enough to cross that bridge, but not today.'

Afterlife

Many believe this life is all; there is no God; death is the end. He respects their belief. However, it is not based on informed choice. Many like me struggle with the question, 'If there is a loving God, why all this pain and suffering in the world?'

Their name may not be in the lamb's book of the living, but their names are in the father's book. Every hair, every sparrow that falls to the ground is in his book.

This is my personal view. You do not have to agree with it.

In my patch, he taught me every grain of sand matters; every person matters. In Haringey, I spent years putting leaflets through people's doors, offering my home and services because God loved them, cared for them. I learnt to care and love them regardless of their response to God or me.

Years later, we had a Nursing Home. My wife and I, every Christmas, made hundreds of parcels. We had undertaken to provide a package for every child with special needs in a three-mile radius of our home. We wanted to make sure no one disadvantaged in life should feel left out at a celebration time. We made an effort to find their names, and each parcel had a name on it.

We gave them the parcels at Christmas. We made presents for local doctors to thank them for the work they did for the communities. We would have done it for every nurse, delivery driver, street cleaner, factory worker, or police officer if we had the resources.

God did not put this into our hearts. We did it because of what he had taught us. Ordinary people are good, decent, hard working, and honest. They have made it possible for us to grow spiritually and physically.

Matthew 25:40, *And the king (Jesus) will answer them, 'Truly I tell you, just as you did it to one of the least of these who are members of my family, you did it to me.'*

Christ's message to humanity. This is my belief.

Out Lord's message to all humanity is, *'because you have fed my little children, clothed them, healed them, driven the taxis, cleaned their streets, I have gratitude towards you. I am sorry for the pain and suffering you endured so that my children, my* **priests**[1], *could mature and be made perfect (**Galatians 4:19,** until Christ, be formed in them). I acknowledge my debt to you.*

'I will provide spiritual sanctuaries in the afterlife supervised by Me and my

---- ☆----

[1]*Exodus 19:6, 'And you shall be to Me a kingdom of priests and a holy nation.'*

.x..x..

362

*chosen and tested **priests.** We will make restitution, make you whole for your pain and suffering on Earth, and reconcile all things in Heaven and Earth.'*

Death

There are countless testimonies of people who say that when a person dies, his soul/spirit goes through a tunnel. At the other end, an angel, a close friend, or relative meets them. These kinds, loving people guide the recent arrival around the garden.

Life goes on, circumstances change.

The vast majority of good decent people in our communities, I believe God will raise them again in the sanctuaries as an act of gratitude: The first resurrection. They have put up with pain and suffering on Earth, fought valiantly to provide for their families and created ideal circumstances (assault course), so we could finish the race set before us.

They did not choose to be part of creation, part of God's plan. Life, creation, was imposed on them.

Therefore, God and we owe them a debt of thankfulness, acknowledgement, gratitude and a moral obligation to make them whole for their contribution in helping us to work out our salvation.

Some people will choose to accept his restitution plan in the sanctuaries; others may decide to return to the grave. Those that choose to accept his plan will live a happier life until the fullness of their time – nothing lives forever.

Selfish and evil people

Selfish and Evil people will spend time in unique sanctuaries with their kind until Judgment Day, without God's restraints or influence. Not a good prospect.

And they should be aware of the second death. ***Revelation 20:6*** *Blessed and holy is he who has a part in the first resurrection.*

Revelation 2:11, *"He who has an ear, let him hear what the Spirit says to the churches. The second death shall not hurt him who overcomes."*

I am a pioneer; those that come after me will be able to do incredible things. With the help of our Heavenly Father, we (Lord, Holy Spirit, and I) have laid the path for others to follow.

Bless you, run the good race.

2 Timothy 2:2, And the things that you have heard from me among many witnesses, commit these to faithful men who will also teach others.

End of Book

Cube Appendix

I have no scientific background, and all I could get was the gist of something that was beyond my present understanding.

APPENDIX. IMAGES OF THE STRUCTURE OF THE UNIVERSE. BING.COM

INSERT THE NUMBERS IN THE CUBE BELOW.

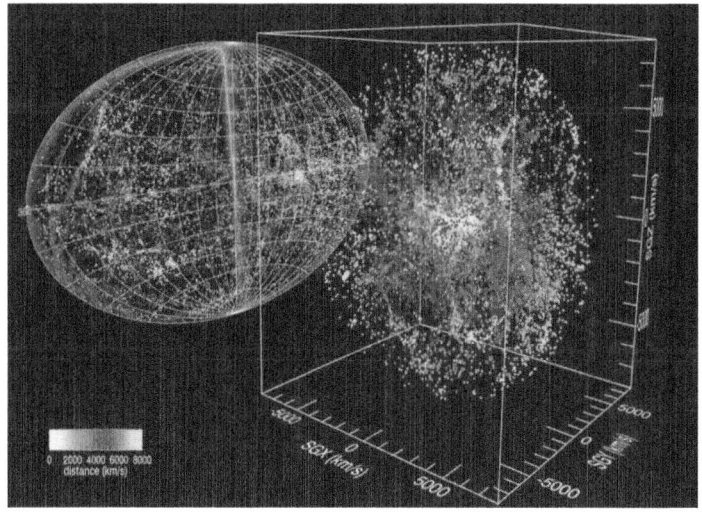

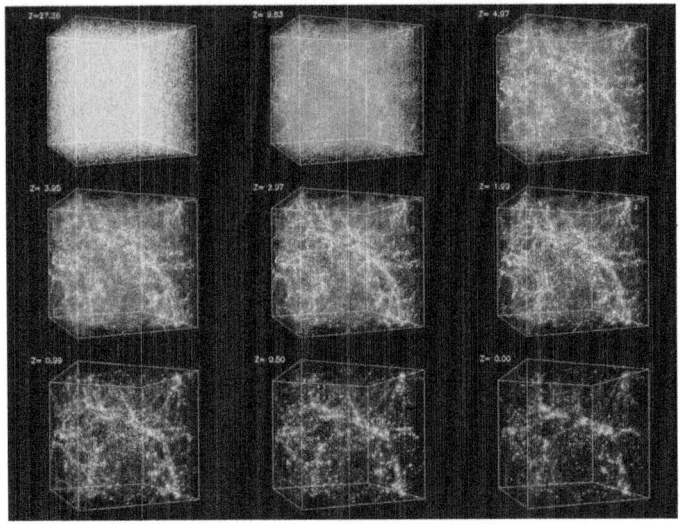

 Size and Scale of the Universe

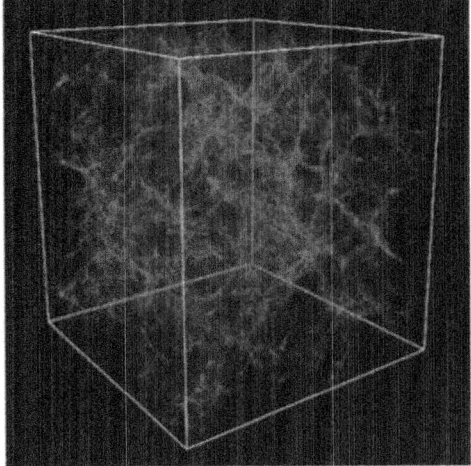

Image Credit: G. L. Bryan, M. L. Norman, UIUC, NCSA, GC3

- Computer simulations also show a similar structure, often called the "Cosmic Web"

THE UNIVERSE
(THE OBSERVABLE PORTION)

- Great walls and filaments of galaxy clusters surrounding voids containing no galaxies

- Probably at least 100 billion galaxies in the Universe

- Surveys of galaxies reveal a web-like or honeycomb structure to the Universe

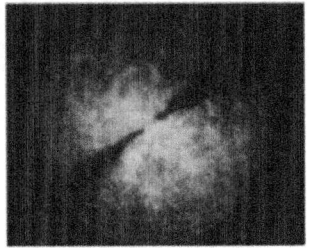

Image Credit: Dr Chris Fluke, Centre for Astrophysics and Supercomputing, Swinburne University of Technology

Appendix. The 10 Outer Dimensions for the Sanctuary. Each cube has 27 sub-cubes, all with eight equal outer forces on the circumference that keeps them intake.

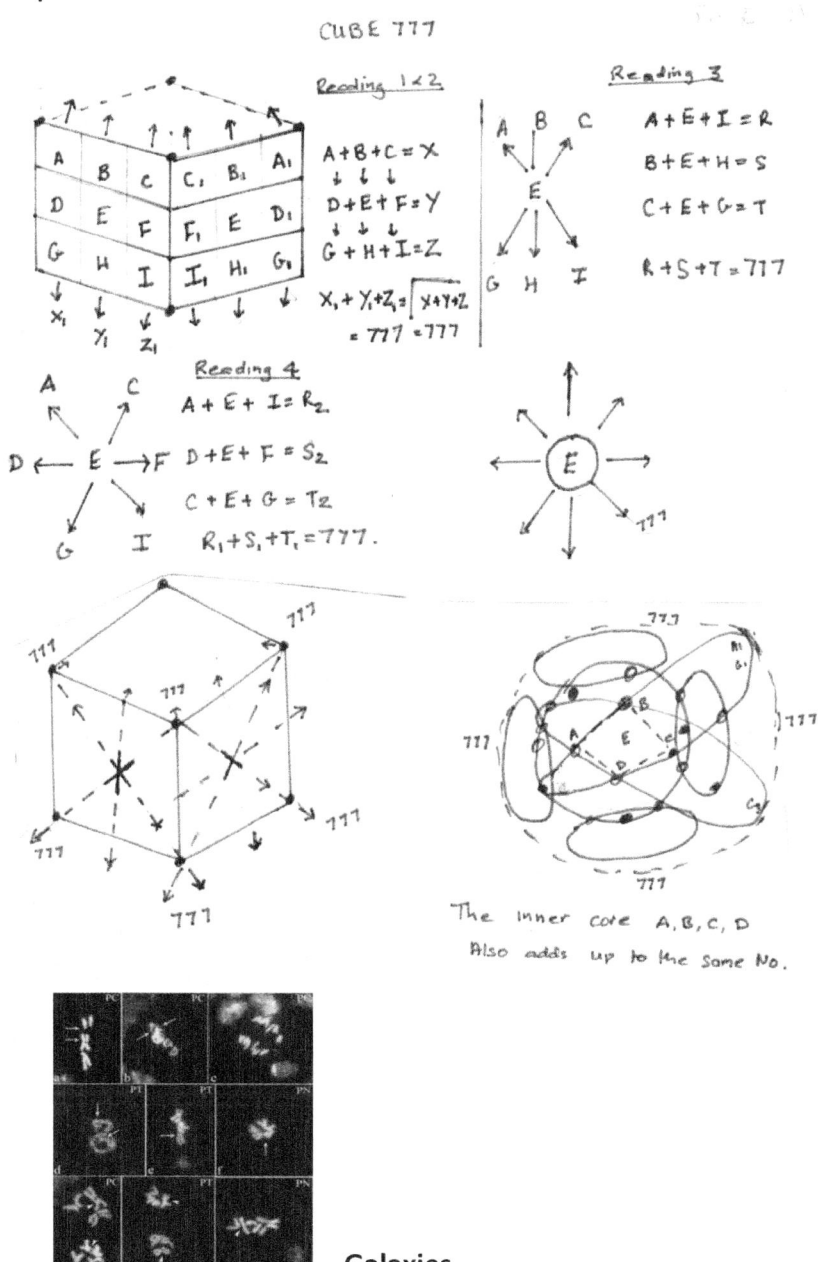

CUBE 777

Reading 1 & 2

$$A+B+C = X$$
$$D+E+F = Y$$
$$G+H+I = Z$$
$$X_1 + Y_1 + Z_1 = \overline{X+Y+Z}$$
$$= 777 = 777$$

Reading 3

$$A+E+I = R$$
$$B+E+H = S$$
$$C+E+G = T$$
$$R+S+T = 777$$

Reading 4

$$A+E+I = R_2$$
$$D+E+F = S_2$$
$$C+E+G = T_2$$
$$R_1 + S_1 + T_1 = 777$$

The inner core A, B, C, D Also adds up to the same No.

Galaxies

Cube 777 Measured from 10 Dimensions

Sides 1-4

Cube 77.7/66.6 inv balanced mxd s1-4 D

Sides 1-4

83.450	67.300	122.200		272.950	B	83.450	67.300	122.200	272.950
222.000	77.700	-66.600		233.100		77.700	77.700	77.700	233.100
72.050	88.100	110.800		270.950		110.800	88.100	72.050	270.950
377.500	233.100	166.400	777.000	777.000		271.950	233.100	271.950	777.000	777.000

Dia

W2   X2   Y2

	C	83.450	222.000	122.200	427.650
		77.700	77.700	77.700	233.100
		110.800	-66.600	72.050	116.250
		271.950	233.100	271.950	777.000	777.000

Sides 2

122.200	65.300	69.050		256.550	B	122.200	65.300	69.050	256.550
-66.600	77.700	222.000		233.100		77.700	77.700	77.700	233.100
110.800	90.100	86.450		287.350		86.450	90.100	110.800	287.350
166.400	233.100	377.500	777.000	777.000		286.350	233.100	257.550	777.000	777.000

Dia

W2   X2   Y2

	C	122.200	-66.600	69.050	124.650
		77.700	77.700	77.700	233.100
		86.450	222.000	110.800	419.250
		286.350	233.100	257.550	777.000	777.000

Sides 3

69.050	88.100	113.800		270.950	B	69.050	88.100	113.800	270.950
222.000	77.700	-66.600		233.100		77.700	77.700	77.700	233.100
86.450	67.300	119.200		272.950		119.200	67.300	86.450	272.950
377.500	233.100	166.400	777.000	777.000		265.950	233.100	277.950	777.000	777.000

Dia

W2   X2   Y2

	C	69.050	222.000	113.800	404.850
		77.700	77.700	77.700	233.100
		119.200	-66.600	86.450	139.050
		265.950	233.100	277.950	777.000	777.000

Sides 4

113.800	90.100	83.450		287.350	B	113.800	90.100	83.450	287.350
-66.600	77.700	222.000		233.100		77.700	77.700	77.700	233.100
119.200	65.300	72.050		256.550		72.050	65.300	119.200	256.550
166.400	233.100	377.500	777.000	777.000		263.550	233.100	280.350	777.000	777.000

Dia

W2   X2   Y2

	C	113.800	-66.600	83.450	130.650
		77.700	77.700	77.700	233.100
		72.050	222.000	119.200	413.250
		263.550	233.100	280.350	777.000	777.000

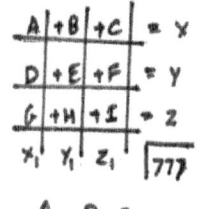

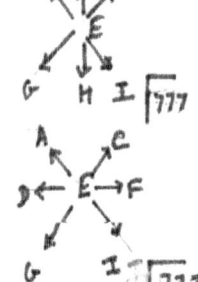

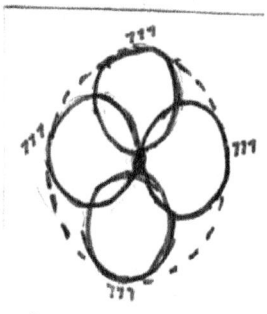

2 Diagonal sides. Their resultant net pull is 777

Diagonal side A

S2	83.450	77.700	69.050		230.200
	222.000	77.700	222.000		521.700
	72.050	77.700	86.450		236.200
	377.500	233.100	377.500	988.100	988.100

B	77.700	77.700	77.700		233.100
	86.450	77.700	72.050		236.200
	164.150	155.400	149.750	469.300	469.300
	W2	X2	Y2		

SUM Dia	988.10	699.50	988.10
	565.90	854.50	565.90
B	1554.00	1554.00	1554.00
Div by 2 =	777.00	777.00	777.00

C	83.450	222.000	69.050		374.500
	77.700	77.700	77.700		233.100
	86.450	222.000	72.050		380.500
	247.600	521.700	218.800	988.100	988.100
	W2	X!	Y2		

Diagonal side B

S3	122.200	77.700	113.800		313.700
	-66.600	77.700	-66.600		-55.500
	110.800	77.700	119.200		307.700
	166.400	233.100	166.400	565.900	565.900

B	122.200	77.700	113.800		313.700
	77.700	77.700	77.700		233.100
	119.200	77.700	110.800		307.700
	319.100	233.100	302.300	854.500	854.500
	W2	X2	Y2		

C	122.200	-66.600	113.800		169.400
	77.700	77.700	77.700		233.100
	119.200	-66.600	110.800		163.400
	319.100	-55.500	302.300	565.900	565.900
	W2	X!	Y2		

2 Cross sides & top / Bottom

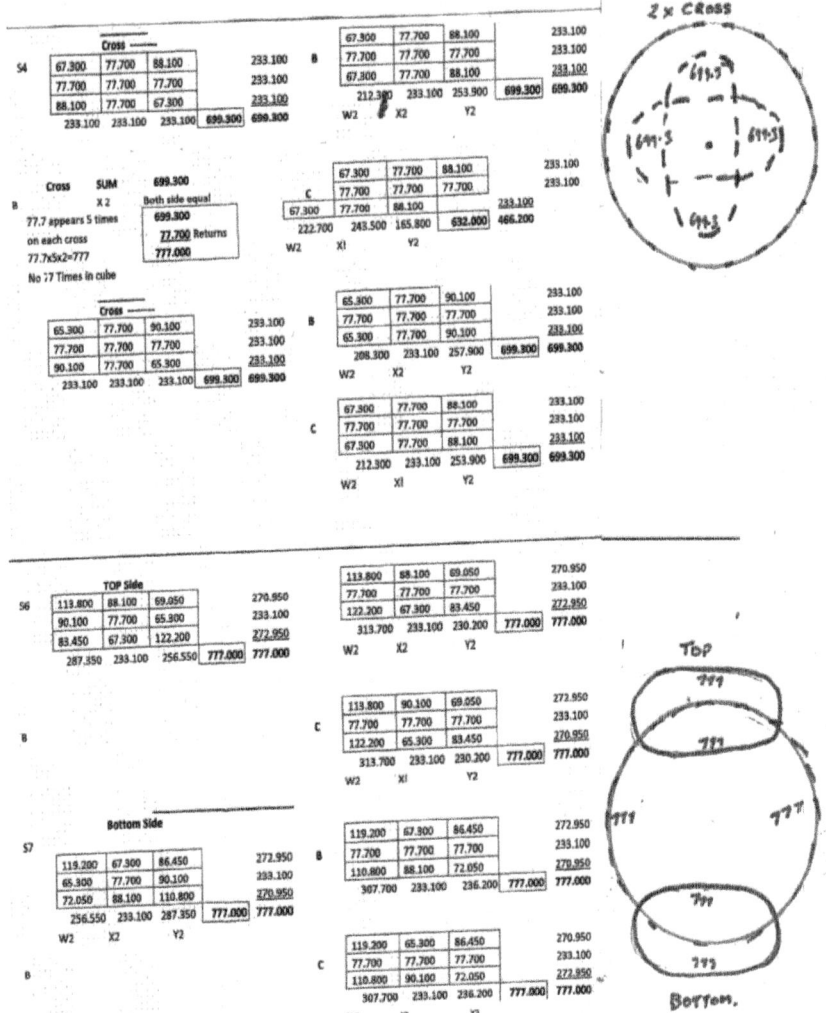

2 x Cross

S4

Cross ——

67.300	77.700	88.100	233.100
77.700	77.700	77.700	233.100
88.100	77.700	67.300	233.100
233.100	233.100	233.100	699.300	699.300

B

67.300	77.700	88.100	233.100
77.700	77.700	77.700	233.100
67.300	77.700	88.100	233.100
212.300	233.100	253.900	699.300	699.300

W2 X2 Y2

Cross	SUM	699.300
	X 2	Both side equal
77.7 appears 5 times	699.300	
on each cross	77.700 Returns	
77.7x5x2=777	777.000	

No 77 Times in cube

C

67.300	77.700	88.100	233.100
77.700	77.700	77.700	233.100
67.300	77.700	88.100	233.100
222.700	243.500	165.800	632.000	466.200

W2 X1 Y2

Cross ——

65.300	77.700	90.100	233.100
77.700	77.700	77.700	233.100
90.100	77.700	65.300	233.100
233.100	233.100	233.100	699.300	699.300

B

65.300	77.700	90.100	233.100
77.700	77.700	77.700	233.100
65.300	77.700	90.100	233.100
208.300	233.100	257.900	699.300	699.300

W2 X2 Y2

C

67.300	77.700	88.100	233.100
77.700	77.700	77.700	233.100
67.300	77.700	88.100	233.100
212.300	233.100	253.900	699.300	699.300

W2 X1 Y2

S6

TOP Side

113.800	88.100	69.050	270.950
90.100	77.700	65.300	233.100
83.450	67.300	122.200	272.950
287.350	233.100	256.550	777.000	777.000

B

113.800	88.100	69.050	270.950
77.700	77.700	77.700	233.100
122.200	67.300	83.450	272.950
313.700	233.100	230.200	777.000	777.000

W2 X2 Y2

C

113.800	90.100	69.050	272.950
77.700	77.700	77.700	233.100
122.200	65.300	83.450	270.950
313.700	233.100	230.200	777.000	777.000

W2 X1 Y2

S7

Bottom Side

119.200	67.300	86.450	272.950
65.300	77.700	90.100	233.100
72.050	88.100	110.800	270.950
256.550	233.100	287.350	777.000	777.000

W2 X2 Y2

B

119.200	67.300	86.450	272.950
77.700	77.700	77.700	233.100
110.800	88.100	72.050	270.950
307.700	233.100	236.200	777.000	777.000

C

119.200	65.300	86.450	270.950
77.700	77.700	77.700	233.100
110.800	90.100	72.050	272.950
307.700	233.100	236.200	777.000	777.000

W2 X1 Y2

B

TOP

777
777
777 777
777

Bottom.

Appendix Fig C   Si Atom

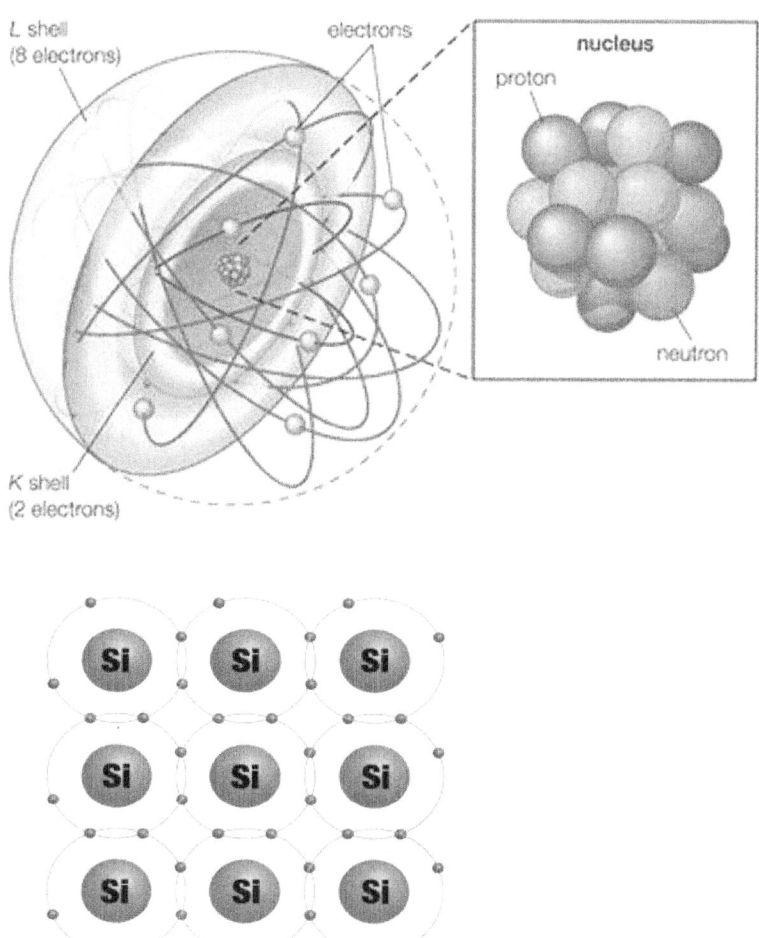

Author's Note. I hope that my testimony encourages you to step out boldly into a new, exciting way of looking at the Bible and its power to transform lives.

Vacancy for church Minister

If I were looking for a new minister for our church, I would point out that Jesus spent 40 days fasting and many nights in prayers as part of his ministry and did miracles. Therefore, the minister applying for the vacant post should prove they are walking in the steps of Jesus.

To be a church leader, the new minister would need to have fasted for at least two weeks. Had at least one precise prophecy and one healing come to pass. Evidence that non-Christians could believe, such as dates and time or medical report etc.

That would be part of my job description for the vacant post.

---- ✠ ----

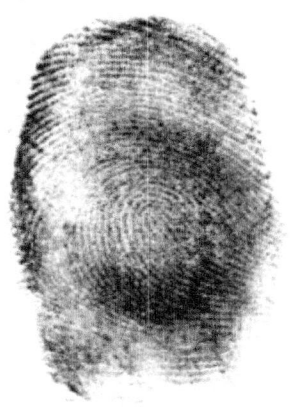

Authors print.

You can contact me at   harxpatel@gmail.com

Book Not for sale.

Following in the steps of Jesus

Property of Author, on Temporary loan to Recipient. I would like feedback on my book; please return to Author or next of kin on request harxpatel@gmail.com

Limited edition of 195 books for distribution in England & Canada.

Book Number ....

Terms of loan.

1. I want as many people as possible to read this book. Please pass on the book to another church leader within seven months.
2. In the 7th year (2026), please return the book to the author with your comments below.
3. Book No 7 is the only book on sale. The first page (chapter 1) and the last page of the book are handwritten by the author, to be sold in 2027.

*Isaiah 55:11 So shall **My word** be that goes forth from My mouth; It shall not return to Me void, But it shall accomplish what I please, And it shall prosper in the thing for which I sent it.*

Date	Comments	Initials

1.

Date	Comments	Initials

2.

3.

4.

Notes

Printed in Great Britain
by Amazon